World As Lover, World As Self

I should not like to have the bodhisattva think this kind of work
hard to achieve and hard to plan out. If he did, there are beings
beyond calculation, and he will not be able to benefit them. Let him
on the contrary consider the work easy and pleasant, thinking they
were all his mother and father and children, for this is the way to
benefit all beings whose number is beyond calculation.

—Subhuti, in *The Perfection of Wisdom in 8,000 Lines*

A NOTE ON USAGE

This book includes many traditional Buddhist terms. For the most part, these terms are used in Pali, the language in which the earliest Buddhist scriptures were recorded. However, for the following terms and proper names, the Sanskrit equivalents are used, as these are already familiar to many Western readers: abhidharma, atman, bodhisattva, chakra, dharma, karma, prajña, nirvana, Sariputra, Siddhartha Gautama, and sutra. Most foreign terms are italicized the first time they appear in the text. Diacritical marks have been omitted. Although there are no footnotes, textual references all appear at the end of the book.

World As Lover, World As Self

Joanna Macy

Parallax Press
Berkeley, California

Printed in the United States of America

Parallax Press
P.O. Box 7355
Berkeley, CA   94707

Cover Design by Gay Reineck
Text Design by Ayelet Maida
Composed on Macintosh in New Baskerville
Cover photo of the Earth from space provided by Kevin Kelly
Back Cover Photo of the author by Catherine Bush Johnson
Illustrations of bodhisattvas on pages *iii*, 1, 51, 117, and 183 are from *The Mystic Art of Ancient Tibet*, by Blanche Christine Olschak in collaboration with Geshé Thupton Wangyal (Boston: Shambhala, 1987). Used with permission.

Library of Congress Cataloging-in-Publication Data

Macy, Joanna, 1929-
       World as lover, world as self / Joanna Macy.
              p.   cm.
       Includes bibliographical references.
       ISBN 0-938077-27-9 : $15.00
       1. Buddhism–Social aspects.   2. Human ecology–Philosophy.
3. System theory.   I. Title.
BQ4570.S6M33 1991
294.3'w2–dc20   91-681
                                                                      CIP

Contents

Foreword

L ife exists only in the present moment. Everything is in this moment—the past, the present, the future, and all beings in all places. When we throw a banana peel or a rose into the garbage, we know that it will decompose quickly and fertilize our garden. We also know that plastic bags and plastic diapers take much longer to break down, perhaps 400 years. And we know that nuclear waste will take the longest time, a quarter of a million years.

In these pages, Joanna Macy shares her lucid understanding through a clear expression of these teachings of the Buddha. "This is, because that is." "This is not, because that is not." "This is like this, because that is like that." Everything exists within this present moment, and all things are interconnected. The poet Walt Whitman said, "I am large, I contain multitudes."

In the *Avatamsaka Sutra,* the Buddha tells us of the bodhisattva who is patted on the head simultaneously by all buddhas, bodhisattvas, and other beings. When we accomplish something crucial for our time, the entire universe congratulates and caresses us. In sharing her insights concerning today's perils and the important role each of us has both in creating these perils and in overcoming them, Joanna Macy speaks the truth with the roar of a lioness, and all beings throughout the universe are patting her head and caressing her in gratitude and appreciation. I am honored to be able to introduce this important book. If we read Joanna's words attentively and put her proposals into practice, we may still have a chance to show our Mother Earth our love for her. Love requires understanding, and *World As Lover, World As Self* helps us understand how we can heal this interconnected, interpenetrating universe.

If we take the hand of a child and look at the small flowers that grow among the grasses, if we sit with him or her and breathe deeply and smile, listening to the birds and also to the sounds of the other children playing together, we will see that that message is exactly the same as the message of this book, and we will know that our future depends on both. Looking deeply into the present moment, we know what to do and what not to do to save our precious planet, and each other. This is real peace education. The deepest teachings of the Buddha are explained here. Let us join the buddhas and bodhisattvas in congratulating Joanna Macy by enjoying this book and by practicing the fruit of her insights.

Thich Nhat Hanh
Kim Son Monastery
Watsonville, California
April 1991

Introduction

One day, when I was a child in New York City, I learned that my grandmother was in the hospital. I could not go see Nonnie, as I called her, because she had pneumonia and people my age were not allowed in the ward for infectious diseases. So, in lieu of a personal visit, I packed a shopping bag that my mother would take to her on my behalf. I remember some of the items I selected to cheer her up and share with her what was important in my life—a doll with roll-back eyes, a favorite book, some acorns from Central Park, a composition I had written for school. I also remember imagining how Nonnie would lift the objects from the bag and turn them in her hands with their heavy rings and yellow, nicotine stains; how she would nod at each one with a short, earthy grunt and know immediately what I was thinking and doing.

World As Lover, World As Self is like that shopping bag. I have put into it an equally varied assortment to convey what I have been about, and with a similar assumption that it will be of interest to someone else. Like the doll with the busy eyelids, this book shares what I have loved; like the carefully corrected piece of homework it shows what I have bent my mind to; and the acorns from the park are here, too, in their own way.

I am happy to have, in a collection that can be lifted with one hand, so many pieces of my life that reflect the pursuits of my heart and mind. Although biographical details are only mentioned in passing, the pulse of experience—of places and faces, scenes, and struggles—gives source to these pages, like roots to a many-branched tree. These talks and writings stem from that portion of my life that has been shaped by Buddhist thought and practice. Yet encounter with the Dharma has the effect of retrieving much that went before, and validating it in a new light. So, in the philosophical reflections of the middle-aged Buddhist scholar, there is also the nine-year-old, exploding out of school and running in Central Park, stuffing acorns in her pocket.

Given the nature of this assortment of pieces, it is not essential that they be read in any particular order. Except for the last section, they did not arise sequentially. Thought and experience recounted in the second and third parts of the book are basic to the perspectives I share in the first. Yet the order in which I have placed these chapters is not random; it means to convey the dynamics by which we make sense of our world and find the capacity to enter it and take action creatively and with authority.

As Part One encourages us, we begin with our own experience, for that is what we know first-hand. The Buddha summoned people to do just that: to rely on the authority of their own experience. *"Ehipassiko,"* he said, "Come see for yourself." And what we're invited first to see, as he made clear in the First Noble Truth, is our suffering. In our collective situation today, with its almost overwhelming social and environmental crises, trusting our own experience means acknowledging our deep, inner responses, our anguish for the world. This pain is ours, it is real. If we are brave enough to confront it and own it, it has much to tell us. It tells us that we are alive and capable of suffering *with* our world—that we are by nature compassionate beings, or *bodhisattvas.* This capacity to suffer reveals our caring and our deep interconnections with all life-forms. From that "interbeing" arises the power to act and the power to heal. Indeed, a fresh perspective on the very nature of power emerges, freeing us from outmoded, hierarchical views. It emboldens us to walk out into the world as into our own hearts.

Joy, too, can reveal the world as lover and as self, but pain is the most patient and powerful of teachers. Our ability to befriend our pain and dance with it is basic to the trainings I have conducted around the world in empowerment for social action. This ability and the power it releases rely on no external dogmas or doctrines, just the sheer capacity to trust our own experience.

Fortunately, conceptual aids are also at hand to shed light on our experience and help us understand and articulate the power of our interbeing in the web of life. We need to train our minds to these understandings, for our society, relentlessly conditioning us to assume that we are separate, isolated beings, catches us up in competitive games fostered by dysfunctional notions of hierarchical power. The Buddha's central teaching of dependent co-arising offers the most elegant ways I know for perceiving the dynamics of interdependent power in our own lives, and for breaking free to reclaim the birthright of our interbeing. This teaching and its import for our lives is presented in Part Two, along with references to general systems theory, a helpful, contemporary perspective arising from Western science and remarkably consonant with the Buddha's teaching of dependent co-arising.

This section, "Rediscovering the Early Buddhist Teachings," may demand more rigorous and sustained attention than other parts of the book. I urge readers, especially Buddhist practitioners, to persist—and allow themselves time to reflect—for these chapters present an important corrective to widespread misconceptions about the Dharma, particularly about the relative reality of self and world, and the nature of liberation. The perspectives presented here have been fundamental to my social action in movements for peace, justice, and the environment, and to my trainings in Despair and Empowerment Work and Deep Ecology Work. Readers of a philosophic bent can acquaint themselves more fully with the Buddha's teaching of dependent co-arising, and its convergence with general systems theory, through my book *Mutual Causality: The Dharma of Natural Systems*. Like the chapters in Part Two, this book is the fruit of the years of doctoral work I did after returning from Asia.

Encounters in Asia first introduced me to the Buddha Dharma and then, in the course of subsequent sojourns and field work, revealed its capacity to transform lives with meaning and courage. Including Tibetans of Vajrayana Buddhism and Indians and Sri Lankans of Theravadin Buddhism, these encounters and relationships have illumined my life. Some of the lessons they gave me are recounted in Part Three, "Learning in Asia." The distant companions referred to are very present to me as I assemble this book. Without them, I suppose, I could still have learned about the Dharma and read the scriptures and practiced the meditations. But it is hard to imagine how, if I had not known them, I would have experienced such delight in the teachings or known the ways they can transform a society.

Part Four, "Opening New Doors," describes just that—how these teachings have swung open new possibilities, new visions and experiences in social action for the healing of our world. Here I have included pieces on the Deep Ecology Work that I developed with Buddhist-oriented colleagues, including the Council of All Beings, to heal our relationship with other life-forms, and on the Deep Time Work and the Nuclear Guardianship Project, to heal our relationship with beings of the future time.

Throughout, at each step, it is evident that action on behalf of life transforms. Because the relationship between self and world is reciprocal, it is not a question of first getting enlightened or saved and *then* acting. As we work to heal the Earth, the Earth heals us. No need to wait. As we care enough to take risks, we loosen the grip of ego and begin to come home to our true nature. For, in the co-arising nature of things, the world itself, if we are bold to love it, acts through us. It does not ask us to be pure or perfect, or wait until we are detached from all passions, but only to care, to harness the sweet, pure intention of our deepest passions, and—as the early scripture of the Mother of All Buddhas says—"fly" like a bodhisattva.

So my heart is full of thanks, as I offer this book. But whom do I thank? In addition to my patient publisher, this book is indebted to countless teachers. If I were to name my Tibetan Dharma brothers and sisters and the Sarvodaya workers, I would need also to mention the Buddha, and the venerable lineages that preserved the teachings, and the nineteenth century British scholars who retrieved the early texts, and then, too, my minister at the Fifth Avenue Presbyterian Church, who also modelled compassion, and my grandmothers Nonnie and Daidee who never heard of the Dharma, and the trees in Central Park that gave me respite from an asphalt world. In this panorama of co-arising it is hard to single out particular beings to thank, for the gratitude seems as big as the world itself—my beloved, generous world.

J.M.
Berkeley, California
March 1991

PART ONE

Trusting Our Experience

CHAPTER ONE

World As Lover, World As Self

Our planet is in trouble. It is hard to go anywhere without being confronted by the wounding of our world, the tearing of the very fabric of life. I return this day from Germany, where I lived in the 1950s amidst the clear waters, rich green fields, and woodlands of Bavaria. Now there is an environmental plague there called *waldsterben*, "the dying of the trees," and the Black Forest is reckoned to be about 50% dead from industrial and automobile pollution.

South of the Black Forest rise the headwaters of the Rhine, which flows on down through Basel, across Europe, and into the North Sea. A 1986 fire at the Sandoz chemical plant in Basel washed 30,000 tons of mercury and dioxin-forming chemicals into that once great, life-bearing artery of Europe. Millions of fish floated belly-up, and the deaths of seals as far away as the North Sea have been traced to the accident. Along this majestic river, requiems were held. On its many bridges, people gathered, banging on pots, pans, and anything that could make a noise, and cried, *"Der Rhein ist tot!"* "The Rhine is dead!"

I went to Germany to lead a workshop, just south of the Black Forest, near the source of the Rhine. We came together to explore the inner resources that are needed to take action in today's world. The corner of Europe where we met, given the prevailing winds in April and May of 1986, received some of the heaviest radioactive fallout from the disaster at the nuclear power plant in Chernobyl. During the workshop, one participant brought out a loaf of bread and said, reverently, "This was made from grains harvested before Chernobyl! We can eat it without fear."

Adapted from the Viriditas Lecture on Spiritual Values and Contemporary Issues, November 1987, Berkeley, California, sponsored by Friends of Creation Spirituality.

In the face of what is happening, how do we avoid feeling overwhelmed and just giving up, turning to the many diversions and demands of our consumer societies?

It is essential that we develop our inner resources. We have to learn to look at things as they are, painful and overwhelming as that may be, for no healing can begin until we are fully present to our world, until we learn to sustain the gaze.

These concerns, obviously, are not limited to Germany. Two weeks before going, I led a similar workshop in England at a neo-Gothic castle in the Lake District. We were fifteen minutes from Barrow, the great ship-building town on the Irish Sea where the new British Trident submarine, with its mammoth load of nuclear warheads, was being constructed. Half an hour up the coast, the dirtiest nuclear reactor ever built, Sellafield, is turning the Irish Sea into the world's most radioactive body of water. Looking for the inner resources to deal with such a world, we felt very deeply the tragedies that are befalling it. As the poisoned winds of Chernobyl and the plutonium being dumped daily into the Irish Sea teach us, there are no boundaries to ecological disasters, no political borders to the perils that threaten us today.

Among the inner resources that we seek for sustaining our action and our sanity are what the Germans call *weltbild*, the way we view our world and our relationship to it. Let us reflect together on our basic posture vis-à-vis our world and how we may come to see it in ways that empower us to act.

By "our world," I mean the place we find ourselves, the scene upon which we play our lives. It is sending us signals of distress that have become so continual as to appear almost ordinary. We know about the loss of cropland and the spreading of hunger, the toxins in the air we breathe and the water we drink, and the die-off of fellow-species; we know about our nuclear and so-called conventional weapons that are deployed and poised on hair-trigger alert and the conflicts that ignite in practically every corner of the world. These warning signals tell us that we live in a world that can end, at least as a home for conscious life. I do not say it *will* end, but it *can* end. This very possibility changes everything for us.

There have been small groups throughout history that have proclaimed the end of the world, such as at the time of the first millennium and again during the Black Plague in Europe. These expectations arose within the context of religious faith, of a belief in a just but angry God ready to punish his wayward children. But now the prospect is spelled out in sober scientific data, not religious belief, and it is entirely devoid of transcendent meaning. I stress the unprecedented nature of our situation, because I want to inspire awe, respect, and compassion for what we are experiencing. With isolated exceptions, every generation prior to ours has lived with the assumption that other generations would follow. It has always been assumed, as an integral part of human experience, that the work of our hands and heads and hearts would live on through those who came after us, walking on the same earth beneath the same sky. Plagues, wars, and personal death have always taken place within that wider context, the assurance of continuity. Now we have lost the certainty that we will have a future. I believe that this loss, felt at some level of consciousness by everyone, regardless of political orientation, is the pivotal psychological reality of our time.

These signals of impending doom bring with them a sense of urgency to do something. But there are so many programs, strategies, and causes that vie for our attention that we may feel overwhelmed. So it is good to pause and ground ourselves, to look at our *weltbild*, at the ways we see and relate to our world, and discover what ways can best sustain us to do what must be done. With this in mind, I would like to reflect on four particular ways that people on spiritual paths look at the world. These are not specific to any particular religion; you can find all of them in most spiritual traditions. These four are: world as battlefield, world as trap, world as lover, world as self.

Many people view the *world as a battlefield,* where good and evil are pitted against each other, and the forces of light battle the forces of darkness. This ancient tradition goes back to the Zoroastrians and the Manichaeans. It can be persuasive, especially when you feel threatened. Such a view is very good for arousing courage, summoning up the blood, using the fiery energies of anger, aversion, and militancy. It is very good, too, for giving a sense of certainty. Whatever the score may be at the moment or whatever tactics you are using, there is the sense that you are fighting God's battle and that ultimately you will win. William Irwin Thompson has called this kind of certainty and the self-righteousness that goes with it, the "apartheid of good."

We see this in many areas of our world today, in Beirut and Belfast, in the Persian Gulf and South Asia, even in my beloved Sri Lanka, a home of the most tolerant of religions. And we see it in our own country. The Jerry Falwells of society evoke the righteousness of this divinely ordained battle, leading, as they see that it must, to Armageddon and the Second Coming of Christ. In this variety of Christian thought, nuclear war may be the catalyst for the millennial dénouement, bringing just rewards to the elect, who will inherit the Earth—and the Bomb itself can appear as an instrument of God's will.

A more innocuous version of the battlefield image of the world is the one I learned from my grandparents. It is the world as a classroom, a kind of moral gymnasium where you are put through certain tests which would prove your mettle and teach you certain lessons, so you can graduate to other arenas and rewards. Whether a battlefield or classroom, the world is a proving ground, with little worth other than that. What counts are our immortal souls, which are being tested here. They count, and the world doesn't. For the sake of your soul, whether you are a Jerry Falwell or an Ayatollah Khomeini, you are ready to destroy.

If you feel our world has seen enough destruction already, this view may be unappealing. But it is strong among monotheistic religions, and it is contagious. Agnostics, too, can feel a tremendous do-or-die militancy and self-righteousness. Even adherents of more tolerant and non-theistic religions betray this kind of fundamentalism, a conviction that you are on the side of the good and, therefore, whatever you do is permitted, if not required. I don't expect many readers to leap to the defense of this view, especially as I am presenting it in so bald and biased a fashion. But it is important that we recognize its presence, its appeal, and its tenacity.

Let us turn to the second view: *the world as trap.* Here, the spiritual path is not to engage in struggle and vanquish a foe, but to disentangle ourselves and escape from this messy world. We try to extricate ourselves and ascend to a higher, supra-phenomenal plane. This stance is based on a hierarchical view of reality, where mind is seen as higher than matter and spirit is set over and above nature. This view encourages contempt for the material plane. Elements of it have entered all major religions of the last 3,000 years, regardless of their metaphysics.

Many of us on spiritual paths fall for this view. Wanting to affirm a transcendent reality distinct from a society that appears very materialistic, we place it on a supra-phenomenal level removed from confusion and suffering. The tranquility that spiritual practices can provide, we imagine, belongs to a haven that is aloof from our world and to which we can ascend and be safe and serene. This gets tricky, because we still have bodies and are dependent on them, however advanced we may be on the spiritual path. Trying to escape from something that we are dependent on breeds a love-hate relationship with it. This love-hate relationship with matter permeates our culture and inflames a twofold desire—to destroy and to possess. These two impulses, craving and aversion, inflame each other in a kind of vicious circle. In the terms of general systems theory, the desire to destroy and the desire to possess form a deviation-amplifying feedback loop. We can see this exemplified in our military arsenal. To back up our demands for the raw materials we want, we threaten their very existence. To sustain our technologies' capacity to destroy, we require increasing amounts of raw materials; and the vicious circle continues, exponentially.

Many on a spiritual path, seeking to transcend all impulses to acquire or to destroy, put great value on detachment. "Let us move beyond all desire or any actions that might inflame desire." And they are reluctant to engage in the hurly-burly work of social change. Some of my fellow Buddhists seem to understand detachment as becoming free from the world and indifferent to its fate. They forget that what the Buddha taught was detachment from ego, not detachment from the world. In fact, the Buddha was suspicious of those who tried to detach themselves from the realm of matter. In referring to some yogis who mortified the flesh in order to free the spirit, the Buddha likened their efforts to those of a dog tied by a rope to a stake in the ground. He said that the harder they tried to free themselves from the body, the more they would circle round and get closer to the stake, eventually wrapping themselves around it.

Of course, even when you see the world as a trap and posit a fundamental separation between liberation of self and transformation of society, you can still feel a compassionate impulse to help its suffering beings. In that case you tend to view the personal and the political in a sequential fashion. "I'll get enlightened first, and then I'll engage in social action." Those who are not engaged in spiritual pursuits put it differently: "I'll get my head straight first, I'll get psychoanalyzed, I'll overcome my inhibitions or neuroses or my hangups (whatever description you give to *samsara*), and *then* I'll wade into the fray." Presupposing that world and self are essentially separate, they imagine they can heal one before healing the other. This stance conveys the impression that human consciousness inhabits some haven, or locker-room, independent of the collective situation—and then trots onto the playing field when it is geared up and ready.

It is my experience that the world itself has a role to play in our liberation. Its very pressures, pains, and risks can wake us up—release us from the bonds of ego and guide us home to our vast, true nature. For some of us, our love for the world is so passionate that we cannot ask it to wait until we are enlightened.

So let us now discuss the third view: *world as lover.* Instead of a stage set for our moral battles or a prison to escape, the world is beheld as a most intimate and gratifying partner. In Hinduism, we find some of the richest expressions of our erotic relationship to the world. In early Vedic hymns, the first stirrings of life are equated with that primal pulse of *eros.* In the beginning there was the sacred, self-existent one, Prajapati. Lonely, it created the world by splitting into that with which it could copulate. Pregnant with its own inner amplitude and tension, it gave birth to all phenomena, out of desire. Desire plays a creative, world-manifesting role here, and its charge in Hinduism pulses onward into Krishna worship, where devotional songs, or *bhajans,* draw on the erotic yearnings of body and soul. Krishna evokes them to bring to his devotees the bliss of union with the divine. As you sing your yearning for the sparkle of his eyes, the touch of his lips, the blue shade of his skin—like the thunderclouds that bring the refreshment and fertility of the monsoon—the whole world takes on his beauty and the sweetness of his flesh. You feel yourself embraced in the primal erotic play of life.

That erotic affirmation of the phenomenal world is not limited to Hinduism. Ancient Goddess religions, now being explored (at last!) carry it too, as do strains of Sufism and the Kabbalah, and Christianity has its tradition of bridal mysticism. It also occurs outside of religious metaphor. A poet friend of mine went through a period of such personal loss that she was catapulted into extreme loneliness. Falling apart into a nervous breakdown, she went to New York City and lived alone. She walked the streets for months until she found her wholeness again. A phrase of hers echoes in my mind: "I learned to move in the world as if it were my lover."

Another Westerner who sees the world as lover is Italian story-teller Italo Calvino. In his little book, *Cosmicomics,* he describes the evolution of life from the perspective of an individual who experienced it from the beginning, even before the Big Bang. The chapter I want to recount begins with a sentence from science. "Through the calculations begun by Edwin P. Hubble on the galaxies' velocity of recession, we can establish the moment when all the universe's matter was concentrated in a single point, before it began to expand in space."

"We were all there, where else could we have been?" says Calvino's narrator, Qfwfq, as he describes his experience. "We were all in that one point—and, man, was it crowded! Contrary to what you might think, it wasn't the sort of situation that encourages sociability..." Given the conditions, irritations were almost inevitable. See, in addition to all those people, "you have to add all the stuff we had to keep piled up in there: all the material that was to serve afterwards to form the universe...from the nebula of Andromeda to the Vosges Mountains to beryllium isotopes. And on top of that we were always bumping against the Z'zu family's household goods: camp beds, mattresses, baskets..."

So there were, naturally enough, complaints and gossip, but none ever attached to Mrs. Pavacini. (Since most names in the story have no vowels, I have given her a name we can pronounce.) "Mrs. Pavacini, her bosom, her thighs, her orange dressing gown," the sheer memory of her fills our narrator

> with a blissful, generous emotion...The fact that she went to bed with her friend Mr. DeXuaeauX, was well-known. But in a point, if there's a bed, it takes up the whole point, so it isn't a question of *going* to bed but of *being* there, because anybody in the point is also in the bed. So consequently it was inevitable that she was in bed with each of us. If she'd been another person, there's no telling all the things that might have been said about her...

This state of affairs could have gone on indefinitely, but something extraordinary happened. An idea occurred to Mrs. Pavacini: "Oh boys, if only I had some room, how I'd like to make some pasta for you!" Here I quote in part from my favorite longest sentence in literature, which closes this particular chapter in Calvino's collection:

> And in that moment we all thought of the space that her round arms would occupy moving backward and forward over the great mound of flour and eggs...while her arms kneaded and kneaded, white and shiny with oil up to the elbows, and we thought of the space the flour would occupy and the wheat for the flour and the fields to raise the wheat and the mountains from which the water would flow to irrigate the fields...of the space it would take for the Sun to arrive with its rays, to ripen the wheat; of the space for the Sun to condense from the clouds of stellar gases and burn; of the quantities of stars and galaxies and galactic masses in flight through space which would be needed to hold suspended every galaxy, every nebula, every sun, every planet, and at the same time we thought of it, this space was inevitably being formed, at the same time that Mrs. Pavacini was uttering those words: "...ah, what pasta, boys!" The point that contained her and all of us was expanding in a halo of distance in light years and light centuries and billions of light millennia and we were being hurled to the four corners of the universe...and she dissolved into I don't know what kind of energy-light-heat, she, Mrs. Pavacini, she who in the midst of our closed, petty world had been capable of a generous impulse, "Boys, the pasta I could make for you!" a true outburst of general love, initiating at the same time the concept of space and, properly speaking, space itself, and time, and universal gravitation, and the gravitating universe, making possible billions and billions of suns, and planets, and fields of wheat, and Mrs. Pavacinis scattered through the continents of the planets, kneading with floury, oil-shiny, generous arms and she lost at that very moment, and we, mourning her loss.

But is she lost? Or is she equally present, in every moment, her act of love embodied in every unfolding of this amazing world? Whether we see it as Krishna or as Mrs. Pavacini, that teasing, loving presence is in the monsoon clouds and the peacock's cry that heralds monsoon, and in the plate of good pasta. For when you see the world as lover, every being, every phenomenon, can become—if you have a clever, appreciative eye—an expression of that ongoing, erotic impulse. It takes form right now in each one of us and in everyone and everything we encounter—the bus driver, the clerk at the checkout counter, the leaping squirrel. As we seek to discover the lover in each life-form, you can find yourself in the dance of *rasa-lila*, sweet play, where each of the milkmaids who yearned for Krishna finds him magically at her side, her very own partner in the dance. The one beloved has become many, and the world itself her lover.

Since, as Calvino reminds us, we were "all in one point" to begin with, we could as easily see the *world as self*. Just as lovers seek for union, we are apt, when we fall in love with our world, to fall into oneness with it as well. Hunger for this union springs from a deep knowing, to which mystics of all traditions give voice. Breaking open a seed to reveal its life-giving kernel, the sage in the *Upanishads* tells his student: "*Tat tvam asi*—That art thou." The tree that will grow from the seed, that art thou; the running water, that art thou, and the sun in the sky, and all that is, that art thou.

"There is a Secret One inside us," says Kabir, "the planets in all the galaxies pass through his hands like beads." Mystics of the Western traditions have tended to speak of merging self with God rather than with the world, but the import is often the same. When Hildegard of Bingen experienced unity with the divine, she gave it these words: "I am the breeze that nurtures all things green...I am the rain coming from the dew that causes the grasses to laugh with the joy of life."

In times like our own recent centuries, when the manifest world is considered less real and alive than ideas inside our heads, the mystic impulse reaches beyond it and seeks union with a transcendent deity. But once the bonds of limited ego snap, that blazing unity knows no limits. It embraces the most ordinary and physical of phenomena. The individual heart becomes one with its world, and expresses it in imageries of circle and net. The fifteenth century cardinal, Nicholas of Cusa, defined God as an infinite circle whose periphery is nowhere and whose center is everywhere. That center, that one self, is in you and me and the tree outside the door. Similarly, the Jeweled Net of Indra, the vision of reality that arose with *Hua Yen* Buddhism, re-vealed a world where each being, each gem at each node of the net, is illumined by all the others and reflected in them. As part of this world, you contain the whole of it.

Today this perception arises in realms of science as well. The founder of general systems theory, biologist Ludwig von Bertalanffy, shows how all self-organizing systems are created and sustained by the dynamics at play in the larger systems of our universe. The part contains the whole, he says, and acknowledges his debt to Nicholas of Cusa. Systems thinker Gregory Bateson describes cognitive open systems, our minds, in terms of a flow-through of information, where no separate self can be delimited. Mind itself is immanent in nature, he says, extending far beyond the tiny spans illumined by our conscious purposes.

The way we define and delimit the self is arbitrary. We can place it between our ears and have it looking out from our eyes, or we can widen it to include the air we breathe, or, at other moments, we can cast its boundaries farther to include the oxygen-giving trees and plankton, our external lungs, and beyond them the web of life in which they are sustained.

I used to think that I ended with my skin, that everything within the skin was me and everything outside the skin was not. But now you've read these words, and the concepts they represent are reaching your cortex, so "the process" that is me now extends as far as you. And where, for that matter, did this process begin? I certainly can trace it to my teachers, some of whom I never met, and to my husband and children, who give me courage and support to do the work I do, and to the plant and animal beings who sustain my body. What I am, as systems theorists have helped me see, is a "flow-through." I am a flow-through of matter, energy, and information, which is transformed in turn by my own experiences and intentions. Systems theory seeks to define the principles by which this transformation occurs, but not the stuff itself that flows through, for that, in the last analysis, would be a metaphysical endeavor. Systems thinkers Kenneth and Elise Boulding suggest that we could simply call it *agape*— the Greek and early-Christian word for "love."

Systems thinking is basic to the swiftly developing science of ecology, and its import for our relationship to the world is expressed most clearly in the movement of thought called "deep ecology." This term was coined in the mid-1970s by Norwegian philosopher and mountain-climber, Arne Naess, to contrast with the environmentalism that still sets the self apart from its world. Environmental efforts that focus on cleaning up the Hudson River or San Francisco Bay for the sake of our own species are inadequate. These tend to be short-term, technological fixes, band-aid approaches to ecological problems, because they do not address the sources of these problems, which is our stance in relation to our world. What is destroying our world is the persistent notion that we are independent of it, aloof from other species, and immune to what we do to them. Our survival, Naess says, requires shifting into more encompassing ideas of who we are.

To experience the world as an extended self and its story as our own extended story involves no surrender or eclipse of our individuality. The liver, leg, and lung that are "mine" are highly distinct from each other, thank goodness, and each has a distinctive role to play. The larger selfness we discover today is not an undifferentiated unity. Our recognition of this may be the third part of an unfolding of consciousness that began a long time ago, like the third movement of a symphony.

In the first movement, our infancy as a species, we felt no separation from the natural world around us. Trees, rocks, and plants surrounded us with a living presence as intimate and pulsing as our own bodies. In that primal intimacy, which anthropologists call "participation mystique," we were as one with our world as a child in the mother's womb.

Then self-consciousness arose and gave us distance on our world. We needed that distance in order to make decisions and strategies, in order to measure, judge and to monitor our judgments. With the emergence of free-will, the fall out of the Garden of Eden, the second movement began—the lonely and heroic journey of the ego. Nowadays, yearning to reclaim a sense of wholeness, some of us tend to disparage that movement of separation from nature, but it brought great gains for which we can be grateful. The distanced and observing eye brought us tools of science, and a priceless view of the vast, orderly intricacy of our world. The recognition of our individuality brought us trial by jury and the Bill of Rights.

Now, harvesting these gains, we are ready to return. The third movement begins. Having gained distance and sophistication of perception, we can turn and recognize who we have been all along. Now it can dawn on us: we are our world knowing itself. We can relinquish our separateness. We can come home again—and participate in our world in a richer, more responsible and poignantly beautiful way than before, in our infancy.

Because of the journey we undertook to distance ourselves from our world, it is no longer undifferentiated from us. It can appear to us now both as self and as lover. Relating to our world with the full measure of our being, we partake of the qualities of both. I think of a poem, "The Old Mendicant," by Vietnamese Zen master Thich Nhat Hanh. In it he evokes the long, wondrous evolutionary journey we all have made together, from which we are as inseparable as from our own selves. At the same time, it is a love song. Hear these lines, as if addressed to you.

> Being rock, being gas, being mist, being Mind,
> Being the mesons traveling among galaxies with the
> speed of light,
> You have come here, my beloved one. . .
> You have manifested yourself as trees, as grass, as
> butterflies, as single-celled beings, and as
> chrysanthemums;
> but the eyes with which you looked at me this morning
> tell me you have never died.

We have all gone that long journey, and now, richer for it, we come home to our mutual belonging. We return to experience, as we never could before, that we are both the self of our world and its cherished lover. We are not doomed to destroy it by the cravings of the separate ego and the technologies it fashioned. We can wake up to who we really are, and allow the waters of the Rhine to flow clean once more, and the trees to grow green along its banks.

CHAPTER TWO

Despair Work

We are bombarded by signals of distress—ecological destruction, social breakdown, and uncontrolled nuclear proliferation. Not surprisingly, we are feeling despair— a despair well merited by the machinery of mass death that we continue to create and serve. What is surprising is the extent to which we continue to hide this despair from ourselves and each other. If this is, as Arthur Koestler suggested, an age of anxiety, it is also an age in which we are adept at sweeping our anxieties under the rug. As a society we are caught between a sense of impending apocalypse and an inability to acknowledge it.

Activists who try to arouse us to the fact that our survival is at stake decry public apathy. The cause of our apathy, however, is not mere indifference. It stems from a fear of confronting the despair that lurks subliminally beneath the tenor of life-as-usual. A dread of what is happening to our future stays on the fringes of awareness, too deep to name and too fearsome to face. Sometimes it manifests in dreams of mass destruction, and is exorcised in the morning jog and shower or in the public fantasies of disaster movies. Because of social taboos against despair and because of fear of pain, it is rarely acknowledged or expressed directly. It is kept at bay. The suppression of despair, like that of any deep recurrent response, produces a partial numbing of the psyche. Expressions of anger or terror are muted, deadened as if a nerve had been cut.

The refusal to feel takes a heavy toll. Not only is there an impoverishment of our emotional and sensory life—flowers are dimmer and less fragrant, our loves less ecstatic—but this psychic numbing also impedes our capacity to process and respond to information. The energy expended in pushing down despair is diverted from more

---

Abridged from the booklet *Despairwork*, (New Society Publishers: Philadelphia, 1981.)

creative uses, depleting the resilience and imagination needed for fresh visions and strategies. Furthermore, the fear of despair can erect an invisible screen, selectively filtering out anxiety-provoking data. In a world where organisms require feedback in order to adapt and survive, this is suicidal. Now, when we urgently need to measure the effects of our acts, our attention and curiosity slacken as if we are already preparing for the Big Sleep. Many of us doggedly attend to business-as-usual, denying both our despair and our inability to cope with it.

Despair cannot be banished by injections of optimism or sermons on "positive thinking." Like grief, it must be acknowledged and worked through. This means it must be named and validated as a healthy, normal human response to the situation we find ourselves in. Faced and experienced, its power can be used, as the frozen defenses of the psyche thaw and new energies are released. Something analogous to grief work is in order. "Despair work" is different from griefwork in that its aim is not acceptance of loss—indeed, the "loss" has not yet occurred and is hardly to be "accepted." But it is similar in the dynamics unleashed by the willingness to acknowledge, feel, and express inner pain. From my own work and that of others, I know that we can come to terms with apocalyptic anxieties in ways that are integrative and liberating, opening awareness not only to planetary distress, but also to the hope inherent in our own capacity to change.

INGREDIENTS OF DESPAIR

Whether or not we choose to accord them serious attention, we are barraged by data that render questionable the survival of our culture, our species, and even our planet as a viable home for conscious life. These warning signals prefigure, to those who do take them seriously, probabilities of apocalypse that are mind-boggling in scope. While varied, each scenario presents its own relentless logic. Poisoned by oil spills, sludge, and plutonium, the seas are dying; when the plankton disappear (by the year 2010 at present pollution rates, according to Jacques Yves Cousteau), we will suffocate from lack of oxygen. *Or* carbon dioxide from industrial and automotive combustion will saturate the atmosphere, creating a greenhouse effect that will melt the polar icecaps. *Or* radioactive poisoning from nuclear reactors and their wastes will accelerate plagues of cancer and genetic mutations. *Or* deforestation and desertification of the planet, now rapidly advancing, will produce giant dustbowls, and famines beyond imagining. The probability of each of these perils is amply and soberly documented by scientific studies. The list of such scenarios could continue, including use of nuclear bombs by terrorists or nation states—a prospect presenting vistas of such horror that, as former Soviet Premier Nikita Khruschev said, "The survivors will envy the dead."

Despair, in this context, is not a macabre certainty of doom or a pathological condition of depression and futility. It is not a nihilism denying meaning or efficacy to human effort. Rather, as it is being experienced by increasing numbers of people across a broad spectrum of society, despair is *the loss of the assumption that the species will inevitably pull through.* It represents a genuine accession to the possibility that this planetary experiment will end, the curtain rung down, the show over.

SYMPTOMS AND SUPPRESSIONS

In India, at a leprosarium, I met a young mother of four. Her leprosy was advanced, the doctor pointed out, because for so long she had hidden its signs. Fearing ostracism and banishment, she had covered her sores with her sari, pulled the shoulder drape around so no one would see. In a similar fashion did I later hide despair for our world, cloaking it like a shameful disease—and so, I have learned, do others. At the prospect of the extinction of a civilization, feelings of grief and horror are natural. We tend to hide them, though, from ourselves and each other. Why? The reasons, I think, are both social and psychological.

When the sensations aroused by the contemplation of a likely and avoidable end to human existence break through the censorship we tend to impose on them, they can be intense and physical. A friend who left her career to work as a full-time anti-nuclear organizer, says her onslaughts of grief come as a cold, heavy weight on the chest and a sense of her body breaking. Mine, which began years ago after an all-day symposium on threats to our biosphere, were sudden and wrenching. I would be at my desk, alone in my study translating a Buddhist text, and the next moment I would find myself on the floor, curled like a fetus and shaking. In company I was more controlled; but even then, in those early months when I was unused to despair, I would be caught off guard. A line from Shakespeare or a Bach phrase would pierce me with pain as I found myself wondering how much longer it would be heard, before fading out forever in the galactic silences.

In a culture committed to the American dream, it is hard to own up to despair. This is still the land of Dale Carnegie and Norman Vincent Peale, where an unflagging optimism is taken as the means and measure of success. As commercials for products and campaigns of politicians attest, the healthy and admirable person smiles a lot. The feelings of depression, loneliness, and anxiety, to which this thinking animal has always been heir, carry here an added burden: one feels bad about feeling bad. One can even feel guilty about it. The failure to hope, in a country built and nurtured on utopian expectations, can seem downright un-American.

In a religious context, despair can appear as a lapse of faith. At a vigil before a peace demonstration at the Pentagon, a noted religious leader spoke of the necessity of hope to carry us through. Others chimed in, affirming their belief in the vision of a "new Jerusalem" and their gratitude for having that hope. After a pause, a young man, who planned to participate in the week's civil disobedience actions, spoke up falteringly. He questioned whether hope was really a prerequisite, because—and he admitted this with difficulty—he was not feeling it. Even among friends committed to the same goal, it was hard for him (and brave of him, I thought) to admit despair. Evidently, he feared he would be misunderstood, taken as cowardly or cynical—a fear confirmed by the response of some present.

Despair is tenaciously resisted because it represents a loss of control, an admission of powerlessness. Our culture dodges it by demanding instant solutions when problems are raised. My political science colleagues in France ridiculed this, I recall, as an endemic trait of the American personality. "You people prescribe before you finish the diagnosis," they would say. "Let the difficulties reveal themselves first before rushing for a ready-made solution or else you will not understand them." To do this would require that one view a stressful situation without the psychic security of knowing if and how it can be solved—in other words, a readiness to suffer a little.

"Don't come to me with a problem unless you have a solution," Lyndon B. Johnson is quoted as saying during the Vietnam War. That tacit injunction, operative even in public policy-making, rings like the words my mother said to me as a child, "If you can't say something nice, don't say anything at all."

In our culture the acknowledgment of despair for the future is a kind of social taboo and those who break it are considered "crazy," or at least "depressed and depressing." No one wants a Cassandra around or welcomes a Banquo at the feast. Nor are such roles enjoyable to play. When the prospect of our collective suicide first hit me as a serious possibility—and I know well the day and hour my defenses against this despair suddenly collapsed—I felt that there was no one to whom I could turn in my grief. If there were—and indeed there was, for I have loving, intelligent friends and family— what is there to say? Do I want them to feel this horror too? What can be said without casting a pall, or without seeming to ask for unacceptable words of comfort and cheer?

To feel despair in such a cultural setting brings a sense of isolation. The psychic dissonance can be so acute as to seem to border on madness. The distance between our inklings of apocalypse and the tenor of business-as-usual is so great that, though we may respect our own cognitive reading of the signs, we tend to imagine that it is we, not the society, who are insane.

Psychotherapy, by and large, has offered little help for coping with these feelings, and indeed has often compounded the problem. Many therapists have difficulty crediting the notion that concerns for the general welfare might be acute enough to cause distress. Assuming that all our drives are ego-centered, they tend to treat expressions of this distress reductionistically, as manifestations of private neurosis. In my own case, deep dismay over destruction of the wilderness was diagnosed by a counselor as fear of my own libido (which the bulldozers were taken to symbolize), and my painful preoccupation with U.S. bombings of Vietnam was interpreted as an unwholesome hangover of Puritan guilt. Such "therapy," of course, only intensifies the sense of isolation and craziness that despair can bring, while inhibiting its recognition and expression.

Some of the biggest money-makers in the film industry, as Andrée Conrad points out in *Disaster and the American Imagination,* are movies that feature cataclysmic events and violent mass death. Earthquakes, rampaging sharks and killer bees, blazing skyscrapers and doomed craft in air and sea, loaded with panicked passengers, vie in imageries of terror. Contrived with technical brilliance, these films draw large crowds and large profits. Their appeal, indeed their fascination, stems from an inchoate but pervasive sense of doom in the American public. The scenarios they present give structure and outlet to unformulated fears of apocalypse, and in so doing provide catharsis. But it is a dangerous catharsis, Conrad observes.

Hooking our anxieties onto isolated and unlikely emergencies, frequently handled with technological heroics, these entertainments give their audience, sitting safely in a comfortable theater, the illusion of having dealt with what is bothering them. On fictitious, improbable themes they air and exercise our dread, while habituating us to prospects of mass death and raising our horror threshold another notch. They blur the boundaries between fantasy and reality, making the next day's news seem like more of the same—alarms to be passively watched until the credits appear and we can stop for a beer on our way to bed.

These entertainments constitute a new version of what Geoffrey Gorer in the 1950s called our "pornography of death." He pointed out that, just as the repression of sex in our puritanically-conditioned culture produces debased expressions of it, so is our repression of the reality of personal death released in fascination with sadistic violence. By analogous reasoning, disaster films can be seen as pornographies of despair. In the same way that X-rated "adult" flicks cheapen the sexual hungers they trade on, the towering infernos and devouring jaws dull and divert us from the true dimensions of our despair.

Until we get in touch with them, our powers of creative response to planetary crisis will be crippled. Until we can grieve for our planet and its future inhabitants, we cannot fully feel or enact our love for them. Such grief is frequently suppressed, not only because it is socially awkward. It is also denied because it is both painful and hard to believe. At the root of both inhibitions lies a dysfunctional notion of the self. It is the notion of the self as an isolated and fragile entity.

Such a self has no reason to weep for the unseen and the unborn, and such a self, if it did, might shatter with pain and futility.

So long as we see ourselves as essentially separate, competitive, and ego-identified beings, it is difficult to respect the validity of our social despair, deriving as it does from interconnectedness. Both our capacity to grieve for others and our power to cope with this grief spring from the great matrix of relationships in which we take our being. We are, as open systems, sustained by flows of energy and information that extend beyond the reach of conscious ego.

VALIDATING DESPAIR

You can hold yourself back from the suffering of the world:
this is something you are free to do, . . .but perhaps
precisely this holding back is the only suffering you might
be able to avoid.

—Franz Kafka

The first step in despair work is to disabuse ourselves of the notion that grief for our world is morbid. To experience anguish and anxiety in the face of the perils that threaten us is a healthy reaction. Far from being crazy, this pain is a testimony to the unity of life, the deep interconnections that relate us to all beings.

Such pain for the world becomes masochistic only when we assume personal guilt for its plight or personal responsibility for its solution. No individual is that powerful. Certainly by participation in society each shares in collective accountability; but the acknowledgment of despair, like faith, is a letting go of the manipulative assumption that conscious ego can or should control all events. Each of us is but one little nexus in a vast web. As the recognition of that interdependence breaches our sense of isolation, so does it also free our despair of self-loathing.

Our religious heritages can also serve to validate despair and attest to the creative role of this kind of distress. The Biblical concept of the suffering servant, as well as an array of *Old Testament* prophets, speaks to the power inherent in opening ourselves to the griefs of others. In Christianity the paramount symbol of such power is the cross. The cross where Jesus died teaches us that it is precisely through openness to the pain of our world that redemption and renewal are found.

The heroes and heroines of the Mahayana Buddhist tradition are the bodhisattvas, who vow to forswear nirvana until all beings are enlightened. As the *Lotus Sutra* tells us, their compassion endows them with supranormal senses: they can hear the music of the spheres and understand the language of the birds. By the same token, they hear as well all cries of distress, even to the moaning of beings in the lowest hells. All griefs are registered and owned in the bodhisattva's deep knowledge that we are not separate from each other.

POSITIVE DISINTEGRATION

The process of internalizing the possibility of planetary demise is bound to bring some psychic disarray. How to confront what we scarcely dare to think? How to think it without going to pieces?

It is helpful in despair work to realize that going to pieces or falling apart is not such a bad thing. Indeed it is as essential to evolutionary and psychic transformations as the cracking of outgrown shells. Polish psychiatrist Kazimierz Dabrowski calls it "positive disintegration." It is operative in every global development of humanity, especially during periods of accelerated change, and, he argues, permits the emergence of "higher psychic structures and awareness." For the individual who, in confronting current anomalies of experience, allows positive disintegration to happen, it can bring a dark night of the soul, a time of spiritual void and turbulence. But the anxieties and doubts are, Dabrowski maintains, "essentially healthy and creative." They are creative not only for the person but for society, because they permit new and original approaches to reality.

What "disintegrates" in periods of rapid transformation is not the self, of course, but its defenses and ideas. We are not objects that can break. As open systems, we are, cyberneticist Norbert Wiener said, "but whirlpools in a river of everflowing water. We are not stuff that abides, but patterns that perpetuate themselves." We do not need to protect ourselves from change, for our very nature is change. Defensive self-protection, restricting vision and movement like a suit of armor, makes it harder to adapt. It not only reduces flexibility, but blocks the flow of information we need to survive. Our "going to pieces," however uncomfortable a process, can open us up to new perceptions, new data, new responses.

ALLOWING OURSELVES TO FEEL

The second requirement in despair work is to permit ourselves to feel. Within us are deep responses to what is happening to our world, responses of fear and sorrow and anger. Given the flows of information circling our globe, they inhere in us already by virtue of our nature as open systems, interdependent with the rest of life. We need only to open our consciousness to these profound apprehensions. We cannot experience them without pain, but it is a healthy pain— like the kind we feel when we walk on a leg that has gone asleep and the circulation starts to move again. It gives evidence that the tissue is still alive.

As with a cramped limb, exercises can help. I have found meditational exercises useful, particularly ones from the Buddhist tradition. Practices designed to increase the capacity for loving-kindness and compassion, for example, are effective in getting us in touch with those concerns in us that extend beyond ego.

In one workshop I led, entitled "Being Bodhisattvas," we did a meditation on compassion, adapted from a Tibetan *bodhicitta* practice. It involved giving oneself permission to experience the sufferings of others (in as concrete a fashion as possible), and then taking these sufferings in with the breath, visualizing them as dark granules in the stream of air drawn in with each inhalation, into and through the heart, and out again.

Afterwards one participant, Marianna, described her experience in this meditation. She had been resistant, and her resistance had localized as a pain in her back. In encouraging the participants to open themselves to their inner awareness of the sufferings of others, I primed the pump with some brief verbal cues, mentioned our fellow beings in hospitals and prisons, mentioned a mother with dried breasts holding a hungry infant...That awoke in Marianna an episode she had buried. Three years earlier she had listened to a recording by Harry Chapin with a song about a starving child; she had, as she put it, "trouble" with it. She put away the record never to play it again, and the "trouble" remained undigested. With her recollection of her experience with the song, the pain in her back moved into her chest. It intensified and hardened, piercing her heart. It seemed for a moment excruciating; but as she continued the exercise, accepting and breathing in the pain, it suddenly, inexplicably, felt right, felt even good. It turned into a golden cone or funnel, aimed point downwards into the depths of her heart. Through it poured the despair she had refused, griefs reconnecting her with the rest of humanity.

Marianna emerged from this with a sense of release and belonging. She felt empowered, she said, not to *do* so much as to *be*—open, attentive, poised for action. She also said that she believed she permitted this to happen because I had not asked her to "do" something about the griefs of others, or to come up with any answers, but simply to experience them.

What good does it do to let go and allow ourselves to *feel* the pain of our planet's people? For all the discomfort, there is healing in such openness, for ourselves and for our world. To accept the collective pain reconnects us with our fellow beings and our deep collective energies.

ALLOWING IMAGES TO ARISE

To acknowledge our pain for the world and tap its energy, we need symbols and images for its expression. Images, more than arguments, tap the springs of consciousness, the creative powers by which we make meaning of experience. In the challenge to survival that we face now, a strong imagination is especially necessary because existing verbal constructs seem inadequate to what many of us are sensing.

At a week long meeting of college teachers and administrators, I chaired a working group on issues of planetary survival, and began to explore ways we could share our concerns on an affective as well as cognitive level. I asked the participants to offer, as they introduced themselves, a personal experience or image of how in the past year the global crisis had impinged on their consciousness. Those brief introductions were potent. Some offered a vignette from work on world hunger or arms. A young physicist simply said, very quietly, "My child was born." A social worker recalled a day her small daughter talked about growing up and having babies; with dull shock she encountered her own doubt that the world would last that long.

Some offered images: fish kill washed up at a summer cottage, strip mines leaching like open wounds. Most encompassing in its simplicity was John's image: the view from space of planet Earth, so small as it glittered there that it could be covered by the astronaut's raised thumb. That vision of our home, so finite it can be blotted out by a single human gesture, functioned as a symbol in our week's work. It helped us cut through the verbiage of reports and the temptations of academic one-upmanship, to the raw nerve in us all—desperate concern.

In the sharing of despair that our imagery had permitted, energy was released. As pent-up feelings were expressed and compared, there came laughter, solidarity, and resurgence of commitment to our common human project.

In that same working group on planetary survival, John showed slides of a trek up Mount Katahdin with some of his Yale students. On a ridge between two peaks was a narrow, knife-edge trail they had to cross. It was scary and dangerous because fog had rolled up, blanketing out the destination and everything but the foot-wide path itself. That picture of the trail, cutting through the clouds into the unknown became a strong symbol for us, expressing the existential situation in which we find ourselves, and helping us proceed with dogged patience, even though we cannot see more than a step at a time.

Recognizing the creative powers of imagery, many call us today to come up with visions of a benign future—visions which can beckon and inspire. Images of hope are potent, necessary: they shape our goals and give us impetus for reaching them. Often they are invoked too soon, however. Like the demand for instant solutions, such expectations can stultify—providing us with an escape from the despair we may feel, while burdening us with the task of aridly designing a new Eden. Genuine visioning happens from the roots up, and these roots for many are shrivelled by unacknowledged despair. Many of us are in an in-between time, groping in the dark with shattered beliefs and faltering hopes, and we need images for that in-between time if we are to work through it.

The first despair work I can recognize as such occurred on a spring weekend toward the end of our military actions in Vietnam. Although I had been active in anti-war protests, I felt sapped that day by a deep sense of futility. To give form to feeling, and tired of words, I worked with clay. As I descended into the sorrow within me, I shaped that descent in the block of clay—cliffs and escarpments plunging into abysses, dropping off into downward-twisting gullies, down, down. Though I wept as I pushed at the clay with fingers and fists, it felt good to have my sense of hopelessness become palpable, visible. The twisted, plummeting clay landscape was like a silent scream, and also like a dare accepted in bitter defiance, the dare to descend into nothingness.

Feeling spent and empty, the work done, my mind turned to go, but then noted what my fingers had, of themselves, begun to explore. Snaking and pushing up the clay cliffs were roots. As they came in focus, I saw how they joined, tough and tenacious, feeding each other in an upsurge of ascent. The very journey downward into my despair had shaped these roots, which now thrust upward, unbidden and resilient. For long moments I traced them, wonderingly, with eyes and fingers.

Quaker-style meetings, where a group sits and shares out of open silence, can let images appear and interact. In one I remember Humpty Dumpty was evoked. Poor old Humpty Dumpty, falling and breaking and all the king's men cannot put him together again. So it is with our outmoded paradigms, our egos and self-concepts: it felt good to give imaginative form to the sense of fragmentation in our time. As we ruminated on that, a voice among us slowly spoke, adding what she saw: From the shattered shell, a bird rose into the air. Eggshells break to reveal new life, I had forgotten that. The very imagery that expressed our pain pointed to the possibility of hope.

Sometimes it takes a while, in the slow alchemy of the soul, for hope to signal, and longer for it to take form in concrete plans and projects. That is all right.

> I said to my soul, be still, and wait
> without hope,
> For hope would be hope of the
> wrong thing.
>
> —*T.S. Eliot*

WAITING

So we wait; even in our work, we wait. Only out of that open expectancy can images and visions arise that strike deep enough to summon our faith in them. "The ability to wait," wrote William Lynch, "is central to hope."

Waiting does not mean inaction, but staying in touch with our pain and confusion *as* we act, not banishing them to grab for sedatives, ideologies, or final solutions. It is, as a student of mine quoted, "staying in the dark until the darkness becomes full and clear." The butterfly, I am told, eats its way out of the cocoon. In despair, if we digest it, is authenticity and energy to fuel our dreams.

Jacob Needleman suggests that part of the great danger in this time of crisis is that we may short-circuit despair, and thereby lose the revelations which can open to us.

> For there is nothing to guarantee that we will be able to remain long enough or deeply enough in front of the unknown, a psychological state which the traditional paths have always recognized as sacred. In that fleeting state between dreams, which is called "despair" in some Western teachings and "self-questioning" in Eastern traditions, a man is said to be able to receive the truth, both about nature and his own possible role in the universal order.

In my own feelings of despair, I was haunted by the question, "What do you substitute for hope?" I had always assumed that a sanguine confidence in the future was as essential as oxygen. Without it, I had thought, one would collapse into apathy and nihilism. It puzzled me that, when I owned my despair, the hours I spent working for peace and environmental causes did not lessen, but rather increased.

One day I talked with Jim Douglass, the theologian and writer who had left his university post to resist nuclear weapons; jailed repeatedly for civil disobedience in this effort, he was leading the citizens' campaign against the Trident submarine base. He had said he believed we had five years left before it was too late—too late to avert the use of our nuclear arsenal in a first strike strategy. I reflected on the implications of that remark and watched his face, as he squinted in the sun with an air of presence and serenity I could not fathom. "What do you substitute for hope?" I asked. He looked at me and smiled. "Possibilities," he said. "Possibilities…you can't predict, just make space for them. There are so many." That, too, is waiting, active waiting—moving out on the fog-bound trail, though you cannot see the way ahead.

COMMUNITY

Despair work is not a solo venture, no matter how alone one may feel. It is a process undertaken within the context of community, even if a community of like-minded others is not physically present. Just knowing that one's feelings are shared gives a measure of validation and support.

Many kinds of community can provide the environment for the kind of sharing that despair work involves. The necessary openness and trust can be found in groups devoted to personal or spiritual growth, and also in groups organized for social action. The "affinity groups" that have emerged in the peace and safe-energy movements, and that are based on strategies of nonviolence, set a high priority on mutual support.

My son had a dream one night about the affinity group he belonged to in the anti-nuclear movement in New England. It conveys something of the sense of strength generated in such community. In the dream he and his affinity group are standing together looking out over a darkened city. All is black and cold. Through their linked hands he feels the current of the group's energy. They chant and the current grows stronger; lights begin to appear and soon the city is aglow, empowered by the energy of their trust and commitment. That, in and of itself, seems a fulfillment.

When we face the darkness of our time, openly and together, we tap deep reserves of strength within us. Many of us fear that confrontation with despair will bring loneliness and isolation, but—on the contrary—in the letting go of old defenses, truer community is found. In the synergy of sharing comes power. In community, we can find our power and learn to trust our inner responses to our world.

CHAPTER THREE

Faith, Power, and Ecology

Yesterday morning at this time I was standing for about an hour in the sweet, gentle, English drizzle. I was in a large meadow with about forty men and women; three of them held toddlers. We stood in a circle and at the center of the circle were two ancient, sacred standing stones. We had come there at the close of a five-day workshop on ecology, and our band included activists from all over the island—social workers, civil servants, artisans, teachers, homemakers—drawn together by a common concern for the fate of our planet.

In the presence of those stones, thousands of years old, we seemed to find ourselves in two dimensions of time simultaneously. One was vast and immeasurable. As we tried to reach back to the ancient Earth wisdom of the culture that erected the stones, we sensed the long, long journey of the unfolding of life on this planet. At the same time, given the focus of the workshop, we were acutely aware of this particular historical moment when forces our culture has unleashed seem to be destroying our world.

Among us were Christians, Jews, Buddhists, Pagans. Yet, despite the differing belief systems to which we belonged, the prayers and affirmations that spontaneously arose in that circle expressed a common faith and fueled a common hope. They bespoke a shared commitment to engage in actions and changes in lifestyle on behalf of our Earth and its beings. They expressed a bonding to this Earth, where we go beyond feeling sorry for the Earth or scared for ourselves, to experience relationship—relationship that can be spiritually as well as physically sustaining, a relationship that can empower.

Fresh from that experience, it seems fitting to address the issue of faith and ecology. Faith is an elusive and questionable commodity

Source: Schumacher Lecture, Bristol, England, October 1986.

in these days of a dying culture. Where do you find it? If you've lost a faith, can you invent one? Which faith to choose? Some of us have retained a faith in a just creator God or in a lawful, benevolent order to the universe. But some of us find it hard, even obscene, to believe in an abiding providence in a world of such absurdity as ours where, in the face of unimaginable suffering, most of our wealth and wits are devoted to preparing a final holocaust. And we don't need nuclear bombs for our holocaust, it is going on right now in the demolition of the great rainforests and in the toxic contamination of our seas, soil, and air.

Faith, in a world like this? The very notion can appear distasteful, especially when we frequently see faith used as an excuse for denial and inaction. "God won't let it happen." Or even, as we hear in some circles today, "It may be God's will," a fearful assertion indeed when it refers to nuclear war itself, seen as the final just and holy battle to exterminate the wicked. The radical uncertainties of our time breed distortions of faith, where fundamentalist beliefs foster self-righteousness and deep divisions, turning patriotism into xenophobia, inciting fear and hatred of dissenters, and feeding the engines of war. If we are allergic to faith, it is with some reason.

Another option opens, however, that can lead to a more profound and authentic form of faith. We can turn from the search for personal salvation or some metaphysical haven and look instead to our actual experience. When we simply attend to what we see, feel, and know is happening to our world, we find authenticity. Going down into a darkness where there appears to be no faith, we can make three important discoveries. I see them as redeeming discoveries that can ground us in our ecology and serve as our faith; and I believe that our survival depends on our making them. These three are: (1) the discovery of what we know and feel, (2) the discovery of what we are, and (3) the discovery of what can happen through us or, as one might express it, grace.

DISCOVERING WHAT WE KNOW AND FEEL

To discover what we know and feel is not as easy as it sounds, because a great deal of effort in contemporary society is devoted to keeping us from being honest. Entire industries are focused on maintaining the illusion that we are happy, or on the verge of being happy as soon as we buy this toothpaste or that deodorant or that political candidate. It is not in the self-perceived interests of the state, the multinational corporations, or the media that serve them both, that we should stop and become aware of our profound anguish with the way things are.

None of us, in our hearts, is free of sorrow for the suffering of other beings. None of us is indifferent to the dangers that threaten our planet's people, or free of fear for the generations to come. Yet when we are enjoined to "keep smiling," "be sociable," and "keep a stiff upper lip," it is not easy to give credence to this anguish.

Suppression of our natural responses to actual or impending disaster is part of the disease of our time, as Robert Jay Lifton, the American psychiatrist who pioneered the study of the psychological effects of nuclear bombs, explains. The refusal to acknowledge or experience these responses produces a profound and dangerous splitting. It divorces our mental calculations from our intuitive, emotional, and biological imbeddedness in the matrix of life. That split allows us passively to acquiesce in the preparations for our own demise.

Joel Kovel, a psychiatrist teaching at Albert Einstein College, says that we are kept subservient and passive by "the state of nuclear terror." This terror is not the fear of nuclear weapons and other means of mass annihilation so much as our fear of experiencing the fear; we are afraid that we might break apart or get stuck in despair if we open our eyes to the dangers. So the messages we tend to hear or give are: "Don't talk to me about acid rain, or the arms race. There is nothing I can do about it. I have a family to support, a job to keep. If I were to take it all in and allow myself to think about it and to *feel* it, I wouldn't be able to function."

The first discovery, opening to what we know and feel, takes courage. Like Gandhi's *satyagraha,* it involves "truth-force." People are not going to find their truth-force or inner authority in listening to the experts, but in listening to themselves, for everyone in her or his way is an expert on what it is like to live on an endangered planet. To help this happen and counter habits of suppression, Interhelp, an international network, has evolved methods and workshops for people to come together to find their own inner authority. Without

mincing words, without apology, embarrassment, or fear of causing distress, participants find they can simply tell the truth about
their experience of this world. A boy talks about the dead fish in a
stream he loves; a young couple wonders about the Strontium 90
in the bones of their children.

Justin Kenrick, an Interhelper in Great Britain, has said:

> We need permission in our minds and hearts and guts to accept
> that we are destroying the Earth and to feel the reality of who we
> are in that context; isolated, desperate, and powerless individuals,
> defeated by our old patterns of behavior before we have even begun
> to try to heal our lives and the Earth. Only then can we give ourselves
> permission to feel the power our culture denies us, to regain our
> intuitive sense of everything being in relation rather than in op-
> position, to regain our intuitive sense of the deep miraculous pattern
> to life that opens to us as we accept it.

When we come to the authority of what we know and feel, when
we acknowledge our pain for the world, we remember the original
meaning of *compassion*, "to suffer with." Suffering with our world,
we are drawn now into the cauldron of compassion. It is there; it
awaits us; and as Kenrick's words suggest, it can reconnect us with
our power.

DISCOVERING WHAT WE ARE

Acknowledging the depths and reaches of our own inner experience, we come to the second discovery: the discovery of what we
are. We are experiencers of compassion. Buddhism has a term for
that kind of being—it is *bodhisattva*. The bodhisattva is the Buddhist
model for heroic behavior. Knowing there is no such thing as private
salvation, she or he does not hold aloof from this suffering world
or try to escape from it. It is a question rather of returning again
and again to work on behalf of all beings, because the bodhisattva
knows there is no healing or transformation without connection.

The *sutras*, or scriptures, tell us that we are all bodhisattvas, and
our fundamental interconnections are portrayed in the beautiful
image of the Jeweled Net of Indra. It is similar to the holographic
model of the universe we find emerging from contemporary sci-

ence. In the cosmic canopy of Indra's Net, each of us, each jewel at each node of the net, reflects all the others and reflects the others reflecting back. That is what we find when we listen to the sounds of the Earth crying within us—that the tears that arise are not ours alone; they are the tears of an Iraqi mother looking for her children in the rubble; they are the tears of a Navajo uranium miner learning that he is dying of lung cancer. We find we are interwoven threads in the intricate tapestry of life, its deep ecology.

What happens for us then is what every major religion has sought to offer—a shift in identification, a shift from the isolated "I" to a new, vaster sense of what we are. This is understandable not only as a spiritual experience, but also, in scientific terms, as an evolutionary development. As living forms evolve on this planet, we move not only in the direction of diversification, but toward integration as well. Indeed, these two movements complement and enhance each other. Open systems self-organize and integrate by virtue of their differentiation, and, vice-versa, they differentiate by virtue of their interactions. As we evolved we progressively shed our shells, our armor, our separate encasements; we grew soft, sensitive, vulnerable protuberances, like eyes, lips, and fingertips, to better connect and receive information, to better know and interweave our knowings. If we are all bodhisattvas, it is because that thrust to connect, that capacity to integrate with and through each other, is our true nature.

In his book *Ecology and Man*, Paul Shepard writes: "We are hidden from ourselves by patterns of perception. Our thought forms, our language, encourage us to see ourselves or a plant or an animal as an isolated sac, a thing, a contained self, whereas the epidermis of the skin is ecologically like a pond surface or a forest soil, not a shell so much as a delicate interpenetration." Paul Shepard is calling us to a faith in our very biology. He goes on to say, "Affirmation of its own organic essence will be the ultimate test of the human mind."

We begin to see that a shift of identification can release us not only from the prison cell of ego, but also from the tight compartment of a solely human perspective. As John Seed, Director of the Rainforest Information Center in Australia, points out, it takes us "beyond anthropocentrism." In his essay by that title, he says that anthropocentrism or human chauvinism is similar to sexism, but substitute "human race" for man and "all other species" for woman. And he says,

> When humans investigate and see through their layers of anthropo-centric self-cherishing, a most profound change in consciousness begins to take place. Alienation subsides. The human is no longer an outsider apart. Your humanness is then recognized as being merely the most recent stage of your existence; as you stop identifying exclusively with this chapter, you start to get in touch with your-self as vertebrate, as mammal, as species only recently emerged from the rainforest. As the fog of amnesia disperses, there is a transformation in your relationship to other species and in your commitment to them...The thousands of years of imagined separation are over and we can begin to recall our true nature; that is, the change is a spiritual one—thinking like a mountain, sometimes referred to as deep ecology.
>
> As your memory improves...there is an identification with all life...Remember our childhood as rocks, as lava? Rocks contain the potentiality to weave themselves into such stuff as this. We are the rocks dancing.

BEING ACTED THROUGH

That leads us to the third discovery we can make in our ecological *Pilgrim's Progress:* the discovery of what can happen through us. If we are the rocks dancing, then that which evolved us from those rocks carries us forward now and sustains us in our work for the continuance of life.

When I admired a nurse for her strength and devotion in keeping long hours in the children's ward, she shrugged off my compliment as if it were entirely misplaced. "It's not *my* strength, you know. I get it from them," she said, nodding at the rows of cots and cribs. "They give me what I need to keep going." Whether tending a garden or cooking in a soup kitchen, there is the sense sometimes of being sustained by something beyond one's own individual power, a sense of being acted "through." It is close to the religious concept of grace, but distinct from the traditional Western understanding of grace, as it does not require belief in God or a supernatural agency. One

simply finds oneself empowered to act on behalf of other beings—
or on behalf of the larger whole—and the empowerment itself seems
to come "through" that or those for whose sake one acts. This
phenomenon, when approached from the perspective of ecology,
can be understood as synergy. This is an important point because
it leads us to reconceptualize our very notion of what power is.

From the ecological perspective, all open systems—be they cells
or organisms, cedars or swamps—are seen to be self-organizing. They
don't require any external or superior agency to regulate them, any
more than your liver or your apple tree needs to be told how to function.
In other words, order is implicit in life; it is integral to life processes.
This contrasts with the hierarchical worldview our culture held for
centuries, where mind is set above nature and where order is assumed
to be something imposed from above on otherwise random, material
stuff. We have tended to define power in the same way, seeing it
as imposed from above. So we have equated power with domination,
with one thing exerting its will over another. It becomes a zero-sum,
or win-lose, game, where to be powerful means to resist the demands
or influences of another, and strong defenses are necessary to maintain
one's advantage.

In falling into this way of thinking, we lost sight of the fact that
this is not the way nature works. Living systems evolve in complexity,
flexibility, and intelligence through interaction with each other. These
interactions require openness and vulnerability in order to process
the flow-through of energy and information. They bring into play
new responses and new possibilities not previously present, increasing
the capacity to effect change. This interdependent release of fresh
potential is called synergy. It is like grace, because it brings an increase
of power beyond one's own capacity as a separate entity.

THE POWER TO CONNECT

I see the operation of this kind of grace or synergy everywhere I
go. For example, I see it in the network of citizens that has sprung
up along the tracks of the "white train" that carries the nuclear warheads
from the Pantex plant in Amarillo, Texas, up to the Trident base
in the northwest on Puget Sound and across the south to the Charleston
Naval Base on the Atlantic. Sitting up late at night to watch the tracks

they telephone to alert each other that the train is coming their way; then these ordinary citizens come out of their homes, to stand by the railroad line and vigil with lighted candles or, on occasion, put their bodies on the tracks to stop the train. Even though this network is scattered across thousands of miles and relatively few of its members have met face to face, it calls itself now the Agape community; for these people have learned to feel each other's presence and support. And the tracks that bear the weapons for the ultimate war have become arteries interconnecting people and eliciting new dimensions of caring and courage.

I see this grace in the Sanctuary movement, where local churches and groups give protective asylum to refugees from the U.S.-supported violence in Central America. In January 1985, the FBI, in an effort to break the movement, which then included 105 centers, brought a number of its members to court and some were jailed. Although the local citizens who participated in decisions to grant sanctuary are largely law-abiding people—middle-aged, middle-class, respected and respectable—the FBI crackdown discouraged few of them. A year and a half later, the number of groups offering protection to Central American refugees, against the will of the Administration, had doubled.

The members of a small Quaker Meeting I know near Philadelphia hesitated to take this step, because they feared they might not be numerous enough or strong enough to provide the constant care and vigilance that is required when you adopt an illegal alien. But, inspired by similar actions elsewhere, they took the risk and granted sanctuary to a young Salvadoran woman. When I visited them a year later, Paz was still with them and the membership of the Meeting itself had become far larger and more active than ever before. By risking action together, action that made them more vulnerable, their power had increased.

There are countless such innovative grassroots actions; they do not make headlines, but taken all together, they amount to an unprecedented, silent explosion of people who are quietly putting the interests of the planet ahead of their personal profit or pleasure. I see it in the growing number of citizens who are refusing to pay taxes for weapons of war; I see it in the thousands of Americans who have been paying their own way to the USSR, simply to connect with their Soviet counterparts so they might begin to know and comprehend each other firsthand. I see it in the bands of eco-warriors who risk their lives to protect marine mammals, and old-growth forests. I see it among the Vietnam veterans who fasted publicly to protest America's undeclared war on Nicaragua, and among the many other veterans across the United States who rallied to support them. As they do this, they expand our understanding of patriotism, demonstrating that love for one's country does not have to exclude the other beings of our planet.

These people show us what can happen through us when we break free of the old hierarchical notions of power. They show that grace happens when we act with others on behalf of our world.

ROOTS OF POWER

What can we do to nourish these efforts and strengthen the bodhisattva in ourselves? Two ways that I know are community and practice.

The liberation struggles in Latin America and the Philippines have demonstrated the efficacy of spiritually-based communities for nonviolent action. These tough networks of trust arise on the neighborhood level, as people strive together to understand, in their own terms and for their own situation, what they need to do to live without fear and injustice. These groups need be neither residential nor elite, just ordinary people meeting regularly in a discipline of honest searching and mutual commitment.

In our own society, too, such communities have been arising in the form of local support and action groups. Here neighbors or co-workers, parents or professionals organize and meet regularly to support each other in action—be it in responding to the poisons leaching from a nearby dump or to the need for a peace curriculum in the local school. Those of us who participate in such "base communities" know that they enhance both personal integrity and our belief in what is possible.

In addition to such external support, we need, in this time of great challenge and change, the internal support of personal practice. I mean practice in the venerable spiritual sense of fortifying the mind and schooling its attitudes. Because for generations we have been conditioned by the mechanistic, anthropocentric assumptions of our mainstream culture, intellectual assent to an ecological vision of life is not enough to change our perceptions and behaviors. To help us disidentify from narrow notions of the self and experience our interexistence with all beings in the web of life, we turn to regular personal practices that range from meditation to the recycling of our trash.

Spiritual exercises for cultivating reverence for life arise now out of many traditions and are welcomed by people regardless of their religious affiliation. I have found adaptations from Buddhist practices particularly helpful because they are grounded in the recognition of the dependent co-arising or deep ecology of all things. Similarly, Native American prayers and ritual forms, evoking our innate capacity to know and live our Earth, are increasingly adapted and included in gatherings for work and worship.

This is a prayer from the Laguna Pueblo people:

> I add my breath to your breath
> that our days may be long on the Earth,
> That the days of our people may be long,
> that we shall be as one person,
> that we may finish our road together.

CHAPTER FOUR

Taking Heart:
Spiritual Exercises for Social Activists

To heal our society, our psyches must heal as well. Haunted by the desperate needs of our time and beset by more commitments than we can easily carry, we may wonder how to find the time and energy for spiritual disciplines. Few of us feel free to take to the cloister or the meditation cushion to seek personal transformation.

We do not need to withdraw from the world or spend long hours in solitary prayer or meditation to begin to wake up to the spiritual power within us. The activities and encounters of our daily lives can serve as the occasion for that kind of discovery. I would like to share five simple exercises that can help in this.

The exercises—on death, loving-kindness, compassion, mutual power, and mutual recognition—happen to be adapted from the Buddhist tradition. As part of our planetary heritage, they belong to us all. No belief system is necessary, only a readiness to attend to the immediacy of your own experience. They will be most useful if read slowly with a quiet mind (a few deep breaths will help), and if put directly into practice in the presence of others. If you read them aloud for others or put them on tape, allow several seconds when three dots (...) are marked, and when more are marked (......), leave additional time, as appropriate.

MEDITATION ON DEATH

Most spiritual paths begin by recognizing the transiency of human life. Medieval Christians honored this in the mystery play of *Everyman*. Don Juan, the Yaqui sorcerer, taught that the enlightened warrior

---

Four of these meditations appear in briefer form in *Despair and Personal Power in the Nuclear Age* (Philadelphia: New Society Publishers, 1983), Chapter Eight.

walks with death at his shoulder. To confront and accept the inevitability of our dying releases us from attachments and frees us to live boldly.

An initial meditation on the Buddhist path involves reflection on the twofold fact that: "death is certain" and "the time of death is uncertain." In our world today, nuclear weaponry, serving in a sense as a spiritual teacher, does that meditation for us, for it tells us that we can die together at any moment, without warning. When we allow the reality of that possibility to become conscious, it is painful, but it also jolts us awake to life's vividness, its miraculous quality, heightening our awareness of the beauty and uniqueness of each object, and each being.

As an occasional practice in daily life:

Look at the person you encounter (stranger or friend). Let the realization arise in you that this person lives on an endangered planet. He or she may die in a nuclear war, or from the poisons spreading through our world. Observe that face, unique, vulnerable...Those eyes still can see; they are not empty sockets...the skin is still intact...Become aware of your desire that this person be spared such suffering and horror, feel the strength of that desire...keep breathing...Also let the possibility arise in your consciousness that this may be the person you happen to be with when you die...that face the last you see...that hand the last you touch...it might reach out to help you then, to comfort, to give water...Open to the feelings for this person that surface in you with the awareness of this possibility...Open to the levels of caring and connection it reveals in you.

MEDITATION ON LOVING-KINDNESS

Loving kindness, or *metta,* is the first of the four "Abodes of the Buddha," also known as the *Brahmaviharas.* Meditation to arouse and sustain loving-kindness is a staple of the Sarvodaya Shramadana Movement for community development in Sri Lanka, and is accorded minutes of silence at the outset of every meeting. Organizers and village workers find it useful in developing motivation for service and overcoming feelings of hostility or inadequacy in themselves and others.

I first received instruction in this meditation from a nun in the Tibetan Buddhist tradition. Here is a version that I have adapted for use in the West.

Close your eyes and begin to relax, exhaling to expel tension. Now center in on the normal flow of the breath, letting go of all extraneous thoughts as you passively watch the breathing-in and breathing-out......

Now call to mind someone you love very dearly...in your mind's eye see the face of that beloved one...silently speak her or his name...Feel your love for this being, like a current of energy coming through you...Now let yourself experience how much you want this person to be free from fear, how intensely you desire that this person be released from greed and ill-will, from confusion and sorrow and the causes of suffering...That desire, in all its sincerity and strength, is metta, *the great loving kindness......*

Continuing to feel that warm energy flow coming through the heart, see in your mind's eye those with whom you share your daily life, family members, close friends and colleagues, the people you live and work with...Let them appear now as in a circle around you. Behold them one by one, silently speaking their names...and direct to each in turn that same current of loving-kindness...Among these beings may be some with whom you are uncomfortable, in conflict, or tension. With those especially, experience your desire that each be free from fear, from hatred, free from greed and ignorance and the causes of suffering......

Now allow to appear, in wider concentric circles your relations, and your acquaintances...Let the beam of loving-kindness play on them as well, pausing on the faces that appear randomly in your mind's eye. With them as well, experience how much you want their freedom from greed, fear, hatred and confusion, how much you want all beings to be happy......

Beyond them, in concentric circles that are wider yet, appear now all beings with whom you share this planet-time. Though you have not met, your lives are interconnected in ways beyond knowing. To these beings as well, direct the same powerful current of loving-kindness. Experience your desire and your intention that each awaken from fear and hatred, from greed and confusion...that all beings be released from suffering......

As in the ancient Buddhist meditation, we direct the loving-kindness now to all the "hungry ghosts," the restless spirits that roam in suffering, still prey to fear and confusion. May they find rest...may they rest in the great loving kindness and in the deep peace it brings......

By the power of our imagination let us move out now beyond our planet, out into the universe, into other solar systems, other galaxies, other Buddha-fields. The current of loving-kindness is not affected by physical distances, and we direct it now, as if aiming a beam of light, to all centers of conscious life...And to all sentient beings everywhere we direct our heartfelt wish that they, too, be free of fear and greed, of hatred and confusion and the causes of suffering...May all beings be happy......

Now, as if from out there in the interstellar distances, we turn and behold our own planet, our home...We see it suspended there in the blackness of space, blue and white jewel planet turning in the light of its sun......Slowly we approach it, drawing nearer, nearer, returning to this part of it, this region, this place...And as you approach this place, let yourself see the being you know best of all...the person it has been given you to be in this lifetime...You know this person better than anyone else does, know its pain and its hopes, know its need for love, know how hard it tries...Let the face of this being, your own face, appear before you...Speak the name you are called in love...And experience, with that same strong energy-current of loving-kindness, how deeply you desire that this being be free from fear, released from greed and hatred, liberated from ignorance and confusion and the causes of suffering...The great loving-kindness linking you to all beings is now directed to your own self...know now the fullness of it.

BREATHING THROUGH

Basic to most spiritual traditions, as well as to the systems view of the world, is the recognition that we are not separate, isolated entities, but integral and organic parts of the vast web of life. As such, we are like neurons in a neural net, through which flow currents of awareness of what is happening to us, as a species and as a planet. In that context, the pain we feel for our world is a living testimony to our interconnectedness with it. If we deny this pain, we become like blocked and atrophied neurons, deprived of life's flow and weakening the larger body in which we take being. But if we let it move through us, we affirm our belonging; our collective awareness increases. We can open to the pain of the world in confidence that it can neither shatter nor isolate us, for we are not objects that can break. We are resilient patterns within a vaster web of knowing.

Because we have been conditioned to view ourselves as separate, competitive and thus fragile entities, it takes practice to relearn this kind of resilience. A good way to begin is by practicing simple openness, as in the exercise of "breathing through," adapted from an ancient Buddhist meditation for the development of compassion.

Closing your eyes, focus attention on your breathing. Don't try to breathe any special way, slow or long. Just watch the breathing as it happens in and out. Note the accompanying sensations at the nostrils or upper lip, in the chest or abdomen. Stay passive and alert, like a cat by a mouse hole.......

As you watch the breath, you note that it happens by itself, without your will, without your deciding each time to inhale or exhale...It's as though you're being breathed—being breathed by life...Just as everyone in this room, in this city, in this planet now, is being breathed, sustained in a vast, breathing web of life......

Now visualize your breath as a stream or ribbon of air passing through you. See it flow up through your nose, down through your windpipe and into your lungs. Now from your lungs take it through your heart. Picture it flowing through your heart and out through an opening there to reconnect with the larger web of life. Let the breath-stream, as it passes through you, appear as one loop within that vast web, connecting you with it......

Now open your awareness to the suffering that is present in the world. Drop for now all defenses and open to your knowledge of that suffering. Let it come as concretely as you can...concrete images of your fellow beings in pain and need, in fear and isolation, in prisons, hospitals, tenements, hunger camps...no need to strain for these images, they are present to you by virtue of our interexistence. Relax and just let them surface...the vast and countless hardships of our fellow humans, and of our animal brothers and sisters as well, as they swim the seas and fly the air of this ailing planet...Now breathe in the pain like dark granules on the stream of air, up through your nose, down through your trachea, lungs and heart, and out again into the world net...You are asked to do nothing for now, but let it pass through your heart......Be sure that stream flows through and out again; don't hang on to the pain...surrender it for now to the healing resources of life's vast web......

With Shantideva, the Buddhist saint, we can say, "Let all sorrows ripen in me." We help them ripen by passing them through our hearts...making good rich compost out of all that grief...so we can learn from it, enhancing our larger, collective knowing...

If no images or feelings arise and there is only blankness, grey and numb, breathe that through. The numbness itself is a very real part of our world...

And if what surfaces for you is not the pain of other beings so much as your own personal suffering, breathe that through, too. Your own anguish is an integral part of the grief of our world, and arises with it......

Should you feel an ache in the chest, a pressure in the rib cage, as if the heart would break, that is all right. Your heart is not an object that can break...But if it were, they say the heart that breaks open can hold the whole universe. Your heart is that large. Trust it. Keep breathing......

This guided meditation serves to introduce the process of breathing through, which, once familiar, becomes useful in daily life in the many situations that confront us with painful information. By breathing through the bad news, rather than bracing ourselves against it, we can let it strengthen our sense of belonging in the larger web of being. It helps us remain alert and open, whether reading the newspaper, receiving criticism, or simply being present to a person who suffers.

For activists working for peace and justice, and those dealing most directly with the griefs of our time, the practice helps prevent burnout. Reminding us of the collective nature of both our problems and our power, it offers a healing measure of humility. It can save us from self-righteousness. For when we can take in our world's pain, accepting it as the price of our caring, we let it inform our acts without needing to inflict it as a punishment on others who are, at the present moment, less involved.

THE GREAT BALL OF MERIT

Compassion, which is grief in the grief of others is but one side of the coin. The other side is joy in the joy of others—which in Buddhism is called *mudita*. To the extent that we allow ourselves to identify with the sufferings of other beings, we can identify with their strengths as well. This is very important for a sense of adequacy and resilience, because we face a time of great challenge that demands of us more commitment, endurance and courage than we can dredge up out of our individual supply. We can learn to draw on the other neurons in the neural net, and view them in a grateful and celebratory fashion, as so much "money in the bank."

This practice is adapted from the *Meditation of Jubilation and Transformation,* taught in a Buddhist text written two thousand years ago at the outset of the Mahayana tradition. You can find the original version in chapter six of the *Perfection of Wisdom in 8000 Lines.* I find it very useful today in two forms. The one closer to the ancient practice is this:

Relax and close your eyes. Open your awareness to the fellow beings who share with you this planet-time...in this town...in this country...and in other lands......See their multitudes in your mind's eye......Now let your awareness open wider yet, to encompass all beings who ever lived...of all races and creeds and walks of life, rich, poor, kings and beggars, saints and sinners...see the vast vistas of these fellow beings stretching into the distance, like successive mountain ranges...... Now consider the fact that in each of these innumerable lives some act of merit was performed. No matter how stunted or deprived the life, there was a gesture of generosity, a gift of love, an act of valor or self-sacrifice...on the battlefield or workplace, hospital or home...From these beings in their endless multitudes arose actions of courage, kindness, of teaching and healing. Let yourself see these manifold and immeasurable acts of merit......

Now imagine you can sweep together these acts of merit...sweep them into a pile in front of you...use your hands...pile them up...pile them into a heap viewing it with gladness and gratitude...Now pat them into a ball. It is the Great Ball of Merit...hold it now and weigh it in your hands...rejoice in it, knowing that no act of goodness is ever lost. It remains ever and always a present resource...a means for the transformation of life...So now, with jubilation and gratitude, you turn that great ball...turn it over...over...into the healing of our world.

As we can learn from contemporary science and visualize in the holographic model of reality, our lives interpenetrate. In the fluid tapestry of space-time, there is at root no distinction between self and other. The acts and intentions of others are like seeds that can germinate and bear fruit through our own lives, as we take them into awareness and dedicate, or "turn over," that awareness to our own empowerment. Thoreau, Gandhi, Martin Luther King, Dorothy Day, and countless nameless heroes and heroines of our own day, all can be part of our Ball of Merit, from which we can draw inspiration and endurance. Other traditions feature notions similar to this, such as the "cloud of witnesses" of which St. Paul spoke, or the Treasury of Merit in the Catholic Church.

The second, more workaday, version of the Ball of Merit meditation helps us open to the powers in people around us. It is in direct contrast to the commonly accepted, patriarchal notion of power as something personally owned and exerted over others. The exercise prepares us to bring expectant attention to our encounters with other beings, to view them with fresh openness and curiosity as to how they can enhance our Ball of Merit. We can play this inner game with someone opposite us on the bus or across the bargaining table. It is especially useful when dealing with a person with whom we may be in conflict.

What does this person add to my Great Ball of Merit? What gifts of intellect can enrich our common store? What reserves of stubborn endurance can she or he offer? What flights of fancy or powers of love lurk behind those eyes? What kindness or courage hides in those lips, what healing in those hands?

Then, as with the breathing-through exercise, we open ourselves to the presence of these strengths, inhaling our awareness of them. As our awareness grows, we experience our gratitude for them and our capacity to partake...

Often we let our perceptions of the powers of others make us feel inadequate. Alongside an eloquent colleague, we can feel inarticulate; in the presence of an athlete we can feel weak and clumsy; and we can come to resent both ourself and the other person. In the light of the Great Ball of Merit, however, the gifts and good fortunes of others appear not as competing challenges, but as resources we can honor and take pleasure in. We can learn to play detective, spying out treasures for the enhancement of life from even the unlikeliest material. Like air, and sun, and water, they form part of our common good.

In addition to releasing us from the mental cramp of envy, this spiritual offers two other rewards. One is pleasure in our own acuity, as our merit-detecting ability improves. The second is the response of others who, though ignorant of the game we are playing, sense something in our manner that invites them to disclose more of the person they can be.

LEARNING TO SEE EACH OTHER

This exercise is derived from the Buddhist practice of the Brahma-viharas, also known as the Four Abodes of the Buddha, which are loving-kindness, compassion, joy in the joy of others, and equanimity. Adapted for use in a social context, it helps us to see each other more truly and experience the depths of our interconnections.

In workshops, I offer this as a guided meditation, with partici-pants sitting in pairs facing each other. At its close, I encourage them to proceed to use it, or any portion they like, as they go about the business of their daily lives. It is an excellent antidote to boredom, when our eye falls on another person, say on the subway, or waiting in the check-out line. It charges that idle movement with beauty and discovery. It also is useful when dealing with people whom we are tempted to dislike or disregard; it breaks open our accustomed ways of viewing them. When used like this, as a meditation-in-action, one does not, of course, gaze long and deeply into the other's eyes, as in the guided exercise. A seemingly casual glance is enough.

The guided, group form goes like this:

Sit in pairs. Face each other. Stay silent. Take a couple of deep breaths, centering yourself and exhaling tension...Look into each other's eyes...If you feel discomfort or an urge to laugh or look away, just note that embarrassment with patience and gentleness, and come back, when you can, to your partner's eyes. You may never see this person again: the opportunity to behold the uniqueness of this particular human being is given to you now......

As you look into this person's eyes, let yourself become aware of the powers that are there...Open your awareness to the gifts and strengths and the potentialities in this being...Behind those eyes are unmeasured reserves of courage and intelligence...of patience, endurance, wit and wisdom...There are gifts there, of which this person her/himself is unaware... Consider what these powers could do for the healing of our planet, if they were to be believed and acted on.........As you consider that, let yourself become aware of your desire that this person be free from fear...Experience how much you want this being to be free from fear, free from greed, released from hatred and from sorrow and from the causes of suffering......Know that what you are now experiencing is the great loving-kindness......

Now, as you look into those eyes, let yourself become aware of the pain that is there. There are sorrows accumulated in that life, as in all human lives, though you can only guess at them. There are disappointments and failures and losses and loneliness and abuse...there are hurts beyond the telling...Let yourself open to that pain, to hurts that this person may never have told another being......You cannot fix that pain, but you can be with it. As you let yourself simply be with that suffering, know that what you are experiencing is the great compassion. It is very good for the healing of our world......

As you look into the eyes of this person, consider how good it would be to work together...on a joint project, toward a common goal...What it could be like, taking risks together...conspiring together in zest and laughter ...celebrating the successes, consoling each other over the setbacks, forgiving each other when you make mistakes...and simply being there for each other......As you open to that possibility, what you open to is the great wealth: the pleasure in each other's powers, the joy in each other's joy......

Lastly, let your awareness drop deep within you like a stone, sinking below the level of what words can express, to the deep web of relationship that underlies all experience. It is the web of life in which you have taken being, in which you are supported, and that interweaves us through all space and time...See the being before you as if seeing the face of one who, at another time, another place, was your lover or your enemy, your parent or your child......And now you meet again on this brink of time...And you know your lives are as intricately interwoven as nerve cells in the mind of a great being......Out of that vast net you cannot fall...no stupidity, or failure, or cowardice, can ever sever you from that living web. For that is what you are......Rest in that knowing. Rest in the Great Peace...Out of it we can act, we can venture everything...and let every encounter be a homecoming to our true nature...Indeed it is so......

In doing this exercise we realize that we do not have to be particularly noble or saint-like in order to wake up to the power of our connection with other beings. In our time that simple awakening is the gift the Bomb holds for us. For all its horror and stupidity, the Bomb, like the toxins we spew into our world, is also the manifestation of an awesome spiritual truth—the truth about the hell we create for ourselves when we cease to learn how to love. Saints, mystics and prophets throughout the ages saw that law; now *all* can see it and none can escape its consequences. So we are caught now in a narrow place where we realize that Moses, Lao-Tzu, the Buddha, Jesus and our own inner hearts were right all along; and we are as scared and frantic as a cornered rat, and as dangerous. But if we let it, that narrow *cul-de-sac* can turn into a birth canal, pressing and pushing us through the darkness of pain, until we are delivered into…what? Love seems too weak a word. It is, as Saint Paul said, "the glory to be revealed in us." It stirs in us now.

For us to regard the Bomb (or the dying seas, the poisoned air) as a monstrous injustice to us would suggest that we never took seriously the injunction to love. Perhaps we thought all along that Gautama and Jesus were kidding, or their teachings meant only for saints. But now we see, as an awful revelation, that we are *all* called to be saints—not good necessarily, or pious, or devout—but saints in the sense of just loving each other. One wonders what terrors this knowledge must hold that we fight it so, and flee from it in such pain. Can it be that the Bomb, by which we can extinguish all life, can tell us this? Can force us to face the terrors of love? Can be the occasion of our birth?

In that possibility we take heart. Even in confusion and fear, with all our fatigues and petty faults, we can let that awareness work in and through our lives. Such simple exercises as those offered here can help us do that, help us to begin to see ourselves and each other with fresh eyes.

Let me close with the same suggestion that closes our workshops. It is a practice that is a corollary to the earlier death meditation, where we recognize that the person we meet may die in a nuclear war. Look at the next person you see. It may be lover, child, co-worker, bus driver, or your own face in the mirror. Regard him or her with the recognition that:

In this person are gifts for the healing of our world. In him/her are powers that can redound to the joy of all beings.

PART TWO

Rediscovering the Early Teachings

CHAPTER FIVE

The Forgotten City:
Turning the Wheel of the Dharma
THE BUDDHA'S TEACHING OF DEPENDENT CO-ARISING

The eight-spoked wheel that graces gateways and temple roofs throughout the Buddhist world symbolizes the teaching of the Buddha. It is called the Wheel of the Dharma, the *Dharma Chakra*. It also represents the central doctrine that his teachings convey: the doctrine of *paticca samuppada* or the dependent co-arising of all phenomena. As the Buddha said, "they who see paticca samuppada see the Dharma, and they who see the Dharma see paticca samuppada."

This centerpiece of the Buddha's teaching is not about a level of reality separate from our daily lives or aloof from the phenomenal world of change. It refers not to any absolute being or essence, but to process itself—to the way things work, how events happen and interrelate. Hence it is often called the Law—the law of causality.

I was drawn to Buddhism long before I grasped the importance of this doctrine. It took me nine years before I realized how remarkable and distinctive this teaching is, and how it casts a clarifying light on every other aspect of Buddhist thought and practice. What had drawn me to the Dharma was the luminous vitality of the Buddhists I knew in South and Central Asia and the meditative practices they taught me. All the while, their discourses on causality struck me as musty and remote. This doctrine seemed either so obvious (everything has a cause) or so abstruse (with scholastic enumerations of causal factors) as to appear irrelevant to my own life. I figured I could bracket that aspect of Buddhist philosophy and devote my studies to more engaging topics, such as the compassionate way of the bodhisattva.

I believed that insights and practices offered in Buddhism could be liberating to Westerners; so after my return from Asia I enrolled

---

For a fuller discussion of the scriptures on which this and the next four chapters are based, along with their counterparts in general systems theory, see *Mutual Causality in Buddhism and General Systems Theory: The Dharma of Natural Systems* (Albany: State University of New York Press, 1991).

in a graduate program at Syracuse University to study Buddhism more formally and obtain credentials to teach in American institutions. I began to study deeply the early scriptures with a particular focus: What was so distinctive in the Buddha's teachings? Why did the moral values and spiritual practices seem so compelling? Other religions upheld similar ideals of compassion and nonviolence, generosity and self-restraint; other faiths acknowledged the same kinds of responsibility and service; but in the Buddha Dharma these ethical norms had a transparent, unburdened quality. Why, in the Buddhist context, did they feel so accessible, so liberating? I sensed that there was something extremely important, but I was unable to bring it into focus.

Related questions arose: According to Western religious thought, ethical values derive from divine commandment. A supernatural source is necessary to provide moral sanction. Without the ontological security of belief in an absolute, everything seems awash, with no clear guidelines, and it's every man for himself. This assumption is so pervasive in the West that many noted scholars judged Buddhism's moral teachings to be weak, since they do not issue from belief in any God. It is true that the Way the Buddha taught is freed from the necessity to believe in any supernatural authority. Indeed, when he was asked by what authority he spoke, he cited again and again the law of dependent co-arising; not any entity ruling our world, but the dynamics at work *within* our world. He cited the interdependence of all phenomena. What did he mean by that? How can radical relativity serve as a moral grounding?

With fascination I studied the early Buddhist texts. I read how the perception of paticca samuppada dawned on the Buddha the night of his enlightenment, and featured in his discourses. I saw how it underlay everything he taught about self, suffering, and liberation from suffering. I noted how it knocked down the dichotomies bred by hierarchical thinking, the old polarities between mind and matter, self and world, that had exasperated me as a spiritual seeker and activist, and as a woman. I saw how it brought the Buddha into conflict with the religious beliefs of his day, distancing him from earlier philosophic thought. I saw it as consonant with the systems thinking emerging in our own era, and important to our understanding of this new process paradigm, so that we can develop it with greater fullness and depth. Indeed I felt as if I had come upon an ancient forgotten city, overgrown by jungle and awaiting rediscovery and restoration.

The Buddha, in speaking of his own initial vision of paticca samuppada, used the same metaphors. (Bear in mind that the Buddha did not speak in the style of Victorian England, but those whose translations are still most extensive did):

> There arose in me vision, knowledge arose, insight arose, wisdom arose, light arose. Just as if, brethren, a man faring through the forest, through the great wood, should see an ancient path, an ancient road traversed by men of former days. And he were to go along it, and going along it he should see an ancient city, an ancient prince's domain, wherein dwelt men of former days, having gardens, groves, pools, foundations of walls, a goodly spot. And that man, brethren, should bring word to the prince or to the prince's minister: "Pardon, Lord, know this....I have seen an ancient city, an ancient prince's domain, wherein dwelt men of former days, having gardens, groves, pools, foundations of walls, a goodly spot....Lord, restore that city." And, brethren, the prince or this minister should restore that city. That city should hereafter become prosperous and flourishing, populous, teeming with folk, grown and thriven.

Note that the Buddha did not create this city; it was already there. As the scriptures tell us, dependent co-arising is the abiding truth about reality which Buddhas, as they appear in the world, rediscover. Having perceived it, as had earlier Buddhas before him, Gautama restored the city for his followers, letting it flourish again as did the prince in his story. Perhaps restoration can be our task, too, in our own era. We can begin by acquainting ourselves with Gautama's reports of his own discovery.

THE INSIGHT THAT AWAKENS

After years of yogic training, Gautama found the religious teachings of his time inadequate to reveal and resolve the canker at the core of human experience. So he sat under the Bodhi tree to plumb for himself the root causes of suffering.

He did not begin with abstractions or generalities, but with the existential factors of life. He named these factors of experience—ignorance, volitional formations, cognition, name and physical form, sensation, feeling, craving and so on—and pursued them relentlessly to determine how they relate to each other. Persistently he questioned, "For this factor to arise, what else must happen? For it to cease, what else must stop?"

Tracing thus the sources of suffering, he did not find a first cause or prime mover, but beheld instead patterns or circuits of contingency. The factors were sustained by their own interdependence. It was then, in that vigil, in the crucible of his attention, that the perception of dependent co-arising swept upon him.

> Coming to be, coming to be!...Ceasing to be, ceasing to be! At that thought, brethren, there arose...a vision of things not before called to mind, and knowledge arose....Such is form, such is the coming to be of form, such is its passing away....Such is cognition, such is its coming to be, such is its passing away. And [he abided] in the discernment of the arising and passing away.

The process nature of reality became clear—its continual flow, the radical impermanence of all things, with no element or entity aloof from change. But the flux was not chaotic or random, for patterns of conditionality emerged. He saw how factors of existence are mutually determined, providing occasion and context for each other's emergence and subsiding.

All the factors of our lives subsist, then, in a web of mutual causality. Our suffering is caused by the interplay of these factors, and particularly by the delusion, aversion, and craving that arise from our misapprehension of them. Hence, the Four Noble Truths: We create our own bondage by reifying and clinging to what is by nature contingent and transient. Being caused in this way, our suffering is not endemic. It can cease. The causal play can be reversed. This is achieved by seeing the true nature of phenomena, which is their radical interdependence. This is made possible by the cleansing of perception through meditation and moral conduct.

Such a vision, however, is hard to convey, because it goes against the grain of both our sensory experience and our desire for security. Recognizing this as he arose from his enlightenment vigil, the Buddha was tempted not to teach.

> I have penetrated this truth, deep, hard to perceive, hard to understand, calm, sublime, beyond logic, subtle, intelligible only to the wise. But this is a race devoting itself to the things to which it clings...And for such a race this were a matter hard to perceive, to wit, that all co-arises interdependently....And if I were now to teach the truth and other men did not acknowledge it to me, that would be wearisome, that would be hurtful to me....This that through many toils I've won—enough! Why should I make it known?

But although he pondered thus, his "heart inclining to be averse to exertion," he remembered the suffering and the need of beings. According to the legend it was the god Brahma who reminded him: "There are those perishing from not hearing the truth; they will come to be knowers of the truth...there are those who will understand." Thereupon, out of compassion, the Buddha set forth to teach.

When he found his former companions and delivered his first teachings, the order and emphasis accorded them in the texts is significant. Note that, of the elements of his sermon, it is paticca samuppada that is identified as unique to the Buddha.

> First he "discoursed in due order,"that is to say, he gave them illustrative talk on generosity, on right conduct, on heaven, on the danger, the vanity and the defilement of lusts, on the advantages of renunciation. When the Exalted One saw that they had become prepared, softened, unprejudiced, upraised and believing in heart, then he proclaimed that Truth which the Buddhas alone have won; that is to say, the doctrine of sorrow, of its origin, of its cessation, and the Path....Whatever has a beginning, in that is also inherent the necessity of passing away.

At this point, his first convert Kondañña was enlightened. "Truly Kondañña perceived it!" said the Buddha.

How was this "it" that Kondañña perceived described as the teachings spread? It was given a name: dependent co-arising, and there were other, similar constructions, like the "conditionality of this to that." One of the earliest formulations was a four-part statement:

> This being, that becomes; from the arising of this, that arises; this
> not being, that becomes not; from the ceasing of this, that ceases.

According to this apparently simple set of assertions, things do
not produce each other or make each other happen, as in linear
causality; they *help* each other happen by providing occasion or locus
or context, and in so doing, they in turn are affected. There is a
mutuality here, a reciprocal dynamic. Power inheres not in any entity,
but in the relationship between entities.

Dependent co-arising was also formulated in terms of the factors
of existence that the Buddha traced during his enlightenment vigil.
Conditioned by ignorance, volitional formations arise; conditioned
by volitional formations, cognition arises; and so forth. Early versions
exhibited some variety in these factors and that made no difference
to the teaching, for what mattered was not the specific factors so
much as the interdependent dynamic between them. As a mnemonic
device in the oral tradition, this formulation became codified into
a particular series of twelve factors; it often appears in conjunction
with the second and third Noble Truths, to show how suffering arises
and can cease. This standardized enumeration of factors, useful no
doubt for rote learning, has had at times the unfortunate effect of
directing attention to the factors themselves, rather than to the dynamic
between them—a dynamic at work between all phenomena.

THE PHILOSOPHIC CHALLENGE

Assumptions about the nature of causality, even when they are
unformulated, shape the values and goals we adopt, and the means
we employ to realize them. In times of paradigmatic change in our
ways of apprehending reality these assumptions become more explicit—
and in the intellectual ferment of sixth century B.C.E. in India, they
were debated with vigor. Many thinkers, from Brahman scholars to
Jain ascetics to materialist philosophers, came to challenge the Buddha
about his teaching of paticca samuppada, for it flew in the face of
beliefs about causation that were current.

It is useful to look at these pre-Buddhist beliefs, both because
each in its own way assumed that if causality exists it must be linear, and because they are comparable to causal notions that have

dominated Western thought. This helps us see how novel and distinctive the Buddha Dharma is even in our own time.

The debates recorded in the early texts show that the Buddha's teaching of paticca samuppada was challenged by three main groups:

—Vedic or Vedanta teachers who held that the phenomenal world unfolds from a divine absolute or unchanging essence.

—the Materialists of the time, who rejected any transcendent spiritual cause and explained events solely in terms of the properties of matter.

—and the Accidentalists who denied any causality at all.

The first view of causality, which imbues the *Upanishads,* the *Bhagavad Gita,* and mainstream Hinduism, stems from a fundamental equation of reality with permanence. Vedic thinkers made the axiomatic move of positing that what is real is immutable, aloof from change. This presupposition cannot be proved or disproved; but it does pose the problem of how to assign reality or value to the existential experience of change. By its logic, novelty is precluded and transformations are seen as mere shifts in appearance. Change itself becomes the realm of *maya,* illusion, which obscures the real and deludes the mind.

Where an absolute is posited as the abode of pure being, it is also the locus of power. Power is seen, then, as an inherent property. It issues forth from its possessor, who is able to affect others without being affected in return. It is a one-way street. And this became in non-Buddhist India, as it did in the West after Plato, the predominant model for causality.

In the sixth century B.C.E., other views of causality contended as well; they arose in reaction to the orthodox Vedic view. Among these were the Materialists. Finding no empirical evidence for a transcendent spiritual essence or entity, they assigned all causal efficacy to matter itself. The reality they perceived adhered to a strict determinism, the remorseless juggernaut of material inevitability.

At the other extreme of non-Vedic thought stood the views of the Accidentalists, who maintained that "the soul and the world arise without a cause." They, too, came to debate with the Buddha, arguing like the others that, unless it derives from an eternal spirit or from matter itself, there can be no causality and all is chaotic, without pattern or meaning.

In these three views of the Buddha's time, we can see analogs to assumptions about causality in the West. Here, too, it has been assumed that if there is no spiritual absolute or prime mover, then causality must inhere in dialectical materialism or be non-existent, with nothing more at work in our world than the random play of chance.

In his dialogues with champions of these views the Buddha expounded and clarified many of his key teachings—teachings about karma and free will, about the nature of consciousness and perception, about the relation of mind to matter and of self to world. When his interlocutors could not share his direct perception of paticca samuppada, and when they remained unpersuaded by his arguments, the Buddha sometimes simply stated as a "bottom line" why he taught it. His reasons were existential and ethical. He said that other views of causality did not allow for novelty and meaningful change; and he had to oppose them because they provided:

> neither desire to do, nor effort to do, nor necessity to do this deed or abstain from that deed. So then, the necessity for action or inaction [is] not found to exist in truth or verity.

SHIFTS IN THE ABHIDHARMA

The radical interdependence of all phenomena is clearly affirmed in the teaching of paticca samuppada that we find in the *sutras* and *vinaya,* the first two *pitaka* or "baskets" of the first Buddhist scriptures known as the *Pali Canon.* This affirmation is eroded by the time of the *Abhidharma Pitaka,* the third basket, which analyzes and systematizes the philosophic elements of Buddhist doctrine. In the theorizing of the Abhidharmist scholastics, some shifts occur which alter the meaning of dependent co-arising in subtle but significant ways. These shifts tend to weaken the moral thrust of dependent co-arising, and blur its distictiveness from the causal views the Buddha contested.

Because the Abhidharma devotes so much attention to causality, it has influenced the way the Buddha's original doctrine has been interpreted. Statements are often made about this doctrine, which in point of fact are only true for the Abhidharma and not for the earlier teachings. The Abhidharma departed from the earlier causal teachings in stating: that phenomena are not only impermanent, but momentary; that nirvana is unconditioned; and that the classic formulation of the twelve interdependent factors refers to a sequence of three lives.

In systematizing the teaching of paticca samuppada, the Abhidharma constructed elaborate theories as to the nature, constitution, and duration of the factors of experience—also known as *dharmas* (small "d," to distinguish from the Dharma as the teaching of the Buddha). This effort tended to substantiate the dharmas as real and discrete entities and divert attention from the dynamic process at work through them. The problem arose as to how to accommodate this substantiation to a dynamic vision of reality. To do that, the dharmas came to be seen as instants, replacing each other with lightning rapidity, too brief to interact or do anything more than succeed each other in time. As a consequence, the Buddha's fundamental notion of impermanence *(anicca)* became momentariness *(khanika)*, and causality was reduced to mere sequence, for the dharmas were seen as too instantaneous to have any connection beyond that of succession.

This is close to the view of causality put forth by British philosopher David Hume, and indeed Hume's view is often taken as similar to the Buddhist. But the similarity extends only to the Abhidharma, and not to earlier Buddhism. There phenomena, impermanent but not momentary, exist long enough to interact with and affect each other. There causality is more than a mere succession of impressions; it is a co-arising that brings forth real change.

In a second shift from earlier teachings, the Abhidharma postulated that there are aspects of reality that are "unconditioned," mainly *nirvana*. This represents a change in the meaning the Abhidharmists assigned to the term *sankhata* and its opposite, *asankhata*.

Sankhata originally meant "put together" or "compounded," and therefore subject to dissolution. When the early scriptures apply its opposite, asankhata, to nirvana it means uncompounded, it does not mean unconditioned. Nothing in pre-Abhidharmist texts is regarded as unconditioned, or *apaticca samuppada*. Even liberation is not seen there as achieved by exiting from causality, but by using it. "I say that liberation is causally associated, not uncausally associated," said the Buddha.

The Abhidharmists' removal of nirvana from the causal realm resulted from their tendency to substantiate the dharmas. When viewed in terms of substances or entities, causality is linear—the production of one thing by another. Since nirvana cannot be considered to be produced in such a fashion, it is made exempt from causality—and in the Abhidharma the term asankhata comes to mean "unconditioned" or "uncaused."

When nirvana is viewed as unconditioned, hierarchical thinking creeps in. Release from suffering is assigned to another level of reality than the world of contingency and need in which we live, and the goal of the spiritual path becomes one of escape. This move erodes the ethical thrust of the Dharma, and the relevance of the Buddha's social teachings.

A third shift in the understanding of causality arose in the way the Abhidharmists interpreted the series of twelve factors, which serves as the classic formulation of dependent co-arising. Varied at the outset, this series had evolved through the oral tradition into a standardized pattern for easy recall. The Abhidharmists, with their habit of focusing on entities more than relations, proceeded to take literally what was originally a metaphoric and mnemonic device, and to see it as portraying a specific, linear progression. They divided the series to represent a sequence of three lives—past, present, and future—showing how actions in one incarnation affect the next. This interpretation in terms of three lives has no basis in the early scriptures. Furthermore, interpreting the causal factors as a linear sequence in time tends to obscure the reciprocal dynamic between them— the way in which, within a given life, indeed within a given moment, one's thoughts, feelings, and actions condition each other.

We can see the drift. To show how the self and its world are impermanent phenomena, empty of "own-being," the Abhidharma analyzed them into their constituent elements or dharmas—and then focused its attention on the dharmas themselves. As a result, the dharmas took on a substantial character; they were enumerated and classified, as if they were autonomous entities.

Eventually a corrective occurred with the first texts of the Mahayana, five centuries after the Buddha. There, in the *Perfection of*

Wisdom literature, a resounding declaration was made: not only is the self empty of own-being, dharmas are empty, too. Emptiness *(sunyata)* became another way of referring to dependent co-arising. And once again as in the early texts, the focus was on process, on relationship, on the dynamics of interdependence. That is why the *Perfection of Wisdom* scriptures are called "the Second Turning of the Wheel of the Dharma."

MARVELOUS AND DEEP

Ananda, the Buddha's beloved disciple and faithful attendant, was full of enthusiasm. "Wonderful, lord, marvelous, lord, is the depth of this causal law and deep it appears," he said. "And yet I reckon it as ever so plain."

"Say not so, Ananda, say not so!" replied the Buddha, "Deep indeed is this causal law, and deep indeed it appears. It is through not knowing, not penetrating that doctrine, that this generation has become entangled like a ball of string and covered with blight, unable to pass over the doom of the waste, the woeful way, the constant faring on."

In exploring the forgotten city of dependent co-arising, I have identified with the words of both Ananda and the Buddha, sharing in the student's delight and sensing the awesome depths of which the teacher spoke. No philosophic tenet has had more impact on me than paticca samuppada. Confirming an intuitive sense I've always felt of the interconnectedness of all things, this doctrine has provided me ways to understand the intricate web of co-arising that links one being with all other beings, and to apprehend the reciprocities between thought and action, self and world. It has led me to see that even my pain for the world is a function of this mutual belonging like a cell experiencing the larger body. Because it shows that causality, or power, resides in relationships rather than in persons or institutions, it offers the courage to resist conformity and to act in new ways to change the situation.

After exploring this teaching in the early Buddhist scriptures, I encountered it in general systems theory, in its explanations of the interdependent, self-organizing nature of open systems. That encounter preoccupied years of my life, as I compared and wove together the Buddhist and systems views of causality. I also encountered it in Sri Lanka, where I went to study the Buddhist-inspired community development movement called Sarvodaya Shramadana. There paticca samupadda is the central operating principle that imbues the ways that strategies are mounted, organizers trained, and villagers work together. Most recently, I encountered paticca samuppada in the field of ecology, especially in what is called "deep ecology," a way of thinking and seeing that takes the logical step of moving beyond anthropocentrism in recognizing the interdependence of all life-forms. I now use the term "deep ecology" as a functional equivalent to dependent co-arising, and I've developed experiential forms that I call "deep ecology work" to empower creative action for the healing of our world.

I doubt that the Buddha's teaching of dependent co-arising would have such an impact on my life and work had I not, in my studies, explored its implications—the perspectives it yields on the ways we know and act and relate. Some of these explorations around the forgotten city are offered in the following chapters.

CHAPTER SIX

Knower and Known

If Lake Erie is driven insane, its insanity is incorporated in
the larger system of your thought and experience.

—Gregory Bateson

One sunny morning on a street corner in Berkeley, where
I live, I ran into a woman I had met at a meditation retreat.
We stopped to talk, calling each other's attention to the
beauty of the day. When she asked, "How are you doing?", I lifted
the newspaper in my hand, with its headlines of troop movements
to the Persian Gulf. "I'm worried sick that we are heading into a
war," I told her.

Ella listened for a few minutes, then shook her head in sweet
concern and smiled. "Those are just passing events," she said, "If
you focus on them like that, you just add to the suffering. From a
higher perspective, it is all in our minds." She went on to tell me
how we "create our own reality" and how I should see through the
material world to know the serenity of the realm of pure spirit.

I started to protest that the events troubling me were as real as
the sun on the sidewalk and as real as the serenity I occasionally
experience. The Persian Gulf crisis was an anguish to me, and I didn't
want it trivialized. But my words turned to laughter, as I realized
that we were taking part in a very ancient conversation. What is real?
Is reality in the world I behold or in the realm of the mind?

The mystery of the relation between mind, which we subjectively
experience, and the world outside it, which we perceive, has teased
humankind since it first reflected on the nature of things. Walking
the Earth with a battery of senses, we see, hear, taste, touch, and
smell it—we know the contours and colors of our world, its texture
and topography. Yet at the same time, it can also appear to us that
we only truly live in the inner realm in which we receive these
impressions and reflect on them.

Is it what I perceive? Am I making it up? These eternal questions bemuse the mind of the growing child. Among philosophers

they engender the pursuit of epistemology, the study of how we know things.

In confronting the riddle of the relation between perceiver and perceived, mainstream Western thought has tended to stress exclusively one or the other. Classical empiricists hold that the world is the cause of our perceptions; taken as incontrovertibly there, it registers its data on passive and neutral sense organs. These data are taken as "given," as philosopher Thomas Kuhn observes:

> Is sensory experience fixed and neutral? Are theories simply [based on] given data? The epistemological viewpoint that has most often guided Western philosophy...dictates an immediate and unequivocal Yes!

In contradistinction, there are those thinkers and traditions who have said "No." Sensing the power of mind, subjective idealists have seen external phenomena as projection only. The cause is mind; therefore, knowledge can be independent of the data perceived.

These two positions, still vying for allegiance in our day, were vigorously debated in ancient India during the Buddha's life. Between these positions, there is no resolution. But Buddhism opens a third alternative: it presents knower and known, mind and world, as dependently co-arising.

It is very important for us to get clear on this interdependent relationship, because as we seek to free ourselves from the reductionism of classical science, which saw only external phenomena as objectively real, we can easily flip over into the opposite and equally one-sided extreme. Like Ella in Berkeley, we can fall into subjective idealism and imagine that we are essentially independent of our world, and that we create it unilaterally.

THE TRANSACTIONAL NATURE
OF PERCEPTION AND CONSCIOUSNESSS

It was the Buddha's view that a clear understanding of the process of perception gives insight into the origin of suffering and the illusoriness of the self. To this end, he and his followers paid attention to the way sensory impressions arise and how they relate to knowing and feeling. The conclusions they drew were very different form the orthodox, Vedic thought of their time.

The *Upanishads,* foundational to Vedic and subsequent Hindu thought, understood sensory perception to be, in the last analysis, a function of the *Atman,* the external, immaterial Self beyond all phenomena. It is the Atman that allows us to perceive the world, for "there is no other seer than he, no other hearer than he..." The *Atman* is the silent witness, the imperturbable rider of the chariot, spectator of all events.

In contrast, the Buddha taught that perception is produced by a convergence of factors. Here sensory perception does not reside in the power of a single agent, but rather in the interaction of three conditions: (1) a sense organ, (2) a sense object coming within its range, and (3) contact between the two. These conditions, especially the first two, constitute the sphere, or gateway *(ayatana),* through which perception occurs.

While consciousness conditions the gateway through which perception occurs, it is conditioned in turn by the objects perceived. It is ignited by them, like a flame.

> Monks, as a fire burns because of this or that appropriate condition, by that it is known: if a fire burns because of sticks, it is known as a stick-fire...and if a fire burns because of grass, it is known as a grass-fire....Even so, monks, when consciousness arises because of eye and material shapes it is known as visual consciousness...when consciousness arises because of mind and mental objects, it is known as mental consciousness.

Consciousness co-arises with sensory activity. It does not exist prior to or independently of its environment, but is called into being and conditioned by that which in turn becomes its object. It is always consciousness *of* something. "Apart from condition, there is no origination of consciousness."

For that reason, the Buddha rejected *a priori* reasoning. He saw no realm of pure logic aloof from or unconditioned by the sensory world. "There exist," he said, "no diverse truths which in the world are eternal, apart from perception." Views arrived at and defended in terms of pure reason alone are suspect in the Buddhist view, because knowing is conditioned by habit and vested interests. The Buddha made this clear:

> Were a man to say: I shall show the coming, the going, the passing away, the arising, the growth, the increase or development of consciousness apart from body, sensation, perception and volitional formations, he would be speaking about something which does not exist.

"Volitional formations" (*sankhara*) are the habits and impulses generated by mental activity; and they, in turn, modify our cognitions, loading them with the freight of past experiences and associations. The series of causal factors used in the teaching of *paticca samuppada* shows how the sankhara shape cognition and how, in turn, perceptions and feelings arise. With feelings of attraction or aversion, ego consciousness arises. There is the sense of something to defend or enhance. And the imagined needs of the ego proceed to impose fabrications on the external world.

Perception, then, is a highly interpretive process. We create our worlds, but we do not do so unilaterally, for consciousness is colored by that on which it feeds; subject and object are interdependent. The Buddha denied neither the "thereness" of the sense objects nor the projective tendencies of the mind, he simply saw the process as a two-way street. The conditioning is mutual.

INFORMATION LOOPS

In our own day, general systems theory gives us conceptual tools for understanding this interaction between knower and known. In the systems view, cognitive activity is seen as a circuit that embraces both the external world and that which perceives it.

Open systems, including cognitive systems like our minds, maintain and organize themselves by virtue of feedback—that is, by monitoring their interactions with their environment. "Monitoring" is a key term in systems theory. All open systems self-monitor; it is like a naturally occurring mindfulness. That is how our blood, for example, or the oceans regulate their levels of salinity. They watch what they are doing and adjust. They do this by a process of matching— matching the observed results of behavior with their inner preestablished goals. It is feedback that just told me to rewrite a sentence because it inaccurately conveyed the meaning I intended. It is feedback that kept my car on the road this afternoon, as I drove home. Instant by instant, so constantly that it is usually unconscious, we steer—which is the root meaning of cybernetics.

Feedback creates causal circuits, or loops of knowing; and in these information circuits our perceptions are conditioned by previous experience. We cannot count the bats in an inkblot, Gregory Bateson said, because there are none, "and yet a man—if he be 'bat-minded'— may 'see' several." In other words, we see by interpreting, and each of us lives in our own assumed form-world. The memories, expectations, and habits carried forward from the past infuse and give shape to our perceptions. They constitute internal codes and constructs by which we order and filter the influx of raw data.

The codes and constructs by which we interpret our world are functional equivalents to the Buddhist notion of sankhara, volitional formations or impulses. The monk-scholar Bhikkhu Nanananda calls sankhara, "the ruts and grooves of our mental terrain." He says that they influence every moment of our living experience. While the Buddhist view highlights, in a way that systems does not, the role of attachment in the perpetuation of these formations, both bodies of thought recognize the role codes play in perception—and both see them as subject to alteration. Formed by experience, these codes are modified by experience.

Our preconceptions not only shape our interpretations of the world, but impinge on the world itself. For the feedback loop extends beyond the subjective realm and circles through the environment "out there." To see how world and mind shape each other, let us look at two main ways feedback works. One is through homeostatic, or negative feedback, by which the world around us is brought into line with our own assumptions and goals. The other, through adaptive or positive feedback, leads to change in the internal codes themselves. Popular usage of the terms negative and positive feedback reverses their meaning in general systems theory, where negative feedback indicates you are on track, with no need for adjustment, and positive feedback signals deviation from objective and the need to correct or alter course.

By the first kind of feedback, we act upon our environment to make it intelligible in terms of our inner pictures and ideas. In this way we are said to "project" our codes upon the environment so that it will continue to confirm our expectations and serve our goals. By such projection the scientist shapes his research to yield the kind of data that can fit his hypothesis, and the architect designs buildings to give body to her dreams. To perpetuate the match between perception and expectation, we impose shapes on our world which then reflects them back. In excavated gardens or fortifications we can read something of the character of an ancient city, for in them its meanings, values and constructs, took form. Notions incarnate. And when we possess a powerful technology, this incarnational capacity is fearsome. Our imaginations erect Pentagons and Disneylands, and even the land itself mirrors back our fantasies, as, gouged and paved over, it testifies to our search for mastery, and our fear of what we cannot control. In the world we create, we encounter ourselves.

The second type of feedback, called adaptive or positive feedback, occurs when there is a persistent mismatch between perception and code—that is, when we can no longer interpret experience in terms of our old assumptions. The cognitive system then searches for new codes by which novel and confusing perceptions can be made intelligible. This search amounts to an exploration of new ways to reorganize itself—and it continues until codes and constructs evolve that can deal with the new data.

Thus do living systems adapt, by transforming themselves, and thus does learning happen. Real learning is not something added, it is a reorganization of the system. New nets and assemblies occur, loops form, alternate pathways develop. The viewed world is different, and so is the viewer. When in the sixteenth century Copernicus and Keppler produced compelling evidence that the Earth revolved around the sun, it was not just additional information. A revolution occurred in our experience of the world and in the ways we see and think. Now, in our own time, the Gaia hypothesis—that the Earth itself is a living system—brings with it a comparable transformation in our understanding of our world and ourselves.

We can recognize here the creative function of cognitive crisis. When old, habitual modes of interpretation become dysfunctional, it is often painful, a dark night of the soul, but that kind of confusion can be fruitful. It motivates the system to self-organize in more inclusive ways, embracing and integrating data of which it had been previously unconscious.

The Zen master, approached for teachings, filled his caller's tea cup till it overflowed—showing in this manner that the new could not be perceived until one has emptied oneself of preconceived notions. Similarly, the Buddha did not pour pronouncements into his followers' heads, so much as invite them to free themselves of habitual ways of seeing. In the meditation he taught, we can engage in the kind of learning that takes us apart and puts us back together again in new ways.

Seen in systems terms, the practice of *vipassana,* or insight meditation, represents a short-circuiting of the codes and constructs we impose upon reality. These are undercut as the mind trains to register perceptions without editorial comment or discursive thought. The application of bare attention allows us to step aside from the mental chatter that perpetuates our preconceptions. Rather than eliminating noise to extract message, the meditator switches off the message in order to attend to the noise. The exercise amounts to a deliberate mismatching, or production, of positive feedback, as awareness widens to the rush of impersonal psycho-physical events, wherein the habitual "I" is no longer discernible. Bare attention to the flow of experience yields no experiencer separable from it, and the Buddha's teaching about the self becomes more than a theory. The absence of a permanent, separate self erupts as a reality that changes the face of life.

THE LIMITS OF COGNITION

If knowing is interactive, it becomes difficult to claim and impossible to prove an ultimate truth. For knowing is relative to the perspective of the knower and conditioned by his past experience.

Gautama was unique among teachers of his time in refraining from establishing a definitive metaphysic. To the puzzlement and exasperation of many of his followers, he refused to define in ultimate terms the way things are "out there" in objective reality, independent of the knower. Theories that define the ultimate source and status of things were suspect, because they are of necessity partial and because they become objects of attachment. Views that claimed exclusive and final accuracy were shunned, dismissed by the Buddha with barely disguised contempt.

> Whatever is esteemed as truth by other folk, amidst those who are entrenched in their own views...I hold none as true or false. This barb I beheld well in advance, whereon mankind is hooked, impaled: "I know, I see, 'tis verily so"—no such clinging for the Tathagatas.

I love this sly and pithy observation. Gautama does not say they are wrong, those who claim they are right and who assert, "I know, I see, 'tis verily so." He just says that they are hooked, they are not free. And he is glad not to be hooked himself—"no such clinging for the Tathagatas" (which is another word for Buddhas). The quote reminds me of "Ari" Ariyaratne, founder of Sarvodaya, the Buddhist-inspired community development movement in Sri Lanka. One day on a visit to a Sarvodaya rural center, we met a New Age Western guru who preached to us the whole time, serenely oozing his certitude of possessing ultimate truth. When Ari and I got back in the car, I began to vent my irritation at the pompous fellow, pointing out emphatically how wrong he was. Ari just laughed and said, "Looks like he's 'impaled on the barb'; but you don't need to be!"

The impossibility of arriving at ultimate formulations of reality does not represent a defeat for the inquiring mind. It is only final assertions that are suspect, not the process of knowing itself. For we each have a valid and important perspective on what is. And to the extent that we can acknowledge the partiality of this perspective, what we say stays clear and true.

OBJECTLESS KNOWING

If knower and known co-arise, and consciousness is transactional, what do we make of those experiences where world and senses fall away? How do we understand the experience of objectless knowing? Ella, for example, spoke with some authority, as if she had experienced an undifferentiated consciousness beyond phenomena. She probably had. The Buddha and his followers experienced it, too, to judge from the scriptures. Ella would probably take exception to my interpretation of paticca samuppada and say that the fact of pure consciousness reveals that there is an unconditioned realm, independent from our world of wars and tribulations. How did the early Buddhists explain this experience?

Their scriptures do not specify a term for pure awareness or objectless consciousness. But they do make clear that the polarity between subject and object can be transcended and that a consciousness can arise that is removed from sensory stimuli and concepts. The nature of such consciousness has puzzled many a disciple. "Could there be such an attainment of concentration," asks Ananda, "that the monk will not be conscious of earth in earth, nor of water in water, [etc.]...and yet he will be conscious?" The Buddha answered,

> Herein, Ananda, a monk is thus conscious: "this is peace, this is excellent, namely, the calming down of all formations. . .the destruction of craving, detachment, cessation, nirvana."

Ananda then directs the same question to Sariputra. The eminent and enlightened senior disciple answers:

> Cessation of becoming is nirvana; cessation of becoming is nirvana: thus, friend, one perception arises in me, another perception fades out in me. Just as, friend, when a pile of sticks is blazing one flame arises and another flame fades out, even so, friend, one perception arises in me: Cessation of becoming is nirvana, and another perception fades out in me: Cessation of becoming is nirvana. At that time, friend, I was conscious of this: Cessation of becoming is nirvana.

According to the replies Ananda elicited, objectless knowing is still a series of momentary events; it partakes of the world of flux and is transitive in the sense that there is still an object of knowing, which is the very cessation of perception.

There are two ways of understanding this kind of consciousness within the context of dependent co-arising: either as transitive (peace or cessation of suffering being the object of cognition) or, if taken intransitively, as a direct experiential validation of the interdependence of subject and object (where the "I" is no longer experienced, neither is the object).

Although this may sound rather abstract, much is at stake in the ways we interpret the experience of pure or undifferentiated consciousness. When it is taken as proof of a metaphysical absolute—an eternal, unconditioned realm, essence, or being—then the radical interdependence or paticca samuppada that the Buddha taught is severely compromised. There arises in our minds the notion of a haven to which we can resort, a haven more real, valuable, and beautiful than the imperfect world around us and the claims of our suffering fellow beings.

Some Buddhists and scholars of Buddhism claim that there is such a realm, and they base this claim on a particular passage in the early scriptures, *Udana 80:*

> There is, monks, that sphere wherein there is neither earth, nor water, nor fire, nor air; wherein is neither this world nor a world beyond, nor moon nor sun. There, monks, I declare, is no coming, no going, no stopping, no passing-away and no arising. It is not established, it continues not, it has no object. This indeed is the end of suffering...Monks, there is a not-born, a not-become, a not-made, a not-compounded. Monks, if (there were not), there would be no stepping out here, from what is born, become, made, compounded.

Please note that the term translated here as "sphere," is ayatana, the gateway that permits the occurrence of perception. It refers to the *means* by which we perceive, or the *way* in which we perceive, rather than to an object of our perception. The knower, then, while out of touch with the environment (in that the six senses are transcended), would be very much *in* touch with what permits his interaction with the environment. He would be conscious of that by which he knows it and , therefore, by which he can "step out," to use the phrase employed, from the fabrications he imposes upon it.

Misconstructions of this passage from the *Udana* derive from confusing a mode of knowing with an object of knowing, and from taking the term "not-compounded" (asankhata) to mean unconditioned (an attribute assigned to no phenomenon in the early teachings).

Note, furthermore, that while *Udana 80* seems to identify this non-discriminatory awareness with enlightenment (saying "this indeed is the end of suffering"), the early scriptures do not. Cessation of perception and feeling is equivalent to the *samadhi* attained by advanced yogis of the time. Learned by Gautama well before he sat under the *bodhi* tree, it was used to attain rest and release from pain, and to develop the concentration requisite to insight. But it is distinct from insight—that recognition of the dependently co-arising nature of existence, that is integral to the enlightenment of the Buddhas and all beings.

WHO IS KNOWING?

Reality appears to be so organized that consciousness of it is hampered to the extent that the distinctions between knower and known are reified. Who, then, is knowing? It is no entity we can isolate, for as soon as distinguished, it is the known, not the knower. Unable to locate an agent, we are driven, in the last resort, to accord that function to the universe itself, which appears to be organized in ways that enable it to observe and know itself.

In early Buddhist teachings, the mental distortions that obscure to us the nature of our being in the world are viewed in a merciless light. At the same time, the idea that we can eradicate and break free of them is proclaimed. Not only is this possibility affirmed, but methods are set forth by which it can be achieved.

In vipassana training, this is done by directing attention not to the things we see, but to how we see them—the co-dependently arising nature of feelings, thoughts, and perceptions. Thus can be gained the "eye of wisdom," that dissolves the hatred and greed we project upon the world. The knower, seeing with the "eye of wisdom," does not seek to extricate herself from the objects of her knowing, so much as to free them from the fabrications she imposes upon them. As the object of knowing seems to disappear in the experience of cessation of perception, so now, with insight practice, the subject seems also to evaporate.

> Then, Bahiya, thus must you train yourself: in the seen, there will be just the seen; in the heard, just the heard; in the sensed, just the sensed; in the known, just the known. That is how, Bahiya, you

must train yourself. Now, when, Bahiya, in the seen there will be just the seen; in the heard, just the heard; in the sensed, just the sensed; in the known, just the known, then Bahiya...you will not be in it. And when, Bahiya, you will not be in it, then Bahiya, you will not be 'here' nor 'there' nor 'midway-between.' This itself is the end of suffering. *(Udana 8)*

Both the "what" that is known and the "who" that is the knower are elusive. Neither can be fixed or pinpointed as static, self-existent entities. Shifting and dancing out of reach as we seek to grasp them, they suggest that there is not knower or known so much as "just knowing."

CHAPTER SEVEN

Body and Mind

The transient Here seems to need and concern us strangely.

—Rilke

The environmental crisis has deep attitudinal roots. To restore our environment we need to heal our relationship with it, and that means healing the split in the psyche that cuts us off from the material world. It means revisioning the relation of mind to matter. The bulldozing of nature and the abuse of our own bodies reveal the depth of this separation, the fear it engenders, and the need to control.

What ways of thinking can help us come home again to the physical world? The materialisms of Marxism, capitalism, and classical science offer little help. They do not heal the separation, because they give no authority to subjective experience. The very values and yearnings within us that would move us toward wholeness are considered peripheral.

When we turn instead to the realm of spirituality, we find that the major religious traditions of our planet are afflicted with the same split—a deadening dichotomy between matter and mind. Behind their theologies and symbol systems, we detect a revulsion against the flesh, as if the mental realm were more real and more valuable than the physical.

Thus the separaton of mind from matter has generated two opposing ways of viewing reality, giving rise to what British novelist and scientist C.P. Snow called the "two cultures" that have divided the modern world. One derives from science, the other from the humanities, and there is little communication between them. As I journeyed between the cultures—from theology to Marxism, from social science back to religion, I encountered in each the split between mind and body. It was hard to find a philosophy or religious system that did not perpetuate it.

After I became acquainted with Buddhism and experienced the luminous beauty of its teachings about the mind, I began to wonder what the Dharma had to say about the body. Did it accord reality and dignity to the physical? Was it free of contempt for matter?

On the surface, it would appear not. There is much in early Buddhism that seems, at first approach, to echo, if not aggravate, the dichotomy between mind and matter. There is a strong ascetic flavor to the Pali Canon. The body is said to be as insubstantial and illusory as a "mass of foam," and the world "a mirage," a "bubble." The monks of the Sangha are counseled to avoid temptations of the flesh by cultivating revulsion for the body. To this end meditative guides are provided in the scriptures, urging the monks to develop aversion by seeing the body in terms of "kidneys, heart, liver, pleura, spleen, lungs, intestines, mesentery, gorge, feces, bile, phlegm, pus, blood, sweat, solid fat, saliva, mucus, synovic fluid, urine."

In Sri Lanka one day I received instruction in this practice from a noted Theravadin meditation teacher. I remember sitting on a mat behind the other students as he gave us guidance in overcoming sense desires. I also recall the scent of jasmine, the feel on my skin of handloomed cotton, and the golden light of late afternoon flickering through the bougainvillea at the window, making delicate, dancing patterns on the floor. "Fresh fruits and curries appear pleasing," said our teacher, "but consider how repulsive the food looks in your mouth when you masticate, and how yet more disgusting it becomes in the stomach…" He went on in this vein, bringing in digestive and intestinal activities, and concluding with the words, "There is nothing coming out of the body that is not disgusting."

He invited questions, but I ducked out, to walk vigorously up and down under the palm trees. "I'll show you three things that came out of my body that aren't disgusting," I muttered into the evening air. "As a matter of fact, I'd like to introduce them to you…"

Still, I could not take too seriously the prudish tone of some of the early texts and of the teachers that expound them. There was more in the Dharma than these pitiful lapses into fear of matter, something bigger and more real and life-affirming. I suspected that it offered an alternative to the two mutually contradictory views of reality that had stymied our culture: materialism on the one hand and ungrounded spirituality on the other, both stemming from the split between mind and body.

"LIKE TWO SHEAVES OF REEDS"

In ancient India, too, there were contending schools of thought as to the relation of mind and body. The materialists reduced mind to matter, and Vedantic thought reduced matter to mind. The Buddha offered a totally new approach. He did not explain one in terms of the other, or question the reality of either. Instead he showed how they interact, how they dependently co-arise.

Their interdependence is given special emphasis in the Buddha's teaching of paticca samuppada. There, in the classic series of twelve conditional factors, name-and-form *(namarupa)* is the factor that represents the body. It arises conditioned by consciousness and conditions, in turn, the arising of perception. In rendering the series, a number of texts pause here and circle back, so to speak, inserting that consciousness itself arises conditioned by name-and-form. Now *all* the factors are implicitly understood to co-arise with each other, but in the case of mind and body a loop occurs to make their interdependence crystal clear.

In referring to mind and body, the preeminent disciple Sariputra likens them to:

> two sheaves of reeds leaning one against the other. Even so, friend, name-and-form comes to pass conditioned by consciousness, consciousness conditioned by name-and-form...If, friend, I were to pull towards me one of those sheaves of reeds, the other would fall; if I were to pull towards me the other, the former would fall.

One day a monk made statements to the effect that consciousness was independent of the material world. The Buddha scolded him with unusual severity, his acrid tone conveying just how crucial he considered this aspect of his teaching to be:

> But to whom, foolish man, do you understand that Dharma was taught by me thus? Foolish man, has not consciousness generated by conditions been spoken of in many a figure by me, saying: Apart from conditions there is no origination of consciousness? But now you, foolish man, not only misrepresent me because of your own wrong grasp, but you also injure yourself and give rise to much demerit which, foolish man, will be for your woe and sorrow for a long time.

If body and mind are to be seen as interdependent, why then the ascetic passages and the cultivation of revulsion in the early texts?

Such passages must be seen within context. Renunciation and sexual abstinence were the norm for all wandering religious movements of the time. The Sangha as a monastic order in India had a stake in helping its adherents maintain celibacy. Given that the scriptures of the Pali Canon represent the views of the most narrowly monastic of the early Buddhist schools, it is not surprising that they feature attitudes which facilitate self-denial and celibacy. Furthermore, and the essential point, these reflections on phlegm, pus, mucus, and so on, did not degrade the body to exalt any higher function or faculty.

The body, although viewed as mercilessly as by any first-year medical student, was not dismissed as less real or less valuable than consciousness, reason, intellect. As the monk was to meditate on the impermanent and composite nature of the body, so was he also to meditate on the composite and transient nature of the mind. Mind, too, was dissected and viewed in terms of the passing flux of thoughts, perceptions, and sensations of which it is constituted. No essence was held up as inherently nobler, purer, or more real than this bag of decaying flesh. The monk's goal, in reflecting on the body, was to become more mindful of it, not to withdraw from it or to alter it.

Therefore, the ascetic flavor of the early Buddhist texts should not mislead us; never is matter presented as less real than consciousness, or as inherently dangerous. Pleasures of the flesh that stimulate our craving are to be shunned, but so are tendentious views and judgments.

Indeed, the body appears to be seen as more innocent and less dangerous than our conceptual reifications. Craving is described in the *Mahanidana Sutta* in terms of four kinds of grasping: "grasping at things of sense...speculative opinions...rule and ritual... theories of the soul." Of the four kinds of clinging, only one is physical, only one involves bodily appetite.

In the *Samyutta Nikaya*, the Buddha says, "The untaught manyfolk, brethren, might well be repelled by this body, child of the four great elements, might cease to fancy it and wish to be free from it, [seeing its] growth and decay." Yet the manyfolk are not repelled by consciousness; they cling to it, thinking, "This is mine, this I am, this is my spirit." But the body persists for years—ten, thirty, fifty, a hundred or longer—whereas consciousness changes ceaselessly. "Just as a monkey, brethren, faring through the woods ... catches hold of a bough, letting it go seizes another, even so that which we call thought, mind, consciousness, that arises as one thing, ceases as another, both by night and by day." These who are repelled by what is transient should hardly prefer mind to matter, he suggests as he concludes: "Therefore, it were better, brethren, if the untaught manyfolk approached this body, child of the four great elements, as the self rather than the mind."

The Buddha himself was scorned by his early ascetic companions for having, in his pursuit of enlightenment, indulged the flesh rather than punished it. Like them, he had mortified the body in grueling austerities. The hunger, filth, and exhaustion he inflicted on himself has been vividly portrayed in Buddhist art. Then, before seating himself in meditation under the bodhi tree, he accepted from a woman a meal of rice and milk. He told later how, when he did this, the yogis, "turned on me in disgust, saying the recluse Gautama has reverted to a life of abundance." And when, after his enlightenment, he went to preach to them, they said, "Here comes the recluse Gautama who lives in abundance...Let us not salute him."

But the woman who brought food to Gautama is honored in carvings throughout the Buddhist world. Kneeling with her bowl beneath the lotus throne, she serves as a reminder that the body is not to be despised as less real or less worthy than mind.

THE LARGER BODY/MIND

If consciousness co-arises with form, can it be limited to the human realm? Is it the unique possession of our species? Does it set us apart from the rest of the phenomenal world?

To these questions, the Dharma says "No." Consciousness pervades all forms of existence. That teaching can begin to free us from the anthropocentrism that we have inherited from the Semitic religions. The English-born monk and scholar Sangharakshita notes that in Buddhism the human is but "one manifestation of a current of psycho-physical energy, manifesting now as god, now as animal, etc." He points out that this belief in psychic continuity underlies the compassion for other creatures, the "boundless heart" that the Buddha exemplified and taught.

Consciousness is throughout, but it is not unitary; it is not, in the Buddhist view, the unchanging oneness we find in Hinduism. There the omnipresence of Brahman, or the pervasiveness of Vishnu, remains changeless and eternal behind the screen of illusion *(maya)*. Awareness of it requires that we see through or strip away the material particularities of life forms. But in the Buddha Dharma, where it co-arises with form, consciousness is, in every instance, particular. It is characterized not by sameness, but by "thatness" or "suchness" *(tathata)*.

While all the worlds and planes of existence teem with consciousness, human mentality presents a distinctive feature: the capacity to choose, to change its karma. That is why a human life is considered so rare and priceless a privilege. And that is why Buddhist practice begins with meditation on the precious opportunity that a human existence provides—the opportunity to wake up for the sake of all beings.

The Dharma vision of a co-arising world, alive with consciousness, is a powerful inspiration for the healing of the Earth. It helps us see two important things: It shows us our profound imbeddedness in the web of life, thus relieving us of our human arrogance and loneliness. And, at the same time, it pinpoints our distinctiveness as humans, the capacity for choice. In appreciating these teachings, I have found systems thinking to be extremely helpful.

BODY/MIND IN SYSTEMS THINKING

Like Buddhism, general systems theory (or, more particularly, in this context as systems philosophy) recognizes that consciousness is endemic to the universe, immanent in all life forms. This pervasive nature of mind is articulated by systems thinkers in a variety of ways. For example, Gregory Bateson refers to "the pattern that connects" in the flow of information or feedback loops that interweave living systems, and Ervin Laszlo speaks of the "interiority" of living systems:

> The phenomenon of mind is neither an intrusion into the cosmos from some outside agency, nor the emergence of something

out of nothing. Mind is but the internal aspect of the connectivity of systems within the matrix. It is there as a possibility within the undifferentiated continuum, and evolves into more explicit forms as the matrix differentiates into relatively discrete, self-maintaining systems. The mind as knower is continuous with the rest of the universe as known. Hence in this metaphysics there is no gap between subject and object...these terms refer to arbitrarily abstracted entities.

Natural systems are both physical and mental. When they are externally observed, says Laszlo, they are material, partaking of our material world. When they are subjectively experienced, they are mind. Mind and body then are two perspectives of the same phenomenon, and you cannot reduce one to the other. Like two sides of a coin or the inside and outside of a house, they are inseparable. And they correspond to each other in complexity—the subjective experience of a cell would be correspondingly simple; and it would be hard to imagine by a brain that is composed of a hundred billion cells. As Laszlo says, its "mind-events must be entirely different in 'feel' from ours, yet they can be mind-events nevertheless, i.e. types of sensations correlated with, but different from physical processes."

One way in which a nerve cell's mind, or a tree's or a dog's would be different in "feel" is that it does not loop back on itself in the complexity of circuits that are required in order to plan ahead and make decisions. Self-reflexive consciousness is an attribute of certain mammals with very large brains. It evolved as the system grew so complex in its organization and behaviors, that it could no longer self-regulate automatically or on instinct alone. Feedback about feedback, in assemblies of loops, had to be consciously monitored. We watch what we do, and decide. Choice enters the scene. We can change our karma.

We exist in nested hierarchies of natural systems, from the molecules and organs that comprise our bodies to the social systems and ecosystems that sustain us from without. Neither the systems inside us nor the systems around us have this self-reflexive consciousness. That capacity to think and choose requires the high degree of internal differentiation and the high degree of organized integration that big brains, like the human and presumably some marine mammals, have developed.

Considering what humans are doing to their world, our use of self-reflexive consciousness is not very encouraging. But the story is not finished. As they have throughout time, systems continue to self-organize and evolve, and new levels of systemic mind can emerge. They can emerge as we work together, in synergy toward common goals, weaving new neural assemblies and feedback circuits. Sometimes, as I behold the ways we attune and support each other in cooperative efforts on behalf of Earth, I imagine that we ourselves are like nerve cells in a larger brain—and that brain is starting to think.

As we take part in the healing of our world, we are supported by the co-arising universe itself. Life pulses through its mind-body, taking countless forms to accompany and teach us. They exist within us in the beautiful homeostatic systems of our "bile, blood, and mucus"; they surround us in the ecosystems of swamp and forest and in the social systems of our neighborhoods and Sanghas. We don't have to go it alone, and we can't. The strength and wisdom we need is not to be concocted on our own, but found in interaction—for that is how they arise, interdependently.

The same is true for our goals and the visions that guide us; they too dependently co-arise. New visions do not come from blueprints inside our heads that are shaped by past experience and old habits of thinking. They are born as we interact with our world, and receive fresh sensations and perceptions. And for that we need Earth and body, the stuff out of which we are made. They remind us that we are not brains on the end of a stick, but an organic, integral part of the web of life. Matter itself, if we attend to it mindfully and gratefully, can help liberate us from delusion; for it is mind, not matter, that is in bondage.

Indeed, the particularity of matter, the thingness of things, is helpful to the mind in returning it to the immediacy of experience. For it is not through its fancies, delusory as they can be, nor through the concepts to which it tenaciously clings, that mind is illumined. It is through attention to the here and now, the immediacy of experiencing what eludes its fabrications, that mind can overleap its old self-enclosing constructs and perceive the living process of which it is a part.

CHAPTER EIGHT

Karma:
The Co-Arising of Doer and Deed

The Buddha's teaching of *anatman,* that there is no permanent abiding self, is central to the Dharma. When I began
to register the meaning of this teaching, it spelled release.
I sensed how it could liberate me from habits of self-concern. It
promised freedom to act—freedom to do what is to be done, without
endlessly taking my own spiritual and psychological pulse before
getting on with it.

I received early lessons in anatman from my first meditation teacher,
Sister Karma Khechog Palmo, an English-born, Tibetan nun in India.
When I made statements like "I cannot sit still," or "I am lazy (or
angry or stupid)," she would immediately cut me short. "Stop!" she'd
say, "Stop saying 'I' in that way, when talking about your experience."
Such 'I' statements work like cement, anchoring passing feelings
into a kind of permanence. Sister Palmo pointed out that it is more
accurate and helpful to say, "Anger is happening," or "Fears are arising."

Her admonishments helped me recognize the burden of a so-
lidified self—and the burden began to lift. The "Joanna" who kept
looking in the mirror to check her rightness, or worthiness or guilt,
seemed to dissolve a little. But the teaching of anatman can seem,
at first approach, to free us from conventional morality as well.

A young woman I knew had been recently exposed to Buddhist
ideas. Nance was leaving a hotel after a conference, when her suitcase
fell open. Along with her clothes and cosmetics, a set of the hotel
towels spilled out on the lobby floor. With an embarrassed shrug,
she handed the towels to the bellboy and proceeded out the door.
Her horrified roommate asked her if she wasn't ashamed of herself.
"What self?" said Nance. "You only get uptight about this if you believe
in the self. At least I am free of *that* illusion."

Her comment may sound blithe, or silly, but it highlights an issue
in Buddhist thought that has been problematic for many. What *is*

there to get uptight about, if we are but a passing flow of psycho-physical events? Does it matter what we do? Are we accountable for our acts? These questions have puzzled some Buddhist scholars too, especially in the West. Pointing out apparent contradictions between the doctrine of anatman and the ethical exhortations of the Buddha, a number have concluded that it weakens any notion of personal accountability.

The basic issue here is the connection between what we do and what we are. Or, if we understand our being as our conscious participation in reality, the question is whether our acts affect that participation—that is, our capacity to know, choose, and enjoy. If not, then notions of responsibility are tangential to one's life, noble but inconsequential. If they do, then distinctions between the pragmatic and the moral dissolve. In the Buddhist perspective of dependent co-arising, this is the case. Here, deeds and doer are reciprocally conditioned, and a notion is affirmed that is central to the Buddha's teaching of karma: What we do not only matters, it molds us. In this teaching, questions of both identity and responsibility are resolved.

THE BUDDHA'S TEACHING OF KARMA

The concept of *karma* is often associated with belief in rebirth or reincarnation, a belief that was almost universally accepted in the culture of the Buddha's time. Many questions addressed to the Buddha concerning the course of the spiritual life, and particularly the nature of personal continuity and the moral effect of deeds, were posed within this context of belief. Not only did the Buddha respond in kind, in terms of rebirth, he is also reported as having acquired on the night of his enlightenment personal recall of former lives. This recall, or retrocognition as it is sometimes termed, is one of the "higher knowledges" which the scriptures recognize, along with such powers as clairvoyance and telepathy. It was said to have enabled the Buddha, and subsequent followers who developed this ability, to perceive the consequences of behavior directly.

The Buddhist approach to rebirth differed radically from other beliefs in survival, because of the doctrine of no-self. The conceptual difficulty of accommodating anatman to the notion of recall of past lives has been a source of concern and speculation. If the self is transient, how can it survive from one life to the next? An early discourse, the *Brahmajala Sutta*, warns that retrocognition can dupe a yogi into belief in an enduring soul, and says that great care should be taken in how this experience is interpreted.

The Buddha did not consider it useful to reflect on the possibility or character of other existences. He said that when the disciple rightly sees the nature of causal arising, it never happens that he will run back to the past, thinking:

> "Did I live in times gone by? Or did I not? What was I in times gone by? How was I then? Or free from being what, did I become what?" Nor will he run toward the times to come, thinking, "Shall I be reborn in a future time, or shall I not? What shall I become in the future? …Why does this never arise? In that the disciple, brethren, has by right insight well seen even as they really are both this causal happening, this paticca samuppada.

Let us, too, decline from musing on other lifetimes and see what the Buddha's teaching of karma can tell us about the effects of our actions within the context of our own experience.

Disciples like Kassapa and Timbaruka often queried the Buddha as to who is responsible for the habits, sufferings, pleasures we experience. Gautama, in reply, refused to say that they are caused by a past actor with whom we have no more connection. One cannot categorically separate the "I" who experiences the result from the "I" who set it in motion; for they are not discontinuous. Yet the Buddha also refused to identify them. One cannot say that "one and the same person both acts and experiences the result," for the person is different, altered. There *is* a continuity, but it is not the continuity of an agent as a distinct and enduring being. The continuity resides in the acts themselves, that condition consciousness and feelings in dependent co-arising. It inheres in the reflexive dynamics of action, shaping that which brought it forth.

For action, the term karma is used. Early on, in pre-Buddhist literature, the word denoted ritual acts; then by extension it meant religiously ordained social duties. In the Buddhist texts, it is broadened to include all volitional behavior—bodily, verbal, and mental. This is what we are. This behavior molds us, as Gautama perceived in the middle watch of the night of his enlightenment. It was then he comprehended that the distinctive character we display at a given point is neither eternal, nor illusory, nor adventitious, but "that beings are mean, excellent, comely, ugly, well-going, ill-going according to the consequence of deeds." As Pali scholar T.W. Rhys Davids points out, "Where others said 'soul', Gautama said usually 'action'."

Our present psycho-physical structure is not that of a continuing self-identical entity, nor is it discontinuous from our past selves. Using the term *kaya*, which often included speech and thought along with body, the Buddha said:

> This body (kaya), brethren, is not your own, neither is it that of any others. It should be regarded as brought about by actions of the past, by plans, by volitions, by feelings.

Kaya, then, appears as a consequence of karma. It is inescapable, for we bear it within ourselves. It is written in the *Dhammapada*:

> Not in the sky, not in the midst of the sea, not if we enter into the clefts of the mountains, is there known a spot in the whole world where a man might be free from an evil deed.

The effect of our behavior is inescapable, not because God watches and tallies, or an angel marks our acts in a ledger, but our acts co-determine what we become.

They do so by means of the *sankharas,* or "volitional formations." These subconscious drives and tendencies condition the ways in which we interpret and react to phenomena. The term means "put together," "compounded," "organized." Sankharas accrue from previous volitional acts and represent the reflexive or recoil effects of these actions—the tendencies they create, the habits they form and perpetuate.

Because the character of a person's experience is affected by these formations, his identity is indistinct from what he does and thinks, has done and thought. He is neither aloof from these acts, nor their victim. They are his identity, continuity, and resource, as the *Anguttara Nikaya* declares.

My action is my possession,
my action is my inheritance,
my action is the womb which bears me,
my action is my refuge.

THE DHARMA AND DETERMINISM

By recognizing the creative interaction between past and present, the Buddha's view of karma diverged from the more deterministic notions of karma current in his time.

According to the contemporaneous Jain theory, each and every former act, regardless of its motivation or circumstance, inexorably bears its fruit; and the subject cannot develop morally or spiritually without personally undergoing all the consequences. Set in motion by the physical effects of deeds, karma represents a kind of substance, or film, an obscuring accumulation that only can be worn away through expiation. This process of wearing away can be hastened by mortification of the flesh. The Ajivika view, also taught in the Buddha's time, is even more deterministic. Considering *every* aspect of present experience, mental and physical, as the result of past action, it sees any human effort whatever as fruitless.

The grim fatalism of these notions of karma, where the past rules the present with a heavy mechanical hand, is evoked vividly by Lama Govinda.

> The idea that the consequence of all deeds, whether of a mental or corporeal kind, must be tasted to the very last morsel, and that through every most trivial action, through the slightest motion of the heart, one is further involved in the inextricable net of fate, is assuredly the most frightful spectre that the human heart, or more correctly the human intellect, has ever conjured up.

By contrast, the Buddha's doctrine of paticca samuppada represents to him a dynamic process of interdependent factors.

> And precisely on this account the entire chain at every moment and from every phase of it, is removable, and is neither tied to "causes lying in an unreachable distant past," nor yet referred to a future beyond the limits of vision in which, perhaps, some time, the effects of these causes will be exhausted.

By virtue of the interdependence of the factors of existence, and particularly the sankharas, dependent co-arising represents release from karmic fatalism. Deterministic views were so strong in his day that the Buddha did not leave this implicit. He repeatedly and specifically countered fatalistic views with his own arguments. The effect of actions cannot be traced in linear causal chains. Their interweavings, he said, are too complex to be so easily comprehended. Inferences drawn from a one-to-one correlation between past and present events can be misleading; therefore, we cannot pinpoint single causes in the past for every present event and condition. It even defies common sense to try, because, as we are aware, we are subject as well to other events—attacks of bile, social vicissitudes, accidents, winds, humors, and seasons. Among these many causal factors, karma, deeds, is just one. In other words, behavior is not the sole determiner of experience; other events condition it also.

The effect of a deed upon a person, furthermore, depends upon the person's character as shaped by other deeds. The Buddha pointed out that the same kind of act performed by different people can yield diverse results, and that different behaviors can produce similar results. An apparent miscreant may end up in bliss, or a reputedly pious person in misery. The growth of a seed depends not just on its own nature but also on the soil into which it is dropped. If a person puts salt into a small cup, the water becomes undrinkable, says the *Lonakappalavagga*, but,

> Suppose that a man, monks, would throw a grain of salt into the river Ganges ... Would this river Ganges also become salty and undrinkable because of this grain of salt? ... In the same way, monks, a man could perform here even a slight sinful action the result of which would lead him to hell. But, again, monks, a man could perform an equally slight sinful action the result of which would be experienced in this very life, and would not appear to be even light, much less grievous.

Finally, in rejecting determinism, the Buddha repeatedly emphasized that the effects of the past can be modified by present action. Because they dependently co-arise, the sankharas themselves can be altered; therefore, change in human motivation can destroy the noxious effects of karma. In confrontation with the Jains, Gautama pointed out that their own present experience is freely chosen, not sentenced by their past. He asked them whether they thought one could alter the outcome of karma by effort. When they in reply denied the possibility of changing karma in any way, the Buddha responded with obvious irony. In referring to the rigorous and painful ascetic pursuits of the Jains, he commented,

> If the pleasure and pain that living beings experience is caused by previous deeds, then, monks, the [Jains] must have been in previous lives doers of evil deeds, for they now undergo such sharp, severe and painful sensations.

If you cannot change karma, the Buddha said, "all effort is fruitless." This he would not allow. He rejected determinist views of karma because he believed that they provided

> neither the desire to do, nor the effort to do, nor the necessity to do this deed or abstain from that deed. So then, the necessity for action or inaction [is] not found to exist in truth or verity.

This "desire to do, and effort to do,"—in other words our volition—modifies the effects of our past, and broadens the scope for present endeavor. This emphasis on will is the most distinctive feature of the Buddhist concept of karma.

> Where there have been deeds, Ananda, personal weal and woe are in consequence of the will there was in the deeds.

That is why the sankharas, which condition our cognitions and perceptions, are understood as "volitional formations"; shaped by our desires, they carry forward the energy of the will. The determinative aspect of past acts resides in the choices that produced them.

A human existence is considered to be incomparably precious precisely because intention is so important and choice so determinative. Animals, ghosts, and gods experience pain and pleasure, but only the human being can affect her experience through decision. Given the astronomical number of other forms of life, this human opportunity is extraordinarily rare and valuable.

Since will determines the effect of acts, for good or for grief, it must be cleansed and exercised, and exertion is required. The early scriptures abound in exhortations to vigorous effort. Those who would "rise up from what is unskilled and establish [themselves] in what is skilled," are summoned repeatedly to be "intent on vigilance," "of stirred up energy, self-resolute, with mindfulness aroused," full of striving and zeal. A cardinal failing, miring one in unskilled ways, is *thinamiddham*, sloth or lethargy. By the same token, *viriya*, energy, resolution, vigor, is seen as essential to the Path and a cardinal virtue in its own right. Its summons presents a vivid contrast to the passivity and fatalism popularly associated with the notion of karma. Here will is primary, and it can be trained.

> Wherefore, brethren, thus must ye train yourselves: liberation of the will through love we will develop, we will often practice it, we will make it a vehicle and a base, take our stand upon it, store it up, thoroughly set it going.

In the early Buddhist view, then, a person's identity resides not in an enduring self but in his actions (karma)—that is in the choices that shape these actions. Because the dispositions formed by previous choices can be modified in turn by present behavior, this identity as choice-maker is fluid, its experience alterable. While it is affected by the past, it can also break free of the past.

THE SYSTEMS VIEW OF KARMA

General systems theory has helped me understand this. In systems thinking also, action appears as choice, and choice as identity.

Because the open system is self-organizing, its behavior cannot be dictated or directly modified from without. External pressures or circumstances can only operate in interaction with the system's internal organization. Past experience, as recorded in the system, is fed back into the making of present decisions. As its organization increases, the system becomes less determined by the environment, more autonomous. Self-reflexive consciousness emerges when the degree of complexity has evolved to the point that self-monitoring is required for evaluating and selecting between alternate courses of action. Freedom enters. As systems thinker Ervin Laszlo puts it,

When a man acts on the basis of his empirical and meta-level reflective cognitions he could always have acted otherwise than he did, for his constructions and cognitions of his environment are not dictated by his environment, but by his present cognitive [cortical] organization.

This "present organization" is a gift of the past. The codes and modes by which the system interprets reality and envisages results are conditioned by previous experience. But the past does not predestine actions, because it functions in mutual interaction with the present. Because it is dynamically self-organizing, the cognitive system "is changing and remaking with each decision in the present," says Karl Deutsch, a systems-oriented political scientist:

Thanks to what it has learned in the past, it is not wholly subject to the present. Thanks to what it still can learn, it is not wholly subject to the past. Its internal rearrangements in response to each new challenge are made by the interplay between its present and its past.

Meta-level reflections arise, and because they do, the individual "could always have acted otherwise than he did." Deutsch goes on to say:

Each of us is responsible for what he is now, for the personality he himself has acquired by his past actions... Nor are we wholly prisoners of any one decision or any one experience. Ordinarily, it takes many repetitions so to stock a mind with memories and habits that at long last lead to the same city, whether it be taken, in religious language, as the City of Destruction, or the City of Salvation.

The parallels to the Buddhist idea of karma are obvious, as also to the sankharas, the memories and habits that "stock the mind" and impel us onward.

The systems view, like the Buddhist, does not see us as victims of our past, hapless pawns of forces and times beyond our reach; rather, as Deutsch continues:

It sees in the actual moment of decision only a *dénouement* in which we reveal to ourselves and to others what we have already become thus far. Each step on the road to "heaven" or to "hell," to harmonious autonomy or to disintegration, was marked by a free decision....The determinate part of our behavior is the stored result of our past free decisions.

So fundamental to the systems view is this notion of choice that it appears as the definition of person. As systems-theologian William Everett puts it, "the self is a decision-center." To systems-psychologist O. H. Mowrer, choice defines consciousness itself. In the context of pointing out the conceptual weakness of behaviorist theory, where consciousness appears as the passive recipient of conditioning, Mowrer says,

I will venture the guess that consciousness is, essentially, a *continuous-computing* device or process. The eternal question is, "What to do? How to act?" And consciousness, as I conceive it, is the operation whereby information is continuously received, evaluated and summarized in the form of "decisions," "choices," "intentions."

Through the operation of feedback, the behaviors we choose and the goals we pursue take root in the psyche. They affect the ways we interpret experience—and these ways constitute who we are. Doer and deed co-arise. Hence our continuity of character, bearing the stamp of repeated choice and habit. Hence also our freedom, for the causal flow of co-arising is altered by each present act of will.

Here then is the answer to our question, "does it matter what we do?" It matters to the extent that *we* matter. Indeed, our acts matter—incarnate—*in* us, for they make us what we are.

This spells both grief and promise for the self we tend to posit and on whose behalf we generally act. Because it is altered by each act, wise or foolish, fearful or brave, the self, even as decisionmaker, is doomed as an enduring entity, ever dying and passing away. Yet in that very evanescence lies hope and promise. For in the flow of decisions and deeds, choices can be made that open broader vistas to perceive and know, wider opportunities to love and act.

CHAPTER NINE

Self and Society

Our own pulse beats in every stranger's throat.

—*Barbara Deming*

After supper at a rural community center, a half dozen visitors stood and talked by the fire. We had enjoyed a delicious and healthy meal of fresh, organic, home-grown produce. Conversation turned to the difficulties in our city lives of procuring food that is not irradiated or adulterated with additives or contaminated with pesticides and herbicides. Some of us had worked with citizen initiatives to pressure legislators and supermarket chains to ensure public access to safe food, and we shared our discouragements.

A woman, who had quietly joined our group and listened to our tales, spoke up. "The best thing to do," she said, "is take control of your own life. Leave the polluted air of the city. Drink pure spring water. Eat produce that you have grown yourself or know firsthand is safe." And I imagined there was an embarrassed defiance in her voice when she said, with firmness, "That's all we can do now, take care of ourselves."

I listened to her attentively, knowing that her logic was impeccable. The urban activists among us had adopted it to some extent, installing water purifying systems in our kitchens and buying from farmers' markets when we could. But her logic made curious our motivation in trying to change our political and economic institutions. I wondered what I could say and what she could hear that could put into question her seemingly accurate conclusion: "All we can do now is take care of ourselves." From her cultivated and deferential manner I assumed that she too had been exposed to religious teachings, and that compassion was hardly foreign to her. She simply believed, apparently, that she could separate herself from society and declare independence from its institutions.

Once again the Buddha's teaching of dependent co-arising rose up in my mind. I groped in vain for a simple, off-hand sentence that could convey the nature of our relationship to the institutions of our society, an interexistence so real that we cannot escape it by going to live in the country and growing our own food. The recognition of this interdependence is of a different order from compassion, which all religions promote and which we all need.

Thanks to his teaching of the radical interdependence of all phenomena, the Buddha set compassion in a context that extends far beyond personal virtue; it affirms the basic nature of our existence. He taught that social institutions co-arise with us. They are not independent structures separate from our inner lives, like some backdrop to our personal dramas, against which we can display our virtues of courage and compassion. Nor are they mere projections or reflections of our own minds. As institutionalized forms of our ignorance, fears, and greed, they acquire their own dynamics. Self and society are both real, and mutually causative. They co-arise or, to use Thich Nhat Hanh's phrase, they "inter-are."

In exploring the early scriptures, I found many passages where the Buddha describes this interdependence between self and society, and its implications for our political and economic behavior. These have moved and instructed me deeply.

THE CO-ARISING OF SELF AND SOCIETY

In ancient India of the Buddha's time, social and political systems were, in the dominant Brahmanical view, preordained. The institution of caste, for example, embodied the cosmogenic act by which the godhead in the form of the *Mahapurusha*, or Primordial Person, created the world out of his head, trunk, and limbs. Hence the divine right of kings, the innate role of priests, and the fixed, subordinate functions of the lower castes. In radical contrast to this venerable view, the Buddha presented such social forms as the impermanent and contingent products of human interaction, according to the law of dependent co-arising.

He illustrated this in the *Aggañña Sutta,* a discourse so popular that it resurfaces again and again in canonical and postcanonical writings and even in the preamble to the Burmese constitution. It is the Buddha's fanciful genesis story, his tongue-in-cheek recounting of the beginnings of things and origins of institutions. It was told pursuant to a discussion of caste, when some Brahmans asked the

Buddha whether caste as a social institution was not divinely ordained. Illustrating the law, or Dharma, by which things co-arise, this story presents self, society, and world as co-evolving forms. Remember, as you read this summary of the sutra, that in the very pretense to know the beginnings of things, the Buddha was poking fun at such metaphysical speculations...

In the beginning of a world cycle neither beings nor their world have solid form or distinctive features. Weightless, luminous, and identical, the beings waft about over a dark and watery expanse. When a frothy substance appears on the waters, they taste it. It is delicious, and for its sweet, honey flavor a craving arises. As the beings consume more and more, both they and their world change, become more distinct. The beings begin to lose to the world their identical luminosity: sun and moon and stars appear, and the alternation of day and night. The beings begin to solidify and vary in appearance. Pride and vanity arise as they compare themselves in beauty, and the savory froth vanishes. The beings bewail its loss: "Ah, the savor of it!" In its place, on earth that is now firmer, mushroomlike growths appear of comparable tastiness—only to disappear as the creatures fatten on them and change. The mushrooms are replaced by vines and these, in turn, by rice. With every new growth the beings crave, eat, grow more substantial and diverse. At each stage their use of the environment modifies it, engenders more solidity and new forms of vegetation, and with such usage they themselves alter, developing more distinctive features. In this interaction both creatures and world progressively differentiate, each gaining in solidity and variety.

When it first grew, the rice was without husk or powder and, when gathered, would grow again in a day. A lazy one, to save effort, decided to harvest two meals at once. Soon beings are harvesting for two days at a time, then for four days, then eight. With this hoarding the rice changes: a husk appears around the grain and the cut stem does not grow again but stands as stubble. So the people divide and fence the land, set boundaries to ensure their source of food. Soon a greedy one takes rice from a neighboring plot. Admonished by the others, he promises to refrain, but he takes again, repeatedly. Since admonishment is of no avail, he is beaten. In such fashion, with the institution of private property, arise theft and lying and abuse and violence.

Soon such acts are so rampant, the scene so chaotic, that the people decide to select one of their own to act on their behalf—"to be wrathful when indignation is right and to censure what rightly should be censured"—and to receive in return for this service a portion of their rice. So arises the *Mahasammata,* the great elected one, and with his rule order prevails. Such is the origin of kingship and the Kshatriya class, and so also evolve, by the assumption and differentiation of roles, the other major divisions of society: the Brahman, Vaisya, and Sudra castes...

Caste or class is not established by divine fiat, but arises from the actions of beings like ourselves and "according to the Dharma," the law of dependent co-arising. These social institutions are circumstantial in origin. Misguided and without foundation, therefore, is "the copious and characteristic abuse" with which the Brahmans revile those of their rank who go over to the Sangha, and with which they denigrate that company of the Buddha for including "the vulgar rich, the swarthy skinned and the menials." While social ranking conditions the lives, skills and hopes of persons, it does not, the scripture affirms, predetermine or foreclose their capacity to live nobly and achieve enlightenment.

The causal dynamics which this story metaphorically expresses underlie the social, economic, and political teachings and practices we find in scripture: the Buddha's rejection of caste discrimination and the egalitarian composition of the Sangha; his distrust of private property and the institution in the Sangha of voluntary poverty, sharing, and alms-begging; his advocacy of government by open assembly and consensus, and the Sangha's rules for debate, ballot, and the settlement of differences. These ideals and practices have been well described in Buddhist scholarship.

My interest here is to stress their profound connection with the doctrine of dependent co-arising. Within that mutual causal perception of reality one is not a self-existent being nor are the institutions of society eternally fixed. They are mutable and they mirror our greeds, as does indeed the face of nature itself. Co-arising with our actions, they, like us, can be changed by our actions. As our own dynamic processes can be transformed, so can they.

This story in the *Aggañña Sutta,* so often repeated in Buddhist writings, has been recognized as the first expression in Indian political thought of a theory of social contract. The beings banded together to make their own government; the Mahasammata was not divinely appointed and anointed, but chosen by his peers to act in their stead and for their purposes. The causality which the story portrays would indicate a difference between the Buddhist view and the Western, Rousseauian notion of social contract. In dependent co-arising, self, society, and world are reciprocally modified by their interaction, as they form relationships and are in turn conditioned by them. The Western idea contrasts with such a view to the extent that it assumes a free association between individuals who remain basically distinct and unaltered by such association.

POLITICAL VALUES AND GUIDELINES

In contrast to the Brahmanical notion of a divinely ordained and eternally valid social order, the Buddha presented political institutions as human-made and transient, subject to the law of dependent co-arising. It is not surprising, therefore, that unlike other wandering religious teachers of his period, he spent much of his career in and around cities, in the company of rulers, on the periphery of political power.

Gautama had grown up to the north of the monarchies in which he taught, in a tribal republic ruled by council or assembly (sangha). The Order he instituted, and called by the same name (Sangha), represented at the outset less a retreat from the world than an alternative community. A vehicle for the transmission of teachings and a locus for the restructuring of consciousness through meditation, it represented as well an embodiment of his social ideals. It served as a model for social equality, economic sharing, and democratic process.

The Sangha accepted persons regardless of caste and was, on that account, the object of some scorn and ridicule. Not only did Brahmans, who had a socially recognized religious vocation, join the Buddha, but merchants as well, and not only the well-born, but Untouchables and runaway slaves. As Jesus did also, the Buddha saw pride in social rank as a kind of spiritual bondage. He is quoted in the *Ambattha Sutta:*

> Whosoever…are in bondage to the notions of birth or of lineage, or to the pride of social position, or of connection by marriage, they are far from the best wisdom and righteousness.

In political organization as well as social complexion, the Sangha represented a contrast to Brahmanical notions. Admittance to the Order involved responsibility, for in its governance, emulating the ancient confederate tribal councils, decisions were to be made by consensus, "in concord." Scriptural passages such as the following represent the first references in Indian thought to rule by assembly.

> So long, O Bhikkhus, as the brethren foregather oft, and frequent the formal meetings of their Order—so long as they meet together in concord, and rise in concord, and carry out in concord the duties of the Order…so long may the brethren be expected not to decline, but to prosper.

Since unanimity could hardly be expected to prevail, and since the repression of beliefs was not to be tolerated, a rule of schism or *Sanghabheda* was instituted, by which dissenting groups formed new settlements within the Order. Within each settlement, select groups or committees, each having its own jurisdiction and procedural rules, were established to deal with matters administrative and doctrinal. The expression of varying opinions in the *Sanghakammas,* or assemblies for decision-making, was facilitated by the taking of ballots *(salaka),* again the first recorded use of such procedure in Indian political history.

While, on the one hand, the value of cohesiveness was stressed in frequency of assembly and rule of consensus, on the other, diversity was facilitated by the allowance of minority views. This was considered more important than ideological solidarity and centralized authority, and the Sangha split into many sects and schools. Given the energy and relative amicability of their interactions, however, this proliferation of forms testifies to strength more than weakness. And given the endurance of the Buddha Dharma over two and a half millennia, it would appear that it hardly required the centralized authority so often deemed necessary for the preservation of religious teachings and practice. Without a Rome or Jerusalem, Buddhism flowered in diversity of forms, while repeatedly renewing, through study and practice, its roots in the teachings of the Buddha.

ECONOMIC VALUES AND GUIDELINES

Early Buddhist scriptures also convey the kinds of economic assumptions and practices that emerge when self and society are seen as interdependent. Central here are the values of non-attachment, sharing, and right livelihood.

The Buddha's teaching that suffering stems from craving (the second Noble Truth) places a high value on self-restraint and low consumption. The traditionally mendicant way of the *bhikkhu* (monk), modelled after the Buddha, underscores the conviction that freedom derives not from wealth or the satisfaction of appetite, but from non-attachment. Liberation can be won from the restless greed to possess and consume, and from the objects, thoughts and habits that stimulate that wanting. Possessions, furthermore, are dangerous to the extent they foster the notion of "mineness" *(mamatta)*, and thus encourage belief in a permanent, personal self who possesses. In the *Aggañña Sutta,* the institution of private property is presented as the occasion for the arising of theft, mendacity and violence. From this perspective, the goal of modern advertising to induce the sensation of need and the desire to acquire is immoral, as, for that matter, is an economic system dependent on ever-widening public consumption of nonessential commodities and artifacts.

As an antidote to attachment and the delusion it engenders, the Buddha preached generosity *(dana)* and organized a community in which private property was renounced, all goods shared in common. The Sangha comprised as its members *bhikkhus* and *bhikkhunis,* terms which literally mean not monk and nun, but "sharesman" and "shareswoman," one who receives a share of something. Their alms-begging was not just a handy means of subsistence. It was sacramental in nature, betokening relinquishment of personal wealth and trusting dependence instead on the resources of society.

The bhikkhus' relation to lay society was reciprocal and symbiotic. In return for material support, the monks and nuns provided counsel, delivered teachings, and exemplified in their own behavior the ideals they taught. They also offered laypeople the opportunity to exercise and experience their own generosity through the giving of alms. In later centuries the Sangha's reciprocity included social services, such as hospitals and orphanages maintained by the bhikkhus, as well as the erection of monuments, libraries and universities, whereby the Sangha, from the gifts it received, created a rich heritage of art and learning.

In the Buddha's teachings, economic sharing was held out as an ideal for the relations between laypersons as well as bhikkhus, and as a prerequisite of a healthy society. While restraint in consumption is seen as salutary, the condition of poverty is not. The Buddha rejected mortification of the flesh, and affirmed the rightful claims of this body "born of the great elements." Indeed, poverty increases attachment; as the Buddha affirmed, a person cannot listen to the Dharma on an empty stomach.

The responsibility given to the individual in working out his own salvation requires an economics of sufficiency, as Emmanuel Sarkisyanz points out in *The Buddhist Roots of the Burmese Revolution*. Because the restructuring of consciousness is essential to the Path, and because no vicarious means of salvation is offered, the ideal social order allows each person the necessary economic base for his spiritual development. Reflecting this assumption, an array of *sutras* and *jataka* tales portray the wise ruler as engaging in broad public works and providing jobs, food, and shelter to the needy.

These scriptures express the economic interdependence that exists between the state and its citizenry, and the extent to which its health and security is a function of the well-being of all its people. When the king, in the *Kutadanta Sutta*, desires to offer a great royal ritual sacrifice to ensure his future welfare, he is reminded of the crime that harries his realm, pillaging towns and making the roads unsafe. His chaplain, who is identified as the Buddha himself in a former life, argues that neither fresh taxation nor arrest and punishment of the miscreants will end the disorder. The one way to stop it is to create productive employment opportunities: to give food and seed-corn to the farmers, capital to those who would engage in trade, and food and wages to those who would enter government service. Then "those men, following each his own business, will no longer harass the realm." And, according to the Buddha's story, not only did that happen, but, with the advent of peace and security, the state's revenues went up.

In the *Mahasudassana Sutta*, the king "of greatest glory" is described—and his magnificence is reflected in the facilities he establishes for the comfort of his people.

> Then, Ananda, [he] established a perpetual grant by the banks of those lotus-ponds—to wit, food for the hungry, drink for the thirsty, raiment for the naked, means of conveyance for those who needed it, couches for the tired, wives for those who wanted wives, gold for the poor, and money for those who were in want.

Many a jataka tale presents the wise ruler as ministering to his realm in similar fashion, offering resources that serve not only humans, but beasts and birds as well, "so as to extend the benefits down to dumb creation." For all hangs together, and when the king is unrighteous that unrighteousness seeps through society, through officers and Brahmans and townspeople, and then even the sun, moon and stars go wrong in their course.

This ideal of concern for the commonweal was most notably demonstrated in the reign of the Buddhist king Asoka. As his pillar and rock edicts witness, public works were instituted, roads, wells, hostels, hospitals—the first social welfare services on historical record.

> Moreover I have had banyan trees planted on the roads to give shade to man and beast; I have planted mango groves, and I have had ponds dug and shelters erected along the roads at every eight kos. Everywhere I have had wells dug for the benefit of man and beast...What I have done has been done that man may conform to the Dhamma.

The inherent right to worthwhile work is reflected in the concept of "right livelihood," a requirement of the Buddha's Eightfold Path. According to the teaching of dependent co-arising, the work a person performs not only expresses his character, but modifies it in turn. High value, therefore, must be placed on the nature of this work. Instead of being considered as a necessary evil to which one is condemned, or as a "disutility," as in the eyes of classical economists, work is a vehicle for the organization and expression of our deepest values.

Meaningful employment is more important than the goods it produces, as the *Kutadanta Sutta* suggests. Unlike consumption, it links the person to her fellow beings in reciprocal relationship, and expresses the interdependence which underlies her existence. The value of her work, then, is beyond monetary measure. Labor policies and production plans that view this work in terms of pay or profit alone degrade it and rob it of meaning. High wages, high dividends, high production or high unemployment payments cannot compensate for the human loss that occurs when assembly-line techniques or joblessness deprive a worker of acquiring and enjoying her skills.

ENDS AND MEANS

As has been repeatedly affirmed throughout human history, moral considerations pertain not only to the goals we try to achieve, but also to the manner in which we go about trying to achieve them. Frequently these appear at odds with each other, like the "war to end all wars." We all are familiar with the moral anguish that arises when worthy objectives seem only attainable by acts which appear, by their nature, to compromise them.

The conflict between ends and means arises from a dichotomized way of thinking; that is when we assume that the goal "out there" has an existence independent of ourselves or the methods we employ. Aristotle, for example, assumed this to be so in explaining his concept of final cause *(telos)*. It is that for the sake of which one acts. And he said in his Nichomachean Ethics (109), "Wherever there are certain ends over and above the actions themselves, it is [their] nature...to be better than the activities." The goal, then, appears as more real and more valuable than the activities it engenders; and acts themselves are merely instrumental to an end whose nature is more final and complete.

Such presuppositions lead to instrumentalist ways of thinking, where concern for ends overrides considerations of the ethical appropriateness of the means. Such considerations come to appear as moral niceties, welcome where they can be accommodated, but in the last analysis, "when push comes to shove," irrelevant to the goal in view—whose attainment may dictate more "pragmatic" and "realistic" choices.

The Dharma of dependent co-arising turns this kind of thinking inside out. It asserts, as indeed have many saints and teachers over the ages, that the goal is not something "out there," aloof from our machinations, but rather a function of the way itself, interdependent with our acts. As doer is interdeterminate with deed, modified by his own thoughts and actions, so are his objectives modified. For however he articulates these objectives, they reflect his present perceptions and interpretations of reality—which are altered, however slightly, by every cognitive event. Means are not subordinate to ends so much as creative of them—they are ends-in-the-making.

The Buddha offered the Dharma, not as a goal to be reached so much as a Way, *magga*. Each step on this way is of intrinsic value, the Dharma being "glorious in the beginning, glorious in the middle, glorious at the end." Value is intrinsic to each act because action (karma) is what we are and what we become. Although we are summoned to strive to transform our lives and our consciousness, we do so with the paradoxical knowledge that, though we may feel very far from where we want to be, there is no place to get to; for we are already there—or, as Jesus put it, "the kingdom of God is within you." This religious paradox, manifest in many faiths, overturns the problem of ends and means. It shows that the goals we pursue are not distant from us in time or space, but present realities, unfolding out of the core of our existence and capable of transforming it in the present moment.

We can never avoid what we seek to escape, least of all the political and economic institutions into which we are born. But by virtue of their dependence on our participation, by vote or consumption, lobby or boycott, they can change. They mirror our intentions, our values and ideals. This is what I would have liked to say to the woman who joined us by the fire that night in the country, because it is what I hear the Buddha's teaching saying to me.

CHAPTER TEN

Mother of All Buddhas:
The Second Turning of the Wheel

A bout five centuries after the Buddha, the Wheel of the Dharma, they say, turned again. The Buddha's central teaching of the dependent co-arising or interbeing of all phenomena, which he had identified as the Dharma itself, was reaffirmed and renewed, clothed in fresh language and imagery. This turning is represented by the scriptures called *Perfection of Wisdom,* or *Prajñaparamita,* which herald the advent of Mahayana Buddhism.

Here the hero figure of the *bodhisattva* appears, no longer limited to former lives of the Buddha, but extending to all beings who are able to perceive the interdependent nature of reality. And here that saving insight itself is personified. Emerging in the same era as did her Mediterranean counterpart Sophia, this wisdom, too, is female. She is the Perfection of Wisdom, the Mother of All Buddhas.

She presents an archetypal structure very different from the feminine attributes we have inherited from patriarchal thought. Freed from the dichotomies which oppose earth to sky, flesh to spirit, the feminine appears here clothed in light and space, as that pregnant zero point where the illusion of ego is lost and the world, no longer feared or fled, is re-entered with compassion.

To get acquainted with her and learn more about the wisdom of interbeing, let us look at one of the richest and most beautiful of the scriptures that honor her, the *Perfection of Wisdom in 8000 Lines,* written down some two thousand years ago.

A DIFFERENT KIND OF WISDOM

As Buddhas, world teachers
Compassionate, are your sons,
So you, O blessed one, are

This piece first appeared in *Anima Magazine,* Fall 1976.

Grandmother of all beings.
…He who sees you is liberated,
And he who does not see you is liberated, too.

The texts which bear her name are central to all major developments in later Buddhism, from Madhyamika philosophy to Vajrayana and Zen. These *Prajñaparamita Sutras* also reiterate tirelessly her categorical difference from earlier and more conventional notions of wisdom.

In the earlier scriptures of the Pali Canon, wisdom was featured, along with moral conduct and meditation, as one of the three essential aspects of the Path, and seen as the knowledge of dependent co-arising, the Buddha's doctrine of causality. Among the Theravadins this doctrine had been primarily understood in terms of the nonsubstantiality of the self. The self was perceived as a congruence of aggregates and these in turn were merely a series of events, or units of experience, known as dharmas. As scholastic Buddhism developed, the nature of these dharmas themselves became a focus of concern; if there was no permanent self, it was a matter of importance and some fascination to understand the flux of dharmas from which the illusion of self arose. They were conceptualized, listed, typed, and classified. Differing views on their nature and interaction engendered different schools of thought. Wisdom became, in short a rational, and analytic exercise, comprising enumeration, categorization, and speculative theory. The debates threatened to go on endlessly when from the wings a new wisdom moved onto the scene.

Because she pointed to a reality which eludes classifications, this wisdom, prajña, was called paramita, which means "gone beyond" or to the "other side," as well as "perfection." To those who were dryly and doggedly analyzing the dharmas, she offered not theories, but paradoxes. "Countless beings do I lead to Nirvana and yet there are none who are led to Nirvana." "The Bodhisattva will go forth—but he will not go forth to anywhere." "In the Buddha's teachings he trains, (but) no training is this training and no one is trained." "In his jubilation he transforms all dharmas, but none are transformed, for dharmas are illusory."

No formula captured her insight, but through the paradoxes shone a light offering release from the self-adhesive nature of human logic. The self is nonsubstantial, true, but so also are its concepts, the very dharmas into which the self was analyzed; they are radically relative, empty, void. In other words, Perfection of Wisdom, freeing us from absolutizing concepts, returned to the Buddha's central insight into dependent co-arising.

In the text it is Sariputra, traditionally revered as the Buddha's most learned disciple, who represents the scholastic mentality. Weighted with logic and literalness, he struggles with the apparent contradictions of the new wisdom, asks the questions that are answered by the Buddha and Subhuti, a follower who is now raised up as an example of one who really sees into the co-dependently arising nature of things. The paradoxes, as Sariputra learns, leave the observing ego no safe place to stand, they knock away the concepts that perpetuate it.

This wisdom, then, is not the kind one can think oneself into; it is a way of seeing. Without it, the very practice of virtue and meditation can be an ego prop, to which we cling in pride or desperation; with it, liberated by it, the world itself *(samsara)* is altered—not suppressed or rejected, but transfigured.

CLEAR LIGHT, DEEP SPACE

The Buddhas in the world-systems in the ten directions
Bring to mind this perfection of wisdom as their mother.
The Saviours of the world who were in the past, and also
    are now in the ten directions,
Have issued from her, and so will the future ones be.
She is the one who shows this world [for what it is],
    she is the genetrix, the mother of the Buddhas.

The mother, like the wisdom she offers, is elusive, "signless." She is barely personalized in the sutra; no stories attach to her, no direct speech is accorded her, no physical descriptions of her are offered—none of the gestures, colors, adornments that will figure in the images made of her centuries later are presented here. The dozen or so anthropomorphic epithets for her in our sutra appear most frequently in passing, as if self-explanatory—"Prajñaparamita, the mother," "Mother of the Tathagatas," "Mother of the Sugatas," "Mother of the bodhisattvas," "instructress of the Tathagatas in this world," "genetrix and nurse of the six perfections."

As children revere the mother who brought them forth, so "fond are the Buddhas of the Perfection of Wisdom, so much do they cherish and protect it. For she is their mother and begetter, she showed them this all-knowledge, she instructed them in the ways of the world... All the Tathagatas, past, future and present, win full enlightenment, thanks to her."

The feminine character of this wisdom is conveyed in many analogies. In his eagerness to learn and his sense that his time has come to experience enlightenment, the bodhisattva is likened to "a pregnant woman, all astir with pains, whose time has come for her to give birth." He is "like a mother, ministering to her only child," in his devotion to the welfare of other beings. "Just as a cow does not abandon her young calf," so does the bodhisattva follow the teacher until he knows this Perfection of Wisdom by heart. In his constant pondering of this wisdom, he is like a man who "had made a date with a handsome, attractive and good-looking woman." "And if now that woman were held back by someone else and could not leave her house, what do you think, Subhuti," asks the Buddha, "with what would that man's preoccupations be connected?" "With the woman, of course," Subhuti answers, "he thinks about her coming, about the things they will do together, and about the joy, fun and delight he will have with her." Just as preoccupied as such a man, says the Lord, is the bodhisattva with thoughts of the Perfection of Wisdom.

And when the bodhisattva meets her, what qualities does he find in her? He finds light, emptiness, space, and a *samsara*-confronting gaze that is both clinical and compassionate.

"The Perfection of Wisdom gives light, O Lord. I pay homage to the Perfection of Wisdom!" cries Sariputra, after listening to Subhuti and the Buddha. "She is a source of light, and from everyone in the triple world she removes darkness...She brings light to the blind, she brings light, so that all fear and distress may be forsaken. She has gained the five eyes, and she shows the path to all beings. She herself is an organ of vision."

As light and insight, she reveals that all dharmas are void, signless, and wishless, not produced, not stopped and non-existent. By the same token, Perfect Wisdom herself is empty, *sunya*. She is "not a real thing"; like dharmas, Buddhas and bodhisattvas themselves she offers "no basis for apprehension." The text recognizes that this is fearful to contemplate. It acknowledges that this teaching is "alarming" and "terrifying." Those who are not distressed, "not frightened on hearing the Mother's deep tenets," "not cowed, paralyzed or stupefied," those "who do not despair, turn away or become dejected," reveal their advancement on the Path, their potential for Buddhahood soon.

While Perfection of Wisdom reveals *sunyata*, the void, in all its awesomeness, she seems to recognize the terror it can initially induce, for she also offers comfort. "In her we find defense and protection." "She offers the safety of the wings of enlightenment." "She helps with the four grounds of self-confidence." The reassurance she gives is symbolized in the *abhaya mudra* of her raised right hand, the fear-not gesture that we encounter in some later Tantric images of her.

Her evident compassion is not seen as a cradling, cuddling, or clasping to the bosom; rather it inheres in her very seeing and is implicit in her clear-eyed vision of the world's suffering. The many eyes, to which Sariputra referred in connection with her illuminating insight, become symbolic of this compassion. When she assumes the form of Tara, these eyes, set in her forehead, hands and sometimes feet, express her caring. It is not surprising that metaphors of sheltering and enclosing are relatively rare for the Perfection of Wisdom and the help she offers. Since, as the bodhisattva is repeatedly reminded, there is no basis, no ground to stand on, the predominant movement is to image her in space, in boundless immensity.

In *akasa*, the infinite expanse of space or ether, the notions of light and void conjoin. In this sutra it is the metaphor *par excellence* for the Perfection of Wisdom. Like space, she is endless, *ananta*. Like space she is immeasurable, incalculable, and insubstantial; like space she cannot be increased, decreased, or confined in categories. Like sheer space, she can terrify, but the bodhisattva must plunge right into it, unafraid and ready to delight. If he is not frightened and trusts her, he becomes "like a bird who on its wings courses in the air. It neither falls to the ground, nor does it stand anywhere on any support. It dwells in space, just as in the air, without being either supported or settled therein."

This space, into which the bodhisattva ventures, is not the old realm of the sky gods, traditionally accorded to the male in the mythical dualities of sky father-earth mother. Attributes of the sky father featured the sovereign heights of his heavens, his astronomic regularity and law, the power of his thunderous downpours. No such references are made to the Mother of the Buddhas, no allusions to the majesty, order, or power of heavenly phenomena. The one attribute she shares with him is that of all-seeing. Furthermore, she is not set in opposition to the recumbent earth; on the contrary, she is, on occasion, metaphorically equated with it as ground of being. "As many trees, fruits, flowers as there are have all come out of the earth... (so have) the Buddha's offspring and the gods and the dharmas issued from Perfect Wisdom." This wisdom is also linked with earth by the act ascribed to the Buddha during his enlightenment vigil, in which he called her to witness. He reached down, touched her, to affirm his right to be there and to destroy Mara's illusions.

The measureless space of the Perfection of Wisdom extends not only outward and up, but also inward and down. It is deep space. "Deep is the Perfection of Wisdom," says Subhuti. And the Lord answers, "Yes, with a depth like that of space." "With the depth of space is this Perfection of Wisdom deep."

THE PREGNANT ZERO

A rich and startling new dimension is added to our understanding of the Perfection of Wisdom, when we learn how some terms used to describe her played a role in the development of mathematics in India, and particularly in the emergence of the concept of zero. The early numerical system developed by the Babylonians was hampered by having no concept and symbol for zero. It was Indian mathematicians in the early centuries C.E. who evolved the decimal system and the crucially important notion of zero. All of this, transmitted to the West by Arab traders, became the basis for European numbering and computation.

Ananda K. Coomaraswamy has pointed out that in India, previous to numerical notations, verbal symbols were used technically. For the concept of zero, in particular, a variety of terms was employed, and these technical verbal symbols for zero had, he maintains, roots in Indian metaphysics. Let us note that several of these terms, including *sunya, akasa,* and *ananta,* were featured as chief attributes of the Perfection of Wisdom, Mother of all Buddhas.

Coomaraswamy says that the apparent contrast between some of these terms, e.g., *purna* (full) along with *sunya* (empty), implies that "to the Indian mind all numbers are virtually or potentially present in that which is without number... (or) that zero is to number as possibility is to actuality." He further reflects that the use of ananta (endless) implies an identification of zero with infinity—"the beginning of all series being thus the same as their end." Akasa represents "primarily not a concept of physical space, but of a purely principial space without dimension, though the matrix of dimension."

This zero space becomes the still center of the turning world. *Kha* and *nabha*, two other terms used technically by mathematicians, originally meant "the hole in the nave of a wheel through which the axle runs." For the wheel to revolve the center must be empty. Hence, presumably, the sign for zero. It is the circle in which end and beginning merge. It is also a sexual sign for the female, linking the feminine and the void, as does the Perfection of Wisdom. Around the sunyata, which she represents, the Wheel of the Dharma turns. That void is, as D.T. Suzuki said, "not an abstraction but an experience, or a deed enacted where there is neither space nor time."

The conjunction of these symbols in the Perfection of Wisdom evokes a similar conjunction in the *Four Quartets* of T.S. Eliot.

> Garlic and sapphires in the mud
> Clot the bedded axle-tree.
>
> At the still point of the turning world
> ...there the dance is.
>
> We must be still and still moving
> Into a further intensity
> For a further union...
> In the end is my beginning

Note the Mother's attitude vis-à-vis this world. The liberation offered by the Perfection of Wisdom is no turning away from samsara. "Those who are certain that they have got safely out of this world are unfit for full enlightenment," says her sutra. The light that she bestows does not dazzle, eclipse, or blind one to mundane phenomena and the traffic of beings; rather clear, cool, it illumines the world "as it is." The capacity to see reality as it is, or *yathabutham*, without denying the multiplicities and particularities of things, is repeatedly stressed as a gift of the Mother of the Buddhas. While the world is often presented in the text as dream, illusion, and magic show, one does not shun it—for there is no dharma that is *more* real or for whose sake or in whose pursuit the bodhisattva would lift his gaze from things-as-they-are.

The Mother of the Buddhas, therefore, does not call the bodhisattva beyond this world, to final nirvana. She retains him on this side of reality, for the sake of all beings. "In this dwelling of Perfect Wisdom...you shall become a saviour of the helpless, a defender of the defenseless...a light to the blind, and you shall guide to the path those who have lost it, and you shall become a support to those who are without support." Here, in such passages as these, the bodhisattva path is, for the first time, fully expressed—as a calling and challenge to all persons. The skill in means *(upaya)*, by which the bodhisattva responds and acts within the realm of contingency and need, is seen as essential to his enlightenment. Upaya, the readiness to reach out and improvise, is the other face of wisdom. Together they constitute both ground for ethical action and basis of delight—revalorizing samsara while assigning no fixed reality to its separate manifestations.

Such is the wisdom of the Mother of all Buddhas, empty of preconception, pregnant point of potential action, beholding the teeming world with a vision which transfigures. When she is later portrayed as Tara and Kwanyin, her gestures will recall this active, compassionate aspect; for the right arm is outstretched to help, and the right leg, no longer tucked up in the aloof serenity of the lotus posture, extends downward, in readiness to step into the world.

NEITHER TEMPTRESS NOR TRAP

To appreciate the distinctiveness of the Perfection of Wisdom, consider the feminine archetype prevailing in Hindu culture. Her symbolizations as wisdom, light, and space run counter to Hindu views and uses of the female principle.

Hindu culture presents a mytho-philosophic worldview rooted in polarities posited between earth and sky, nature and consciousness, matter and mind. The aboriginal pre-Aryan culture provided the basis in its worship of a goddess representative of fertility. Like other neolithic societies dependent on agriculture, it worshipped the productivity of nature (seen as female because of its birthing capacity), while recognizing its remorseless vegetative cycle of growth and death. The goddess of the Indus valley and Dravidian culture was driven underground by the invading Aryans and their chariot-driving, warrior sky-gods. Centuries later she resurfaced, clothed in respectability, in the Samkhyan philosophy, which had a profound and formative effect on subsequent Indian thought. Samkhya re-established her in the form of the eternally evolving and fecund *prakrti* (nature principle). She is dynamic and unconscious, in contrast to *purusa*, the conscious spirit. The individual soul finds himself entrapped in prakrti's turbulent world of change and materiality, and it is only in extricating himself from her that transcendence and release can be won.

The ancient matriarchal element also reasserted itself in the later development of the Devi and her cult. Represented variously as Durga and Kali, and other female forms, she is essentially one—Devi, the "goddess." Whether adorned with peacock feathers or garlanded with skulls, she is the ceaselessly active one, prakrti, *maya, shakti.* She is the restlessness of primal matter, the fecund and cruel mother. As the creative power of the male gods, from whom she issues, she complements their pure, passive intelligence.

The goddess is both indulgent and terrible. The ambivalent feelings about the mother figure which she reflects can be related to the dual status of women in traditional Hindu society. As a sexual partner, the woman tends to be seen as a dangerous and enfeebling seductress, a semen-stealer; but as a mother—the mother of a son, that is—she is revered and accorded prerogatives denied her as a person. Childbirth, then, can serve the cause of self-assertion. Consequently, the indulgence that a mother lavishes on her son is not unmixed, as anthropologist Richard Lannoy puts it, "with her feeling of maternal love co-exist feelings of envy and retaliation." Lannoy, studying this phenomenon, links it persuasively with the prevalence of the "terrible mother" in Hindu myth, and finds its imagery expressive of both dependence and aggression.

In any event, there are philosophic grounds for this image of the feminine in the Hindu tradition. Differing apprehensions of reality lie at the root of the contrast between the Devi and the Perfection of Wisdom. The positing of a metaphysical dichotomy between consciousness and nature leads to a vision of spirit as struggling to be free from the toils of matter. In such polarization matter comes to be seen as polluting and binding, her fertile nature as arbitrary, lavish, cruel.

James Hillman, the Jungian psychologist, shows that a love-hate relationship with matter is endemic in the Great Mother complex and evident today in contemporary values. When the archetypal mother is linked with the chthonic in opposition to the psyche, a dual response is elicited from the son, the spirit. Either the spirit rebels (devalorizing and eradicating matter, be it by mortification of the flesh or defoliation of the land), or it seeks to seduce and possess the mother (in accumulation and consumption of goods). Either way, matter, mater, exerts her power and fascination.

Even when *maya* is understood as derivative of the transcendent One, as in Vedanta, it is perceived as both binding and maternal. As Krishna says in the *Bhagavad Gita* (VII.14-5): "For all this (nature) is my creative power (maya)...hard to transcend. Whoso shall put his trust in me alone shall pass beyond (it)." The noted scholar R.C. Zaehner, commenting on this passage, says the spirit "is made flesh in the womb of nature...but matter binds; and *like any mother, is unwilling to let her son go free:* hence she does all she can to deceive him; as such she is maya which, at this stage of the language, means both 'creative power' and 'deceit.'" [Emphasis added].

The Perfection of Wisdom, Mother of all Buddhas, escapes this role and presents a radically different feminine archetype. The doctrine of dependent co-arising permits no polarization of consciousness and nature. Matter, seen as co-emergent with mind, is neither temptress nor trap. Faith in this wisdom mother is very different, therefore, from devotion accorded to the Devi. The Perfection of Wisdom is not a mother to be placated and cajoled. Faith in her is not a seeking of favors, but a letting go, a falling into emptiness. It is the release of one's clutching onto dharmas and concepts, a venturing outward, a leaning into space. It is a self-naughting, a passing through the zero point. Because such a zero experience is a kind of birth, generative of new worlds, it is fitting that she who leads us through it is seen as "genetrix" and mother.

Centuries later, in profusion of graphic imagery, the Perfection of Wisdom plays a dominant role in Buddhist Tantrism. She is the prototype of all the female figures featured in Buddhist Tantric interplay. With serene aplomb she copulates with upaya, skill in means; her "other face," compassionate action, has become her male consort.

Scholars and art lovers have wondered and debated why, in these Buddhist figures, the sexual roles are reversed from the Hindu brand of Tantrism. There in connubial embrace is Shiva, who is the sublimely passive partner, and his consort Shakti, who represents dynamism. We now understand why the Perfection of Wisdom cannot, without misrepresentation, be equated with Shakti, or even Shiva for that matter. The Buddhist *yab-yum* (mother-father embrace) embodies a different vision altogether.

The fundamental difference is ontological: Perfection of Wisdom is empty, devoid of independent being, whereas Shiva as wisdom is the ultimate essence with which, by aid of Shakti, the adept would merge. In the Hindu pair, maya (material manifestation) is subsumed into *moksha* (spirit and release). In contrast to this, the Tantric symbolism of Buddhism represents not a cancelling of one pole, but the continual interplay of both. These poles are not moksha and maya or pure consciousness over against energy/matter, but rather two kinds of consciousness/energy. In the embrace of prajña and upaya, wisdom and skillful means, life's dialectic modes of vision and action are held in balance, complementary and mutually essential. That numinous copulation expresses the Buddha's insight into the codependently arising nature of reality.

Appearing both as luminous space and compassionate caller of bodhisattvas, Prajnaparamita, the mother of all Buddhas, conveys a transforming vision of the world. In her and through her the central insight of the Buddha is rediscovered and reaffirmed; and that is why the scriptures that honor her are known as the Second Turning of the Wheel of the Dharma.

Learning in Asia

CHAPTER ELEVEN

Three Lessons in Compassion

I thought I knew what compassion was—it is a familiar concept, common to all religions. But in that first summer I spent with the Tibetans, it appeared in dimensions new to my experience. I wasn't a student of Buddhism then, when I lived in India with my husband and children, and when in January 1965 I encountered Tibetan refugees in the foothills of the Himalayas. Nor was it, I thought, interest in the Dharma, that drew me back to them the following summer—back to that ragtag collection of monks and lamas and laypeople who, with their leader Khamtul Rinpoche, had come out from Kham in Eastern Tibet. I simply wanted to be around them. I felt a kind of wild gladness in their company, and imagined I could be of some use.

Despite their colorful, stirring ceremonies, they were in difficult straits. Prey to diseases unknown in Tibet, they were living hand to mouth, crowded into rented, derelict bungalows in the hill station of Dalhousie. With no remunerative livelihood or land of their own, they were fearful of being separated from each other and shipped off by Indian government authorities to different work projects, road gangs, camps, schools, orphanages, and other institutions being set up for the thousands of refugees from Chinese repression in Tibet. So, along with an American Peace Corps volunteer, I worked to help them develop an economic base that would enable them to stay together as a community. When my children were free from school in Delhi, we moved up to Dalhousie for the summer.

Our goal was to help the refugees draw on their rich artistic heritage to produce crafts for sale, and to set up a cooperative marketing scheme. In the process friendships took root that would change my life.

It was clear that the Rinpoches, or venerable incarnate lamas of the community, were great masters of Tibetan Buddhism, but I did not ask for teachings. Given the conditions with which they were coping, and the demands on their attention and health, that seemed presumptuous. I wanted to ease their burdens, not add to them. The precious hours when we were free to be together were devoted to concocting plans for the community, applying for government rations, or choosing wools, dyes, and designs for carpet production. Walking between my rented cottage with four children above Dalhousie's upper circle road and the Khampa community on a lower ridge a mile below, there was not time anyway for reading scriptures or learning meditation. But the teachings came anyway. They came in simple, unexpected ways. Three incidents live vividly in my memory.

One day, after my morning time with the children, I was walking down the mountain to meet again with my Khampa friends. On the way I had accompanied my oldest, eleven-year-old son to a Dharma class for Westerners at a school for young Tibetan lamas. The English-speaking nun in charge was teaching and she said, "So countless are all sentient beings, and so many their births throughout time, that each at some point was your mother." She then explained a practice for developing compassion: it consisted of viewing each person as your mother in a former life.

I played with the idea as I walked on down the mountain, following a narrow, winding road between cedars and rhododendron trees. The astronomical number of lifetimes that the nun's words evoked boggled my mind—yet the intent of this quaint practice, for all of its farfetched fantasy, was touching. What a pity, I thought, that this was not a practice I could use, since reincarnation hardly featured as part of my belief system. Then I paused on the path as the figure of a coolie approached.

Coolies, or load-bearing laborers, were a familiar sight on the roads of Dalhousie, and the most heavily laden of all were those who struggled up the mountain with mammoth logs on their backs. They were low-caste mountain folk whose bent, gaunt forms were dwarfed by their burdens, many meters long. I had become accustomed to the sight of them, and accustomed as well to the sense of consternation that it triggered in me. I would usually look away in discomfort, and pass by with internally muttered judgments about the kind of social and economic system that so exploited its own population.

This afternoon I stood stock still. I watched the slight, bandy-legged figure move slowly uphill towards me, negotiating its burden—which looked like the trunk of a cedar—around the bend. Backing up to prop the rear of the log against the bank, and ease the weight of it, the coolie paused to catch his breath. "Namasté," I said softly, and stepped hesitantly toward him.

I wanted to see his face. But he was still strapped under his log, and I would have had to crouch down under it to look up at his features—which I ached now to see. What face did she now wear, this dear one who had long ago mothered me? My heart trembled with gladness and distress. I wanted to touch that dark, half-glimpsed cheek, and meet those lidded eyes bent to the ground. I wanted to undo and rearrange the straps that I might share her burden up the mountain. Whether out of respect or embarrassment, I did not do that. I simply stood five feet away and drank in every feature of that form—the grizzled chin, the rag turban, the gnarled hands grasping the forward overhang of log.

The customary comments of my internal social scientist evaporated. What appeared now before me was not an oppressed class or an indictment of an economic system, so much as a distinct, irreplaceable, and incomparably precious being. My mother. My child. A thousand questions rose urgently in my mind. Where was he headed? When would he reach home? Would there be loved ones to greet him and a good meal to eat? Was there rest in store, and songs, and embraces?

When the coolie heaved the log off the bank to balance its weight on his back again and proceed uphill, I headed on down the mountain path. I had done nothing to change his life, or betray my discovery of our relationship. But the Dalhousie mountainside shone in a different light; the furnishings of my mind had been rearranged, my heart broken open. How odd, I thought, that I did not need to believe in reincarnation for that to happen.

The second incident occurred soon after, on a similar summer Dalhousie afternoon. It was one of the many tea-times with Khamtul Rinpoche, the head of the refugee community from Kham, where with two younger tulkus or incarnate lamas we were devising plans for their craft production center. As usual, Khamtul Rinpoche had a stretched canvas propped at his side on which, with his customary, affable equanimity, he would be painting as we drank our tea and talked. His huge, round face exuded a serene confidence that our deliberations would bear fruit, just as the Buddha forms on his canvas would take form under the fine, sable brush in his hands.

I, as usual, was seized by more urgency in pushing through plans for the craft cooperative and requests for grants. I could not know then that this work would eventuate in the monastic settlement of Tashi Jong, where in a few years, on land acquired up Kangra Valley in the Himalayan foothills, the 400 member community of Khampa monks and laypeople would sink their roots in exile.

On this particular afternoon a fly fell into my tea. This was, of course, a minor occurrence. After a year in India I considered myself to be unperturbed by insects—by ants in the sugar bin, spiders in the cupboard, and even scorpions in my shoes in the morning. Still, as I lifted my cup, I must have registered, by my facial expression or a small grunt, the presence of the fly. Choegyal Rinpoche, the eighteen-year-old tulku who was already becoming my friend for life, leaned forward in sympathy and consternation. "What is the matter?"

"Oh, nothing," I said. "It's nothing—just a fly in my tea." I laughed lightly to convey my acceptance and composure. I did not want him to suppose that mere insects were a problem for me; after all, I was a seasoned India-wallah, relatively free of Western phobias and attachments to modern sanitation.

Choegyal crooned softly, in apparent commiseration with my plight, "Oh, oh, a fly in the tea."

"It's no problem," I reiterated, smiling at him reassuringly. But he continued to focus great concern on my cup. Rising from his chair, he leaned over and inserted his finger into my tea. With great care he lifted out the offending fly—and then exited from the room. The conversation at the table resumed. I was eager to secure Khamtul Rinpoche's agreement on plans to secure the high-altitude wool he desired for the carpet production.

When Choeyal Rinpoche reentered the cottage he was beaming. "He is going to be all right," he told me quietly. He explained how he had placed the fly on the leaf of a branch of a bush by the door, where his wings could dry. And the fly was still alive, because he began fanning his wings, and we could confidently expect him to take flight soon...

That is what I remember of that afternoon—not the agreements we reached or plans we devised, but Choegyal's report that the fly would live. And I recall, too, the laughter in my heart. I could not, truth to tell, share Choegyal's dimensions of compassion, but the pleasure in his face revealed how much I was missing by not extending my self-concern to *all* beings, even to flies. Yet the very notion that it was possible gave me boundless delight.

My third lesson that summer also occurred casually, in passing. In order to help the Tibetans I wanted to tell their story to the world— a story I was just beginning to discover. I had stunning photos of the Tibetans in exile, of their faces and crafts, and the majestic lama dances of their lineage. I envisaged an illustrated article for a popular periodical, like the *National Geographic;* but to hook Western sympathies and enlist Western support, such an article, I figured, should include the horrors from which these refugees had escaped. Stories of appalling inhumanity and torture on the part of the Chinese occupation had come to me only peripherally, in snatches, from laypeople and other Westerners. The Rinpoches themselves were reluctant to describe or discuss them.

I presented my argument to Choegyal Rinpoche, the most accessible and confiding of the tulkus. He had been a mature thirteen-year-old when the Chinese invaded his monastery, and he had his own memories to tap of what they had done to his monks and lamas. I suspected a voyeuristic element in my eagerness to hear the ghastly tales—a voyeurism bred by the yellow journalism of Sunday supplements in my New York childhood, and by horror movies of arcane Chinese torture; still I knew that such tales would arrest the attention of Western readers and rally support for the Tibetan cause.

Only when I convinced Choegyal that sharing these memories with the Western public would aid the plight of Tibetan refugees, did he begin to disclose some of the details of what he had seen and suffered at the hands of the Chinese before his flight from Tibet. The stories came in snatches of conversations, as we paused outside the new craft production center or walked over to the monastery in its temporary, rented quarters. Then only did he divulge some elements of what had occurred. Many of these elements, the forms of intimidation, coercion, and torture employed, have become by now, over a quarter of a century later, public knowledge. Reports now available through agencies like Amnesty International and the International Council of Jurists, may not have the poignant immediacy of Choegyal's words, but they give the gist.

The lesson I learned, however, and that will stay forever with me, is not about the human capacity for cruelty. I was standing with Choegyal under a rhododendron tree, the sunlight flickering on his face through the leaves and the blossoms the color of his robes. He had just divulged what perhaps was the most painful of his memories—what the Chinese military had done to his monks in the great prayer hall, as his teachers hid him on the mountainside above the monastery. I gasped with shock, and breathed hard to contain the grief and anger that arose in me. Then I was stilled by the look he turned on me, with eyes that shone with unshed tears.

"Poor Chinese," he murmured.

With a shudder of acknowledgment, I realized that the tears in his eyes were not for himself or for his monks or for his once great monastery of Dugu in the land of Kham in Eastern Tibet. Those tears were for the destroyers themselves.

"Poor Chinese," he said, "they make such bad karma for themselves."

I cannot emulate that reach of compassion, but I have seen it. I have recognized it. I know now that it is within our human capacity. And that changes for me the face of life.

CHAPTER TWELVE

Shramadana Means Sharing Energy

I t does not require oil, gas, coal, or nukes. It empowers people not machines. It is *shramadana.* Literally meaning "the giving (dana) of human energy (shrama)," this source of power is widely used in rural Sri Lanka. In more than 2,000 villages over the past twenty-two years, that is how roads have been built, irrigation canals dug, markets and meeting halls erected. Note the name: neither the purchase of energy through tariffs, taxes, tolls, nor the forced conscription of human labor, shramadana is rather its free gift—*dana* denoting both the gift and the virtue of generosity itself, the supreme and most meritorious "perfection" in the ancient Buddhist tradition of this land. Over the centuries the notion of *dana* had become largely identified with almsgiving to the Sangha or order of Buddhist monks. It was almost forgotten that long before the colonial rulers came with their Western ways, the great irrigation systems that had made of this island the "granary of the East" were constructed and maintained through the voluntary sharing of human energy. This was recalled, however, as a glory of the past that could be reappropriated when, in 1958, A.T. Ariyaratne organized the first shramadana work camp in one of the island's poorest, most backward communities. This launched a campaign that has grown into a national movement for community development.

Any day, any week, there will be several shramadana work camps underway around the island—one or two may go on for months but most occur on Sundays, when folks are free from jobs and school. You can cut a two-mile road through the jungle on three Sundays if you rally enough people. And "people" does not mean just able-bodied men, but children too, and mothers and grandparents, everybody can contribute. If you are not big and strong enough to

---

This is adapted from an article in *CoEvolution Quarterly,* Spring 1980.

wield the heavy earth-slicing hoe or to loosen, lasso, and pull over a palm tree, you can rake the dirt or carry the kettle of hot sweet tea that goes the rounds. Except for the elephant borrowed on the first Sunday to haul out the heaviest trees, all the power is people power. There is no roar of bulldozer or drill to compete with the music that blares from the loudspeaker set up in the temple compound—or with the laughter. Toward the temple's open preaching hall, pots full of rice and curries, with fresh banana leaves tied on for tops, are carried from each household. Come noon, you drop your tool and converge there with the others for a cooperative meal and the traditional Sarvodaya "family gathering." Then you sit on a straw mat as the hottest part of the day slips by, sharing the curry a neighbor cooked and the songs and prayers and talks which follow.

Then it is back to work to see if you all can finish the section of road as far as the paddy field before you quit until next Sunday's shramadana. As you collaborate to lever up some roots, you may find yourself in a team with someone you hardly know. He may be from the other side of the village and from a caste different from yours. But you work together now, learning to know and trust each other's strength, and, as you heard in the "family gathering" and were urged to do, you call him *malli*, brother.

Shramadana campaigns proved so effective in organizing villagers, that in the mid-1960s the government started conducting some of its own. It even briefly formed an office of National Shramadana Service. To ensure that people showed up to work and to keep them at it, material rewards were sometimes offered, in cash or kind—perhaps a ration of rice or some powdered milk. According to Sarvodayans they were not very successful. Those camps, they say, lacked both discipline and laughter; people did not sing together or call each other brother and sister; they did not choose the project themselves or take charge of their own work. When the project is one the villagers want—and know they want, having chosen it—additional rewards can be unnecessary and even counterproductive. The two-mile road that will connect the village of Jambureliya to the Colombo Road means an hour's less walk to buses and schools, two hours less wait when a doctor must be fetched. That meaning can be present in each shovel-load of dirt—along with pride in the doing of it and gratitude for each other.

Last Sunday's shramadana in the hill town of Avissawella was one of a series to clean and beautify the grounds of the district hospital. A committee of long-term patients had asked local Sarvodayans to help them organize an action, get the trash picked up and construct a lotus pond by the front entrance. Unlike cutting a road or digging a canal, this had no economic merit; no one's livelihood or convenience would be benefited—yet the spirit was the same. The long line I joined to pass down the pans of dirt excavated for the pond was hot, sweaty, and high spirited. Ten and twelve-year-olds, including a little girl on my left in a lacy pink party-dress, kept up the pace and younger children raced the empty pans back to the diggers. Young bucks in stylish Sunday bellbottoms or more sensible sarongs, showed off a bit, tossing and twirling the pans to each other, while saried ladies in their sixties joined the brigade for shorter spells. So did patients from the hospital and nurses in starched white saris, neither group showing concern for the loose red soil that would spill on them. To my right I slung the dirt to a public official from the Ministry of Health. Discovering my interest in Buddhist philosophy, he engaged me in a disjointed discussion of the doctrine of "no-self." "Ah, see," he said, half joking, "with every load of dirt, I wear away the illusion of ego." He was also a little annoyed that Sunday visitors to the hospital would watch us without joining in. For me, however, still relatively fresh to shramadana, it was wonder enough that *we* were doing it.

Veteran Sarvodaya organizers say that it is sometimes questionable whether the actual work accomplished in a camp is worth the amount of time, effort, and frequent subsidiary costs that are required to set it up. What is considered definitely worth the price, however, are the other results of shramadana. These are manifold and nonmaterial. They are reflected in the Sarvodayan saying, "We build the road and the road builds us." If the villagers now have a road where there was no road before, they have also that which the road built—a new sense of unity across the caste, class, and political barriers that so frequently fracture village life. A widow of forty with three children, having moved here two years back, had decided to leave and seek elsewhere to settle. Now, after the village's first shramadana, she and her family choose to stay. They have friends now, she tells me, and it is a better place to be. After shramadana in the nearby village of Galapitemadama, the young people now draw lots each week to select the house where they will work together—fixing the well or repairing the roof.

What gets built then is a new sense of power and possibility. This is evident in the local Sarvodaya *haulas,* or committees, that often constellate in the course of the first shramadana or two—youth committees, elders' committees, or committees of mothers to start a preschool or community kitchen. The collective action combined with the fresh respect it breeds for manual labor can generate a personal commitment to the development of the village that no government programs or foreign aid projects appear able to duplicate. Public reforestation schemes, for example, often founder because villagers neglect the seedlings, letting goats and cattle eat them. But when undertaken as shramadana, with the sense of ownership and responsibility that that brings, the plants are watered and protected.

With the experience that the Sarvodaya movement has accrued with more than 3,000 shramadana camps, and well over a half million participants, certain methods have evolved as most effective for long-term results. Here is how—if you are a Sarvodayan in Sri Lanka—you organize a shramadana:

1. Go to a village and start making a survey of its needs. Go from house to house and then get folks together, say in the temple or in the school, to talk about what they want. Talk until agreement is reached on the choice of an initial project.

2. Contact district government officials to see if they can provide needed material—tools, seeds, truck. They are usually not hard to persuade when you have a lot of free labor to offer.

3. If cement, bricks, elephant, or right-of-way over a piece of land are needed, ask wealthier parties in the village to offer them. In the course of your meetings with them, they often will, to their own surprise and out of competition or desire for good will.

4. Be sure to involve the local priest. Usually ready to bless so generous an effort, his presence both legitimates and inspires.

5. Meanwhile a local family or two will be taking the lead in organizing the day's collective meal. A mass potluck is always fun and sometimes the start of a community kitchen, which can make a real difference in awareness of nutrition needs.

6. See which city folk and foreign visitors to Sarvodaya headquarters want to join the shramadana. They often enjoy this contact with village life and in the eyes of the locals their presence—and their actual physical labor—adds lustre to the occasion.

7. When the day comes, start early while it is cool; this also saves time for the midday and evening "family gatherings." Begin with a brief meeting for meditation and chant. It helps collect the energy that will be given this day.

8. At the family gatherings, as folks relax, speak about the meaning of dana, the power of the free gift, the merit of generosity. Remind people they can remake their world out of their own caring and power. Recall for them the glories of the past when Sri Lanka was *Danyagara* and *Dhammadvipa,* "granary of wealth" and "island of righteousness." These can be restored when they work as brother and sister; as you have from the start you continue, of course, to address them in these terms and treat them in this fashion.

9. Remember to provide in these gatherings both space and encouragement for the participation of the villagers. They enjoy this opportunity to perform for their neighbors in song or dance, which, of course, is great for community spirit; and the experience of giving an impromptu talk on their perception of village needs raises their awareness of their own leadership capacities.

10. When it is all over, stay in close touch—for shramadana is just the beginning.

It is just the beginning because people have tasted what they can do together—and there is no limit to that. As a visitor from a faraway land, I tasted it too. It stirred in me old memories of my grandparents telling about husking bees and barn-raisings, stirred also more recent memories of the potlucks and collective gardens we started in upstate New York. In America, too, there was shrama-dana and there also the sanity of the past is being reappropriated. Not having seen it, though, on a scale like this, I find myself wondering if we could not move more systematically and full-tilt into the giving of human energy. There is healing, hope and deep community in such sharing, perhaps because, in the last analysis, that is what we are—pure energy.

CHAPTER THIRTEEN

Sarvodaya Means Everybody Wakes Up

W hat has religion to do with economic development? Not much, in the eyes of most planners and administrators who design programs to alleviate poverty in the "Third World." Conventional Western economists consider the religious traditions of a given society to be peripheral. Indigenous belief systems and practices are generally viewed as hangovers from a pre-colonial past that have little relevance for modernization. They have even been seen as obstacles to overcome in freeing people from apparent superstition and passivity, and in transferring the technology that would bring them unencumbered into the marketplace of the late twentieth century.

This transfer of technology has turned out, as we know, to be not so simple a process. Unexpectedly, it boomerangs, exacerbating local inequities, creating patterns of dependence, and leaving behind, along with rusting, unused equipment, an increased sense of frustration and powerlessness. Aid programs have followed blueprints that may be rational in the minds of Western university-trained planners. But too often the only "growth" they bring to the local population is in the wallets of a small urban elite and in a mounting national debt.

WHAT *IS* DEVELOPMENT?

At the end of the second decade of such development efforts, at a meeting of the Society for International Development in Colombo, Sri Lanka, in 1979, these problems were openly acknowledged. In a moving expression of honesty and humility, some economists and

---

Material for this chapter is drawn from *Dharma and Development* (West Hartford, Connecticut: Kumarian Press, 1985), from field work in Sri Lanka 1979-80 and 1984, and from "What Do We Really Need?" *Creation Magazine*.

planners questioned the very assumptions on which aid programs had been built. "Do we need a new definition of development?" some voices asked. They pressed for understandings that go beyond Western-style modernization and industrialization.

Sri Lanka was an appropriate place to raise such questions, for it is the home of Sarvodaya Shramadana Sangamaya, a Buddhist-inspired community development movement that, involving over 5,000 participating villages, is the country's largest non-governmental organization. And this movement, with its extraordinary record of popular participation, has its own definition of development. Having come to Sri Lanka to spend a year with Sarvodaya, I had heard it from trainers and village workers and seen it put into action in many a grassroots project. Now at this international meeting in Colombo, amidst the suits and ties of Western and Westernized development "experts," A.T. Ariyaratne, founder and president of Sarvodaya, mounted the platform in his white cotton shirt and sarong to convey views that were as different from the prevailing mode as was his dress. I found myself wishing that the audience could also hear Sarvodaya's voices from the villages and know that what Ari spoke was not one man's rhetoric but a living reality to many village workers in his Movement.

In my mind I still hear the local Sarvodaya workers, in their village meetings and district training centers: Development is not imitating the West. Development is not high-cost industrial complexes, chemical fertilizers, and mammoth hydro-electric dams. It is not selling your soul for unnecessary consumer items or schemes to get rich quick. Development is *waking up*—waking up to our true wealth and true potential as persons and as a society. That is what the Buddha did under the bodhi tree and that is what we can do—wake up. Sarvodaya's name conveys that. Originally coined by Gandhi to mean "the uplift or welfare of all," it was adopted by Ari and his colleagues and given a Buddhist twist: for as, in the Sanskrit, *sarva* means "all," *udaya* connotes awakening, as well as being raised up.

So Sarvodaya means "the awakening of all" or "everybody wakes up." "Everybody" includes the landless laborers as well as the farmers, the school dropouts as well as the university trained; the women and children and old people along with the merchants, managers, and civil servants. What they call "awakening" happens when, prompted by local Sarvodaya organizers, they meet together, plan, and carry out joint community projects. They wake up to their real needs, to their capacity to work together, and to their power to change.

In the decade following the Colombo meeting a terrible civil war has racked Sri Lanka. Conflict between the two main ethnic groups of Sinhalese and Tamils erupted in bloody violence—aided by external supplies of arms—and fractured the society at every level. But the Sarvodaya movement has continued its village programs. Because it had, from the beginning, engaged Buddhists and non-Buddhists alike, it has provided inter-communal communication in the midst of the conflict. Much of its efforts have been diverted from economic development to the relief and rehabilitation of refugees from strife-torn areas, be they Tamils or Sinhalese. Yet the lessons it has provided over its thirty-year lifespan, and especially its understanding of what "development" can mean, are still valuable to us all.

THE MOVEMENT

A young woman greeting her friends as she returns to her remote village after attending a training program…families assembling and weaving palm fronds to thatch a roof for a preschool…toddlers learning songs, getting vaccinated, bringing matchboxes of rice to share…mothers preparing food in a community kitchen, starting a sewing class, pooling rupees for a machine…a procession of villagers with picks and banners heading out to cut a road through the jungle…a monk in orange robes calling on government officials in their file-filled offices, inviting them to join a work party and supply the cement for culverts…police cadets in the city coming to training courses on community awakening…prisoners released from jail to work with neighborhood families to clear parks and playgrounds for their children…school dropouts organizing masonry workshops in a corner of a temple compound…monks and laypeople chanting sacred verses as a new community shop is opened, as a mile of irrigation canal is dredged of weeds, as a hand-built windmill is erected and begins to pump…while in the temple's preaching hall villagers gather to hear their children sing ancient songs and to discuss the construction of community latrines.

What can such a multiplicity of scenes and actors have in common? Each is a fragment of the larger whole that is Sarvodaya, woven together by a philosophy of development based on indigenous religious tradition, that is, on the Buddha Dharma.

The movement began in 1958 when a young science teacher at a prestigious Buddhist high school in Colombo organized a two-week "holiday work camp" in a remote and destitute village. "Ari" demonstrated that people could work together and learn from each other in mutually enriching ways, discovering new dimensions within themselves and new promise for their society. This involved discomfort and hard work, and yet it released an enthusiasm that spread and soon constellated into a nationwide self-help movement. From the outset it engaged Buddhist monks, for the awakening it ignited was spiritual as well as economic, and it took inspiration from the social teachings of the Buddha. It also drew considerable assistance from foreign agencies impressed by this new model of development.

Within a decade it had, from its headquarters and main training center in Moratuwa near Colombo, established a dozen regional centers and lively programs in health, preschool education, agri-culture, cottage industry, and village technology. By the time I came to live and work with Sarvodaya, in 1979 and 1980, its full-time volunteers numbered nearly 100,000.

The Movement asserts that development can only be meaningful in terms of human fulfillment. While this fulfillment involves the production and consumption of goods, it entails a great deal more—such as unfolding the potential for wisdom and compassion. While contemporary conditions neither reflect nor encourage this potential, it is real and can be awakened.

Since udaya means awakening, and sarva means all, or total, the Movement's name is given a dual meaning. In addition to the awakening of everybody, it denotes the awakening of the total human personality. Indeed, the transformation of personality—the "building of a new person"—is presented as the chief aim of the Movement. Ariyaratne consistently stresses this, declaring that:

> This definition of development goes beyond those that confine themselves to measuring gross national products, growth rates, per-capita income, and even the latest measure called the Physical Quality of Life Index...It represents the process [necessary for] total happiness.

AWAKENING TO INTERDEPENDENCE

Poverty engenders a sense of powerlessness, and is aggravated by it in turn. The Sarvodaya Movement sees any development program as unrealistic that does not recognize and alleviate the psychological impotence gripping the rural poor. It believes that by tapping their innermost beliefs and values, one can awaken people to their *swashakti* (personal power) and *janashakti* (collective or people's power).

Sarvodaya sees this awakening taking place, not in monastic solitude, but in social, economic, and political interaction. While many capitalists and Marxists take spiritual goals to be quietistic, drawing one off onto private quests, Sarvodaya's awakening pulls one headlong into the "real" world and into the Movement's multifaceted programs to help people meet their basic needs.

Furthermore, in working together to meet these needs, people gain wisdom about the interdependence of life. Given the Buddha's teaching of dependent co-arising, this is important to Buddhists even in development work. As Ariyaratne says: "A Sarvodaya worker learns to understand intellectually and to experience spiritually the interrelationship that exists between different manifestations of the living world."

Because reality is seen as dependently co-arising, or systemic in nature, every act is understood to have an effect on the larger web of life, and the process of development is perceived as being multidimensional. One's personal awakening *(purushodaya)* is integral to the awakening of one's village *(gramodaya)*, and both play integral roles in *deshodaya* and *vishvodaya*, the awakening of one's country and one's world. Being interdependent, these developments do not occur sequentially, in a linear fashion, but synchronously, each abetting and reinforcing the other through multiplicities of contacts and communications, each subtly altering the context in which other events occur.

As I watched and listened to Sarvodaya organizers at work, I saw them challenge the villagers to become more than they were—in their self-image and in their relations with others.

> Your village may boast of having a post office, telephones, electricity...but that is not what constitutes being developed. Development is in your head, your mind.

Here you find out what you can become. Leave behind your
old conflicts, fears, and laziness, and discover your real strength
and unity.

It's not enough to parrot Sarvodaya philosophy, we've got to
live it. Our revolution has got to be spiritual; no amount of tricking
will get us there.

This belief in the spiritual nature of the revolution is what appears
to distinguish Sarvodaya in the eyes of its own organizers, especially
those who were formerly communist.

I tell my communist friends, I know how you work, because I was
one of you. It is all talk, talk, talk. In Sarvodaya we *act...now...*we
make shramadanas, training programs, preschools. We don't divide people, we show them how they can change.

The notion that real social change requires personal change,
a notion conveyed in songs, slogans, murals, training courses, and
organizing methods, is anchored in Sarvodaya's creative interpretation of traditional religious doctrine. It can be seen as a "social
gospel" form of Buddhism, stressing the socio-economic aspects of
the Buddha's teachings and presenting them as a challenge for villagers
to take responsibility for their lives.

THE FOUR NOBLE TRUTHS

The Movement's distinctive approach can be seen in the way it features
and interprets the Buddha's Four Noble Truths. The dictum of the
First Noble Truth, that "there is suffering," is translated concretely
into "there is a decadent village" and used as a means of consciousness-
raising. It serves to help the villagers focus on the actual conditions
prevailing in their community, on its poverty, conflict, and disease.
The importance of confronting these facts of life is reflected in
Sarvodaya's style of organizing. Instead of coming in to present a
predetermined project or "solution" to local problems, organizers
first instigate a village gathering where the village people, out of
their own experience, consider together their own situation and
needs. Meeting with the object of selecting a common work project,
the "family gathering" serves as a lens through which all those present

can see more clearly—and through each other's eyes as well—the present conditions of the village, including the scope of its needs and internal conflicts.

The Second Noble Truth, which in Scripture declares that craving *(tanha)* is the cause of suffering, is presented by the Movement in terms of the egocentricity, greed, distrust, and competition that erode village energies. Each of these factors comes down to the individual's sense of separateness and selfishness. In the training of village organizers, these human failings are noted as having been exacerbated by the practices and attitudes of former colonial powers, and especially by the acquisitiveness bred by capitalism.

The Third Noble Truth, as traditionally formulated, affirms that craving, and therefore suffering, can cease—it is the hope at the heart of Buddhism. Sarvodaya presents this hope concretely in affirming that the village can reawaken and find its potential as a vigorous, unified, and caring community. No inexorable fate condemns people to live in apathy, sloth, distrust, or greed; for their actions, like their thoughts and words, are ultimately of their own choice. Action, choice—Ariyaratne reminds his Movement—are the original meaning of karma: just as our lives are conditioned by past deeds, so can they be remade by our present acts. All hinges on our will, on the choice that is present to us moment by moment.

The Eightfold Path, which constitutes the Fourth Noble Truth, offers the principles by which to make such choices. Right Understanding and Right Intention arise as we understand the systemic nature of life, the interdependence between self and other, mind and body; and Right Speech arises as we give expression to this with honesty and compassion. Right Action, Right Livelihood, and Right Effort are no longer abstract notions, but become as immediate and tangible as today's collaboration in cleaning the village well or digging latrines, and Right Mindfulness is given a similarly social thrust. As a Sarvodaya trainer expresses it:

> Right Mindfulness—that means stay open and alert to the needs of the village....Look to see what is needed—latrines, water, road...Try to enter the minds of the people, to listen behind their words. Practice mindfulness in the shramadana camp: Is the food enough? Are people getting wet? Are the tools in order? Is anyone being exploited?

The last aspect of the Eightfold Path, Right Concentration or *samadhi*, is made present to the Movement through the moments of meditation that precede every meeting as well as through the meditation courses offered to its full-time workers.

The Four Noble Truths as reformulated are not taught to the people as a catechism; rather they are presented in symbols and graphics, on murals and posters, as reminders of what the people experience already as they engage in the Movement's activities.

> Let them see first, listen second. Our philosophy is better understood in a shramadana than in a speech. Afterwards we give words to what they have experienced.
>
> *(District coordinator)*

DANA AND THE FOUR ABODES

How do you know if you are waking up? How, for that matter, do you go about that process? You practice *dana*, you enter the abodes.

Even more central to lay Buddhists than the Four Noble Truths is the concept and practice of dana, a venerable term that means generosity, the act of giving, and the gift itself. Considered the most meritorious of all virtues, dana had, over the centuries, come to be identified with almsgiving to the Sangha or Order of Monks. Sarvodaya reclaimed its original scope by interpreting it to include the sharing of one's time, skills, goods, and energy with one's community. Villagers are not given sermons so much as opportunities to experience their own innate generosity. Whether it is a small child bringing her matchbox of rice to the Sarvodaya preschool, or a landowner invited to give right of way for an access road through his tea estate, the operative assumption is that the act of giving empowers the giver and is the soil out of which mutual trust and respect can grow.

> Of course, her family is poor and of course we do not really need her little bit of rice or her betel leaf. But in giving it, she gets a new idea about herself.
>
> *(Shramadana organizer)*

Most frequently on the lips of Sarvodaya organizers and participants, and evoked at village gatherings, are the Four Abodes of the Buddha, the *Brahmaviharas.* Both the means and the measure of personal awakening, these are *metta* (loving-kindness), *karuna* (compassion), *mudita* (joy in the joy of others), and *upekkha* (equanimity). Like the Four Noble Truths, each of these is portrayed in terms of social interaction.

Metta or loving-kindness is presented by the Movement as the fundamental attitude that must be cultivated to develop motivation for service, capacity to work harmoniously with others, and, above all, nonviolence. The Movement promotes it through sermon, song, and slogan, and also through the practice of the metta meditation, which is expected of all participants and accorded silence at the outset of every meeting, be it a community "family gathering" or a committee session on latrines. Summoning participants to develop the "boundless heart" of the Buddha, it serves to ennoble menial tasks, defuse conflict, and inspire the giving of energy.

Metta is taken, furthermore, as an instrument for affecting the behavior of others. A young Sarvodaya-trained monk went to settle and work in a village that had been a Communist stronghold. Over half the villagers initially opposed him through ostracism, open threats, and depredations on the newly reopened temple. His explanation to me of how he finally won their support did not feature any particular organizing strategy. Rather, he said,

> It was doing the metta meditation...every day before I went out and every night when I came back, sending the power of loving-kindness to my opponents. After two years, most of the village was with me.

Compassion (karuna) the second Sublime Abode, is seen by the Movement as the translation of metta into action on behalf of others. It is concrete service and "self-offering" in tangible projects that improve the village life.

> Feeling sorry for people is not enough. Act to help them.
>
> *(Shramadana guideline)*

> Nonviolence is more than not walking on insects in the road. It is to be of service to our fellow beings.
>
> *(Sarvodaya organizer)*

Mudita, as defined by the Movement, is the joy one reaps in beholding the effects of this service. Whether these results are seen in a completed road to the village or in the altered lives of its inhabitants, they constitute the most tangible external reward gained by most Sarvodayans. But the Movement urges its workers not to be dependent on even these rewards, for their work may fail and is bound, in any case, to displease some parties and arouse opposition; hence the importance of the fourth abode, upekkha, equanimity in the face of praise or blame. It is a notion which helps preserve Sarvodaya workers from "burn-out."

> Don't be discouraged if they [villagers] seem not to care. We will teach them by *our* caring.
>
> *(Young trainer)*

> Upekkha is dynamite. It is surprising the energy that is released when you stop being so attached....You discover how much can be accomplished when nothing is expected in return.
>
> *(District coordinator)*

A plethora of Buddhist stories, many drawn from the Jataka tales about earlier human and animal incarnations of the Buddha, illustrate these virtues in action. They are familiar to Sri Lankan Buddhists, and Sarvodaya monks often recount them again in preschools, youth groups, festive ceremonies, and the "family gatherings" that punctuate the work camps. They add substance and flavor to the notion of personal awakening.

If the Four Abodes are taken as signs and means of personal awakening, the Dharma also specifies four principles of social behavior *(Satara Sangraha Vastu),* which Sarvodaya upholds as pathways to community awakening. In addition to dana, whereby people come alive again to their capacity to give and receive from each other, these principles include *priyavachana,* literally translated as pleasant speech. Sarvodaya takes it to stress the subtle, far-reaching importance of the everyday language we use, in helping to avoid divisiveness and violence and in promoting mutual respect and a sense of equality. The third principle, *samanatmatha,* is social equality itself. Ariyaratne, who initiated his Movement in an outcaste village, reminds his fellow-Buddhists that discrimination on the basis of caste or class is a moral outrage that was rejected by the Lord Buddha humself. Over the centuries, under the influence of the Hindu subcontinent, caste practices insinuated into South Asian Buddhism, but they are rejected by Sarvodaya, where social equality remains fundamental to development work. The fourth and last of these ancient principles of social conduct is *arthachariya* or constructive work. Symbolized in the shramadana work camps, the sharing of labor is viewed as essential if persons and communities are to awaken to their potential and capacity for self-reliance.

AWAKENING TO THE POWER OF SELF-RELIANCE

Global economic patterns, with the centralizing effect of their markets, technologies, and capital investments, render rural populations poorer and more dependent; and large-scale assistance programs seem to increase this dependence on external factors. Recognizing these trends, Sarvodaya stresses the importance of local self-reliance— and draws on the Dharma to do so.

In Sarvodaya, self-reliance is set within the larger goal of awakening:

> The ideas of self-development, self-fulfillment, and self-reliance, all are understood in the single word *udaya* (awakening)....This is consistent with the Buddhist principle that salvation lies primarily in one's hands, be it an individual or a group.

In appealing to Buddhist principles as fundamental to self-reliance, Ariyaratne is on firm ground. Of the world's great religious teachers, the Buddha was probably the least authoritarian and the most emphatic in urging his followers to rely on their own experience and on their own efforts. Both on the economic level, through his teachings of Right Effort and Right Livelihood, and on the spiritual level through his admonitions to "Come see for yourselves" and "Be ye lamps unto yourselves," he urged people to take responsibility for their lives. These admonitions are echoed now in the words of Sarvodaya trainers—and this despite the traditionally hierarchical cast of Sinhalese culture. To quote one of them, as he expounded Sarvodaya concepts to a group of new trainees, "Don't take *my* word for it. Think it out for yourselves. You will see how it works."

To help villagers move out of patterns of apathy and dependence, Movement organizers challenge the villagers, from the moment of the first meeting, to participate in decision-making and to take some action—no matter how small or menial—in meeting a local need. When the action is finite enough for its success to be predictable and measurable, it can begin to build a sense of power—both personal power (swashakti) and people's power (janashakti).

> You say you have waited two years for the government to clean that canal. You can keep on waiting, while your fields bake. But where is your power? You won't find it sitting around till the government does it for you. Your power is not in Colombo; it is in you, in your heads and hands.
>
> *(Shramadana organizer)*

Given its emphasis on local self-reliance, it is not surprising that Sarvodaya has been a pioneer of appropriate village-level technology in Sri Lanka, constructing and experimenting with windmills, biogas generators, gravity-fed water systems. The Movement appeals to the Buddhist virtues of thrift and self-restraint in consumption, as it urges its workers to use cheap local resources. Out of an abundantly available weed it has developed the nutritious conjee-leaf soup for its community kitchens, out of banana-tree juice a tough mortar for mudwalled housing, out of palm products ingredients for roofing sheets and laundry soap. The Buddha's teaching of Right Livelihood is, of course, relevant to the Movement's efforts to develop the village industries and community shops that make and sell such products, and to keep their overhead low so that they can survive in today's market.

Self-reliance is also a goal in Sarvodaya's work with children. Preschool programs (under way in over two thousand villages) have long been a dominant feature of the Movement. They are non-controversial and easy to mount, and they serve as an opening wedge for community organizing. But they are also undertaken because they build the "psychological infrastructure" which Ariyaratne and his colleagues see as essential to long-term development. This last objective is conspicuous in their innovative, non-authoritarian methods. Contrasting with educational styles found elsewhere in the country, these methods foster the child's self-reliance in three ways: (1) through creative, energetic play using messy materials and large motor-muscles, (2) through the repeated offering of choice, and (3) through opportunities to perform and help at village work camps. Even Sarvodaya workers who are uninvolved with children's services recognize the importance of this approach; to quote two, both male:

> Just as we work from the village up to make Sri Lanka strong again, so we must work from the infant up. All the world's great men were little once, got their start in infancy. The little child can understand a lot, he's got a good head. Give him the experiences he needs to develop his mind.
>
> *(Shramadana trainer)*

> Don't do for the child what he can do for himself. Don't over-help. That way he can find his swashakti [own power].
>
> *(Shramadana organizer)*

Sarvodaya headquarters has been dependent on foreign assistance, and its self-help and appropriate technology programs supported by Dutch, German, and American agencies. So the question arises as to how seriously the Movement takes this matter of self-reliance. In reply to this question, Ariyaratne makes several points. In the light of the structural inequalities at work in our world today, and considering the state of material and psychological dependence existing in the impoverished countries, self-reliance, he says, is a relative term, and not to be equated with financial independence. Until a just economic order prevails, such independence is a chimera, and "for the haves to turn towards the have-nots and tell them to be self-reliant is a very superficial statement."

AWAKENING TO NATIONAL SELF-ESTEEM

It is hard for a community or a people to release its energies—and experience its self-reliance—if it is pervaded by a sense of unworthiness and cultural inferiority. Sarvodaya's summons to "wake up" goes hand in hand with a reaffirmation of the strength and beauty of Sri Lanka's indigenous culture. It fosters pride in the religious heritage that bred the grandeur of this culture.

In traditional, postcolonial societies, the affirmation of culture and the affirmation of religion are commensurate. The revival of Sinhalese Buddhism that took place in the late nineteenth century had a nationalist flavor; challenging the people to cast off their emulation of the colonizers' ways, it drew on the need for cultural pride and renewed it. In similar fashion, Sarvodaya's community-development form of Buddhism presents itself as a reclamation of the nation's heritage. The glories of the past, when Ceylon was *Dhammadveepa* (island of righteousness) and *Dhanagara* (treasury of wealth, or "granary of the East" as it was known abroad), are evoked in speeches and songs which summon the population to the noble task of building anew on its ancient strengths.

> People laughed to see me working like a coolie, especially when the sacks of milk powder I was carrying leaked down my back. But I remembered I was working for Dhammadveepa and Dhanagara, and the ridicule did not bother me.
>
> *(Young trainer to new recruits)*

These images are explicitly used to counter the feelings of cultural inferiority that often result from contact with "developed" countries, through tourism and imported goods and advertising. The great Ceylonese reformer, Dharmapala, who at the turn of the century called on his countrypeople to reject slavish imitation of Western dress and manners, is an oft-quoted inspiration to Sarvodayans. They see their prestigious leaders appear in banian and sarong; they hear their trainers remind them:

> How silly it is to ape ways that are not suitable....as foolish as using forks instead of fingers, or wearing the tight trousers. Sarongs are more comfortable and efficient. They are cooler in the heat, easier for movement and for answering the calls of nature.

The cultural affirmation is not only national but *rural*, for villagers' feelings of backwardness result also from contact with urban, Westernized Sri Lankans. Even among Sarvodaya staff-persons the lure of "modern" appearance and behavior is strong. Some are tempted to acquire status, in their own and the villagers' eyes, by imitating bureaucratic behavior—using staff vehicles, dressing Western, flaunting "official files." But these are usually criticized, and ridiculed:

> J. and E. used a Sarvodaya jeep to go to Kandy, when they could have gone by bus or train. They were just showing off. That is not the Sarvodaya spirit.

> K. came to the shramadana, but he wanted to stay clean and go around carrying his papers and checking off lists of names. We said he could leave, because there is no room in Sarvodaya for a "file Mahattea" [file gentleman].

The Movement builds cultural self-esteem through repeated allusions to past glory (in speeches and songs about Dharmadveepa and Dhanagara), through efforts to clean and restore indigenous monuments (from village temple compounds to the sacred precincts of the ancient royal stupas), and through emphasis on traditional custom (from village rituals, like the blessing of the fields, to the practicing of "reverencing" one's parents). All of these have religious roots and religious flavor.

In addition to these, another factor now fosters a sense of cultural pride among Sarvodayans, especially the more sophisticated and thoughtful of the organizers. That is the knowledge that their work in the Movement has meaning for the rest of the world, in revealing the true nature of development. For vishvodaya or world awakening—and not just for itself—Sri Lanka can become again, they would believe, an "island of righteousness."

AWAKENING TO OUR SOLIDARITY

A chief cause of village stagnation, in the eyes of the Movement, lies in the conflicts that fragment human energies and discourage joint action, conflicts bred by caste, class, and especially party politics. Feuding and backbiting, and petty politics at the local level, often mire even the best public programs.

I spoke with villagers in over thirty localities, and I asked how Sarvodaya differs from other organizations. Almost unanimously their replies singled out, as the Movement's most distinguishing feature, its nonpartisan character. It fostered, they said, a sense of community within the village. The Movement's nonpartisan nature is clearly basic to its effectiveness in engaging the trust of the people. This is particularly significant in a country and under a regime where local social and economic efforts are heavily politicized.

> We turned to Sarvodaya and asked the District center to help us organize our rebuilding, because everyone else, including the Gram Sevaka [government extension agent at village level], had his own party interests and his own party favorites. The fighting kept us at a standstill. When Sarvodaya came in, we could work together.
>
> *(Member of model village)*

The high priority Sarvodaya puts on unity stems from its vision of the "awakening of all." Inspiration is drawn from the Buddha,who in his own time assailed social divisions bred by caste or class, by narrow allegiances or doctrinaire opinions. His inclusivity and tolerance are reemphasized as essential to successful community action.

Sarvodaya organizers urge village workers to not get embroiled in party politics:

> Never invite a politician to your first shramadana. Wait till the villagers have a sense of their own power, otherwise he's likely to make them feel dependent on him.
>
> No, I never tell villagers how I voted.
>
> *(District coordinators)*

AWAKENING TO OUR TRUE ECONOMIC NEEDS

Awakening entails economic pursuits that foster self-respect and self-reliance and that serve to integrate, rather than disperse, the energies of the local community. From the perspective of the Dharma, economic goals include not only production and profit, but also their human and environmental impact. The conservation of material resources, their humane use, and their equitable distribution are taken as preeminent concerns.

The Movement is critical of capital-intensive development schemes and free-trade manufacturing zones that draw workers away from their villages. Jobs in remote workplaces are not truly "economic"; for they erode the villagers' true security, which is inseparable from their family and community relations. It is this security, along with the self-respect and harmony generated by constructive work, that is seen by Sarvodaya as the essential value of economic endeavor. The Movement upholds not an economics of growth, with endless and doomed pursuit of an ever-increasing Gross National Product, but an economics of *sufficiency* (to use the term coined in Buddhist Burma and taken up by E.F. Schumacher in his book *Small is Beautiful*). Sufficiency in this context means an economic base adequate to the pursuit of enlightenment. It entails modest consumption, or simple living, and Right Livelihood that contributes to the welfare of all.

The Buddhist and Sarvodaya principle of *arthacharya*, or constructive activity, includes both voluntary and remunerative work. It gives equal dignity to unpaid efforts, and indeed exalts them as dana or gifts to the public weal. While Sarvodaya seeks to promote income-generating activities in the villages, recognizing their desperate and growing penury, it declines to judge the value of human energy in terms of cash earned. It sees the free sharing of labor, skills, and time ennobling and necessary for both the individual and society. Thus it erodes the division between the formal and non-formal sectors of the economy, which has in our time robbed non-remunerated work of its dignity.

> We had traditions based on trust, like *rajakariya*, where we gave to the common good. Now people only want to work for wage and profit. And look! That does not enrich us, and it does not satisfy us either.
>
> *(Sarvodaya trainer)*

Such a vision of development—with its rejection of a capital-intensive, high-technology, and import-based economy—is clearly at odds not only with classical Western notions, but also with the policies pursued by the recent Sri Lankan government. It is noteworthy that Sarvodaya's use of religion in conveying this vision permits it to do so in a way that appears less oppositional and less threatening. It is hard to take issue with invocations of Buddhist teachings, especially when the party in power also seeks to cloak itself in an aura of Buddhist piety.

THE TEN BASIC HUMAN NEEDS

For training and guidance in its work, the Movement came up with a list of ten basic human needs. Sarvodaya specified these needs in order to help its people keep their intentions clear and their priorities straight. For social and political action, even on the grassroots level, involves hard choices, and these choices in turn involve trade-offs. It's easy, even on the village scene, to get caught up in power plays and party politics. So this roster of human needs was agreed upon, written down, and put to use. I saw it in the hands or heard it on the lips of many a Sarvodaya worker. In English translation it is a small four by five inch pamphlet: *Ten Basic Human Needs and their Satisfaction* by the Sarvodaya Movement, Sri Lanka.

Recently, years after my sojourn in Sri Lanka, I had occasion to study this pamphlet again for the preparation of an article. Riding in a limousine bus to Los Angeles International Airport, waiting in the air conditioned terminal, and drinking my plastic cup of soda, as the jet lifted up through the smog, I read it and made the following notes.

1. Environment–Among the factors conducive to the fullest personality development a clean and beautiful environment takes pride of place....Well swept pathways and rooms, gardens and latrines ...unpolluted air and soil...freedom from factors such as noise which impede concentration and contribute to mental disturbances. *(The airport shuttle inches its way through the fumes and din of downtown traffic, waits bumper to bumper on the freeway ramp.)*

2. Water–Every individual requires water for drinking, for bathing, for washing clothes, watering the garden....Necessary to sustain life, it can also destroy life, spreading typhoid, cholera, dysentery, hepatitis if contaminated...so the wells and tanks must be clean. Have a separate rope and bucket for drawing drinking water. *(As we take off over Los Angeles, I see through the haze, between the miles on miles of concrete, oa-*

sis-like enclaves dotted with turquoise swimming pools, golf courses, and cemeteries kept emerald green by sprinklers. I think of the fight to divert more water from Northern California, of the industrial wastes leaching into the wells, of the leaks from off-shore oil rigs.)

3. Clothing–Clothing is necessary to protect oneself from heat and cold and from flies and mosquitoes....We believe every individual should be possessed of six sets of clothing: two for daily home wear, two for school or the workplace, one for nightwear and the other for ceremonial wear...See that they are kept clean. If no money is available for soap, dirt can be removed with water mixed with the ash of coconut branches.

4. Food–All living beings exist on food. *(It's noontime, but no lunch; I consider showing this list to the airline.)* Sarvodaya workers should strive to establish conditions to supplement dietary needs of young children, expectant and lactating mothers, invalids and old people. Rice and millet for energy; lentils and dairy for growth; yams and oranges, papaw, pumpkins for protection... *(My favorite dish in my Sri Lankan village was pumpkin curry. The stewardess hands me a minuscule packet of peanuts that I can't open; I try tearing the plastic with my teeth.)*

5. Housing–A house with adequate light and ventilation, affording protection against sun, rain, heat, cold, and mosquitoes is a basic human need. If bricks or stone cannot be afforded, walls can be built of rammed earth or wattle and daub, plastered and lime coated...for roofing, if tiles are too costly, palmleaf thatching is very adequate...floor of cement or, failing that, rammed earth kept clean with fresh cow dung. *(Sleek office buildings rise in my city, their entryways at night littered with rags, papers, huddled figures sleeping.)*

6. Health Services–Health care activites that can be undertaken at the community level are many and varied. Give priority to training local Health Sevakas (servants) and to preventive and rehabilitational as well as curative measures, especially to the malnourished and the young. Boil the drinking water. Keep hands and utensils spotlessly clean. Include recreation and leisure in daily routine; remain se-

rene and smiling in the midst of any trouble, for mental well-being is essential to physical health.

7. Communication–A roadway to every village and at least a footpath to every house is essential. For transport all should have access to bus, and use of cart and bicycle...The media of communication include the temple bell, the conch, bonfires, birds and letters, as well as telephone, radio, television. Place notice boards in public places. Establish a public library to be open at least an hour a day. Disseminate news in the village through a tom-tom beater. Hold village meetings at least once a month to discuss matters of common concern. Train a group of youths to go from house to house and explain relevant matters to the people.

8. Fuel–Join in our work to evolve efficient means to generate energy from solar rays, wind and water, methane gas from dung and nightsoil. Meanwhile, to meet the basic needs for heat, light and cooking fuel, we must conserve sawdust and paddy husks for burning in the hearth and plant more trees, such as the "Mara" tree, for eventual firewood. *(The pilot announces our descent into Oakland Airport. I look down over denuded hills, see San Francisco Bay appear in the distance and dimly through a brown veil, fed by streams of smoke from the Richmond refineries, the hazy outlines of the city.)*

9. Education–Lifelong education is a basic human need. Speaking from our Buddhist philosophy, this is an education to liberate oneself from sorrow. From birth to death, all types of experiences a person goes through can be regarded as having an educational value. Begin with programs for children under three years, in cooperation with their mothers, to look after their health and their emotional and social adjustment...A preschool for children between three and six...Adult education programs for those who have missed formal schooling. Create the necessary infrastructure so that community members can educate each other for economic, social, and political growth. Hold lectures and seminars. Provide classes to learn a language other than the mother tongue.

10. Cultural and spiritual development–Even when material and social needs are met, human life is incomplete without a cultural and spiritual base....Have the elders perpetuate folklore and folksongs and proverbs to the younger generation. Keep traditions alive with festivals, pageants, drama and dance....Arrange facilities for learning methods of meditation, and also the essence of other religions as well, giving due respect to those religions.

The plane taxied up to the gate, passengers reached for bags and briefcases, pushed past each other down the aisle, their pace quickening as they moved on out through the airport. I hurried too, by habit, and headed for the parking lot, trying to remember where I left the car. I didn't have a car in Sri Lanka and I didn't hurry either. I had more time.

Is Sarvodaya's list of basic needs too basic for our sophisticated appetites, our complicated comforts and ambitions? Perhaps. But, at the same time, it seems almost utopian. Caught in a rat race that compels us to acquire more and more, we neglect many of our simplest requirements. Safe food, pure water, clean air appear to be scarce luxuries now.

Is it realistic in our modern world to suppose that there is enough to go around? Gandhi said, "There is enough for everyone's need, but not for everyone's greed." Perhaps in our case addiction is a more accurate term than greed. If needs like serenity and community were honored, we might be less compulsive in our patterns of consumption. We might be less inclined to measure our worth in wages and possessions.

Maybe it is not only addictive greed, but denial too that leads us to enslave ourselves to ever-new conveniences and diversions. We may be trying to protect ourselves from confronting the conditions of our world, to block out the knowledge of the figures in the downtown doorways. For even at a subliminal level that awareness hurts. If the hunger and homelessness were not out there, we might relax, might drop the armor and busy-ness that shields us from their pain.

Looking at Sarvodaya's list of basic needs, politicians and lobbyists would find a glaring omission. What about defense? What about national security? It has become axiomatic in our society that military protection and preparedness is a fundamental requirement, clearly more important than schools, housing, health. And here it is not even mentioned by Sarvodaya, even though Sri Lanka is torn by warring factions and terrorist attacks.

Ask a Sarvodaya organizer about this omission and he or she might well answer in terms of what people can awaken to. It is what we are beginning to suspect, as we experience the social, economic, spiritual costs of our military budget. It is that a country's security depends in the last analysis on how well it takes care of its people.

So it seems as relevant to us as it is to those community development workers in South Asia, to think in terms of what we humans really need. We can ask that of ourselves, we can ask it of each other and our elected officials. When we do, when we consider and acknowledge those needs and begin to act on them, we too might "wake up."

CHAPTER FOURTEEN

The Dharma, the Serpents, and the Ex-Untouchables

After living in India with my family in the mid-1960s, I returned there on my own in 1976, taking a three-month break from my doctoral studies to make a pilgrimage to the most ancient shrines of the Dharma. Leaving husband, children, and books behind, I was ready to follow my heart into the world of the first Buddhists. In the cave temples in the Western ghats, in Sanchi, Sarnath, and Bodh Gaya, I studied the stones they carved, traced them with eyes and fingers, felt their age-old exuberance. But another kind of pilgrimage emerged as well, weaving the ancient strands of Dharma into the turmoil of present-day India.

It beckoned as soon as I landed in Bombay and met, in that teeming Hindu and Parsee city, a fellow-Buddhist. Born an Untouchable and still treated as one, he was, I learned, an Ambedkarite. This means a follower of Dr. Ambedkar, the constitutional lawyer who led millions of his fellow-Untouchables into Buddhism. So my new friend was also called a *neo-Buddhist*. That felt pretty companionable to me; I was a new Buddhist myself and had engaged in a civil rights movement in my own country.

The threads of that second pilgrimage, interlacing the one that took me to hallowed, sylvan ruins, brought me into crowded, urban slums, into the more genteel poverty of their Dharma teachers' homes, and into the schools and colleges that Ambedkar founded. It brought me new friends for whom the Buddha Dharma was not only a spiritual pursuit, but a lifeline to sanity and self-respect. And, on the eve of my departure for home, it brought me to Nagpur.

There in 1956, in that center-most point of the subcontinent, Dr. Ambedkar and over 300,000 of his followers embraced the Buddhist

Adapted from "Tradition and Innovation in Contemporary Indian Buddhism," *Studies in History of Buddhism* (Delhi: B.R. Publishing Corp., 1980), A.K. Narain, ed., pp. 133-154.

faith. Here it started, the conversion movement that drew many millions more and brought the Buddha Dharma into the slums and hearts of the despised and outcaste ones. Babasaheb Ambedkar was dead, but Bhadant Anand Kausalyayan, a man who knew the story and helped make it, was still alive—and I had come to meet him.

Nagpur means "the city of serpents," *nagas*, the aboriginal name of the tribal people from whom, Dr. Ambedkar believed, the Dharma first came. That is why he chose this place for the historic event. Now, decades later, the *deeksha bhumi* or initiation ground is an empty, littered lot, the stands and canopies dismantled, the flags and flowers gone. On its far side, as I approached by motor rickshaw, stood Niwas Bhavan, the modest bhikkhu training center and the quarters of its teacher Bhadant Kausalyayan.

Unlike the people to whom he has devoted his life, Anand Kausalyayan was never an Untouchable. Born into a privileged, caste-Hindu family in the Punjab, he was ordained a Buddhist monk by the Sangha in Ceylon before I was born. Despite his elite origins and orthodox training, he had been ready to throw in his lot with the oppressed, and support B.R. Ambedkar in his search to find freedom in the Dharma. And now, with Ambedkar dead, he continued to serve Ambedkar's people, the *dalit*, the "broken ones."

So I entered Niwas Bhavan with some shyness and reverence, touching Bhadant Kausalyayan's feet in homage. He was livelier for his age than I expected; and his greeting, I imagined, was as warm as it would be for Eleanor Zelliot herself, the American historian I had read and admired for her studies of the new Indian Buddhists. He had obviously read my letter and grinned in anticipation of a good talk.

In the course of that good talk, he told me of a conference on the history of Buddhism to which he had been invited to speak, but since it was to take place in Madison, Wisconsin, he would be unable to attend. That was regretable, since the story he could tell deserved to be told. I did not know then that I would go in a few months to that conference myself, to present along with Eleanor Zelliot a paper of my own on the new Buddhists of India.

I realized that many Buddhists and Buddhist scholars of more venerable, unbroken traditions of the Dharma, looked down on this upstart, "neo-version" and its departures from some hallowed beliefs. So I endeavored, in the paper that follows, to acknowledge these departures, while also conveying the kind of liberation my new ex-Untouchable friends found in the Dharma, a liberation that moved me deeply and taught me much.

* * *

On October 14, 1956, in an open field in Nagpur, B.R. Ambedkar and some 300,000 of his followers embraced the Buddhist faith. The deeksha (initiation) sparked a series of mass conversions, creating more thousands, then millions of Indian Buddhists. The event was not unexpected. Ambedkar, born of the Untouchable Mahar community, a lawyer, political leader, and architect of the Indian constitution, had publicly despaired of progress for the Untouchables so long as they remained within the Hindu fold. He had been drawn to Buddhist teachings since his days as a student; further reflection and voracious reading fueled his conviction that the path to social equality and psychological liberation lay in the Buddha Dharma. With his conversion and that of his followers, the Buddhist religion became once again a mass movement in the land of its birth.

This movement, still largely limited to ex-Untouchables, with the Mahar community constituting a large majority, holds distinctive views of Buddhist history and doctrine. No established organization, foreign or indigenous, was present to mediate more traditional teachings, so the movement, very much on its own, started out with its own version of the Buddha Dharma. This was evolved largely by Ambedkar himself. His perspectives on the faith which he transmitted molded to a large extent the converts' understanding of the Buddhist past and Buddhist teachings.

SETTINGS AND SOURCES

Buddhism was an option for Ambedkar, because its revival in India had long since begun. The roots of this revival trace back to archaeological discoveries of British civil servants, to the recovery and translation of texts by nineteenth-century European scholars, and Anagarika Dharmapala's founding of the Maha Bodhi Society, dedicated to the rehabilitation of ancient shrines and the renaissance of the faith on its native soil. By the early decades of this century the beginnings of a revived Indian Buddhism were evident—in limited but influential conversions at both extremes of Indian society. These included, at the lower end of the social scale, Tamil-speaking *pariahs* in the South and, emerging from caste-Hindu society in the North, a trio of Buddhist scholars: Rahula Sanskrityayan, Anand Kausalyayan, and Jagdish Kashyap. The writings of the Tamil Buddhists, especially of P.Lakshmi Narasu, made a strong impact upon Ambedkar, while the leading and enduring role played by the latter three is continued today by Anand Kausalyayan in his training center for bhikkhus in Nagpur.

The numbers of Indian Buddhists are difficult to estimate. The Government Census of 1971 set the total of Buddhists at 3,812,325, which represents a growth of over three and a half million since the Nagpur deeksha. But even then members of the movement itself believed their numbers to be higher, arguing that converts are often reluctant to identify themselves officially as Buddhists and thereby forfeit, in all States but Maharashtra, benefits to which they are entitled as members of the Scheduled Castes. Nyanajagat, head of the All India Bhikku Sangha, estimates that there are fourteen million of these converts in India. Anand Kausalyayan himself puts the figure at twenty million. Whether or not these higher figures are accurate, the movement represents a historic return of the Buddhist presence in India.

The converts' background, as Untouchables in caste society, colors their views of the faith they espouse—casting into bold relief the social teachings of the Dharma and those interpretations of the Buddhist past that speak to their need for self-respect. These perspectives were afforded them by Babasaheb Ambedkar, whose authority is unquestioned by most converts. A few even refer to him as a "Second Buddha" and the Nagpur deeksha has been described as a new Turning of the Wheel of Law. This new Turning gives the Law a distinctive flavor. As a scholar of political theory and champion of the downtrodden, Ambedkar projected upon the Dharma his own faith in rationalism and his overriding concern for social reform. The chief vehicle for transmitting and interpreting the new faith is his book *The Buddha and His Dhamma,* written in English at the end of his life, published posthumously, and subsequently translated into Hindi and Marathi. Ambedkar's aim was to produce a "Bible" (the volume's books, parts, sections, and sentences are numbered, to facilitate reference; this also gives it a scriptural flavor) and so it has served and continues to serve in modern Buddhist India, where it is held in reverence and gratitude. For many illiterates, it is the only one they hear, read aloud to them in villages and city slums, bearing in their eyes the authority of sacred scripture.

The Buddha and His Dhamma is not intended to be scholarly. The Buddha's life and teachings are narrated freestyle, with great independence exercised in selection, amplification, and interpretation. The volume is unencumbered by textual references; no effort is made to distinguish Ambedkar's commentary from scriptural material, and the liberties taken with the Pali Canon have excited the criticism of many scholars and traditional Buddhists.

In his Hindi translation of the volume, Bhadant Anand Kausalyayan has identified the original texts from which Ambedkar drew. Queried about departures from canonical scripture, Bhadant Anand, a Pali scholar, commented that *The Buddha and His Dhamma* represents a "new orientation, but not a distortion" and that all central doctrines are present. Ambedkar himself offers a rationale by which differences can be explained. He points out that oral transmission of the teachings gave scope for error even during the Buddha's lifetime. Identifying five such cases in the Sutras, he notes that mistaken views appear "common with regard to karma and rebirth," and are likely to have continued, especially, since they represent Brahmanical reinterpretations. "One has, therefore, to be very careful," Ambedkar concludes, "in accepting what is said in Buddhist canonical literature as being the word of the Buddha." Ambedkar sets forth the criteria by which he determines authenticity:

> There is one test which is available. If there is anything which can be said with confidence, it is: He was nothing if not rational, if not logical. Anything, therefore, which is rational and logical, other things being equal, may be taken to be the word of the Buddha. The second thing is that the Buddha never cared to enter into a discussion which was not profitable for man's welfare. Therefore, anything attributed to the Buddha which did not relate to man's welfare cannot be accepted to be the word of the Buddha.

The religious implications of taking reason and logic as ultimate authorities, and the implications for historical scholarship of taking them as criteria for accuracy, did not appear to concern Ambedkar. His emphasis upon rationalism reflects in part the situation in which converts find themselves vis-à-vis the dominant Hindu culture. To lend authority to their rejection of Hindu belief structures, they have no God or divine revelation to point to, nor an ecclesiastical institution whose age and grandeur could serve to validate belief. Deification of the Buddha would simplify this problem of ultimate authority, but was out of the question, for it would lend credibility to the Hindu belief that the Buddha was an *avatar* of Vishnu. In battling the ideas of God, soul, and reincarnation upon which they see the institution of caste ultimately resting, Ambedkar and his followers appeal, in the last analysis, to no other authority than that which resides in human reason itself.

VIEW OF BUDDHIST ORIGINS

Ambedkar's chief departure from the traditional view of the historical origins of the Dharma lies in his account of the circumstances prompting the Going Forth of Gautama and the ethnic character of the mass of his followers. Both these points of divergence lay emphasis on the nature of the Dharma as rationalistic social gospel and both dramatize the role of non-Aryan elements in its birth and dissemination.

The cause for Gautama's renunciation of his princely life is no longer taken to be the traditional Four Passing Sights, which confronted the young Sakya with the fact of human suffering. Ambedkar found it an affront to common sense to suppose that a man of twenty-nine would not have been exposed earlier to the presence of sickness and death.

> These are common events occurring by the hundreds and the Buddha could not have failed to come across them earlier. It is impossible to accept the traditional explanation that this was the first time he saw them. The explanation is not plausible and does not appeal to reason.

The judgment is literalistic, betraying no recognition that this story could have a symbolic truth or that the Four Passing Sights could be interpreted as metaphors for human transience and pain.

Ambedkar did not question the appropriateness of applying "reason" and plausibility to mythic material.

As the circumstance prompting the Great Going Forth, Ambedkar offers Gautama's refusal to support a Sakya military action against the Koliya tribe in a feud over water rights. Determined not to participate in war, Gautama went into voluntary exile as a *parivrajaka*, a wandering religious mendicant. His moral stand lent courage to those Sakyas opposed to the use of force and the feuding parties were reconciled. When alerted of this outcome and invited to return home, Gautama reflected and refused; this decision constituted his great renunciation.

> He had left home because he was opposed to war. "Now that the war is over is there any problem left for me? Does my problem end because the war is ended?" On deep reflection he thought not. "The problem of war is essentially a problem of conflict. It is only a part of a larger problem. This conflict is going on not only between kings and nations but between nobles and Brahmans, between householders....The conflict between nations is occasional. But the conflict between classes is constant and perpetual. It is this which is the root of all sorrow and suffering in the world....I have to find a solution for this problem of social conflict."

Ambedkar's references to "class conflict" and "class struggle" do not betray an allegiance to Marxist ideology so much as an effort to compete with it. As he said near the end of his life in an address on "The Buddha and Karl Marx," he saw their goals as similar, but Marxism and Buddhism differed radically in their perception of means. To reform the world, he said, the mind of man must be reformed and the Buddhist way, while tedious, was the safest, soundest, and most democratic way for this to happen.

Ambedkar may have derived his version of the Going Forth from the writing of Dharmanand Kosambi, a Brahman from Goa, who had become a Buddhist monk and the first modern Indian scholar of Pali. In his *Bhagvan Buddh*, published originally in 1940, Kosambi criticized the credibility of the story of the Four Passing Sights. To help explain Gautama's renunciation he turned to the Rohini water dispute that is described in the *Kunala Jataka*, in which the Buddha intercedes and recites the *Attadanda Sutta* decrying conflict and the use of force. Kosambi suggests that the original event occurred before the Buddha's enlightenment and that, while revulsion for the world and hope for nirvana were part of Gautama's motives for going forth, the Sakya-Koliya river dispute probably constituted the main reason.

In previous scholarship, inquiring into the roots of Untouchability, Ambedkar had concluded that India's aboriginal stock had common ethnic roots, which he identified as Naga, which literally means serpent. Subjugated by the Aryans, the Nagas, he believed, became Buddhist in large number. They were progressively excluded from the mainstream of society and eventually cast out as "broken men," the ancestors of the Untouchables. Before their extreme degradation, while still bearing the dignity of their past and rich in culture, these people were patrons and disseminators of the Buddha Dharma. In his conversion speech, Ambedkar pointed to the Nagas as chief propagators who "spread the teachings of Bhagvan Buddha all over India." The Koliyas, to whom Gautama was related on his mother's side, belonged to this ethnic stock. So the Nagas were connected to the Dharma's origins through blood (Gautama's mother) and water (Rohini), as well as being instrumental in its spread.

The paucity of historical evidence to document this view does not diminish its impact on many converts, and they see a symbolic significance in the choice of Nagpur, city of the Nagas, for the event that heralded the return of Buddhism to Indian soil. It is a part of a new mythic identity and history. This vision of their past affords roots and dignity, a historical role in which they find continuity and pride in being the "true Buddhists." The early Buddhist sanctuaries, and especially the cave temples and *viharas* of Maharashtra, which are close to many Mahar Buddhists, speak to them of their ancient relationship with the Dharma. There, carved on wall and pillar, cobra-crowned Nagas hold the stem of the lotus-throne supporting the seated Buddha. Those snake-kings are for the converts a reminder and proof of their past role in a faith to which they now return.

This vision is receiving support from contemporary scholarship. Anthropological, linguistic, and archaeological researches combine to reveal additional evidence that non-Aryan elements played a key role in the rise of Buddhism. Even on the popular level of mainstream Indian culture, such a view is becoming acceptable, as is exemplified by a recent magazine article entitled "Was the Buddha an Aryan?" Giving an overview of some of the relevant evidence it asserts that "Buddhism has always been a religion of the non-Aryan indigenous people of India" and concludes: "It may be discovered (by future scholarship) that many of our national heroes, besides the Buddha, belong to the hitherto despised aboriginal strata."

VIEWS ON THE SANGHA

Ambedkar's perspective on Buddhist history plays down and occasionally criticizes the distinctiveness and importance of the Sangha. To correct an impression that the Buddha addressed himself primarily to the bhikkhus, Ambedkar argues that "the Buddha clearly had the laity in mind when he preached." He judges by their content that the Five Precepts and the Eightfold Path are addressed to householders.

To rationalize the existence of the Sangha, Ambedkar offers the view that it was instituted by the Buddha to serve as a model and show that the ideals he preached were practicable. The monk has a role to play in social uplift and example.

> Is the bhikkhu to devote himself to self-culture or is he to serve the people and guide them? He must discharge both functions. Without self-culture he is not fit to guide....A bhikkhu leaves his home. But he does not retire from the world. He leaves his home so that he may have the freedom and the opportunity to serve those who are attached to their homes, but whose life is full of sorrow, misery and unhappiness and who cannot help themselves....A bhikkhu who is indifferent to the woes of mankind, however perfect in self-culture, is not at all a bhikkhu. He may be something else, but he is not a bhikkhu.

Ambedkar emphasizes that the differences between monks and *upasakas*, lay followers, were essentially formal—homelessness, freedom from possessions, celibacy, initiation, ceremony, and accountability for vows. "Except on [these] points there is no difference between the life of the bhikkhu and the upasaka." In describing their reciprocal rights and responsibilities, he stresses that the laity could bring complaint of any monastic mischief or misconduct. He draws no explicit comparison with the status of the Brahman priest, but does claim that lay complaints occasioned amendments to monastic rules and that "the *Vinaya Pitaka* is nothing but redress of complaints of the laity."

The difference between upasakas and bhikkhus as to initiation or deeksha turned out to be a grievous one, in Ambedkar's view.

> Sangha-Diksha included both initiation into the Sangha as well as into the Dhamma. But there was no separate Dhamma-Diksha for those who wanted to be initiated into the Dhamma, but did not wish to become members of the Sangha....This was a grave omission. It was one of the causes which ultimately led to the downfall of Buddhism in India.

It was this "grave omission" that Ambedkar amended, when he invented the Dhamma-Diksha ceremony.

The Sangha, in Ambedkar's view, although instituted to teach, demonstrate, and serve, had become often derelict in these duties. He publicly expressed the opinion that the majority of modern bhikkhus had "neither learning nor service in them," and urged monks to follow the example of Christian missionaries in outreach to the masses. Shortly before his death he held a closed meeting at Sarnath with monastic leaders; according to former colleagues who were present, he took the occasion to criticize the modern Sangha for its apparent espousal of the *arahant* ideal.

Ambedkar's historical view of the Sangha, whether accurate or not, has some relevance for a period when many Indian Buddhists have little or no contact with a monk. Bhikkhus, especially native-speaking ones, are still rare, and Ambedkar's emphasis on the dignity and role of the laity helps foster an attitude of religious self-reliance. Although the need to train more monks is expressed, there also is talk of the need to develop an upasaka or lay Sangha and of its appropriateness now in a time and community that lack the economic base for a full-time Order. The activity of young college students, teaching the Dharma in the villages, can be seen as an embryonic form of such an upasaka Sangha. In the Ambedkar and Milind Colleges in Aurangabad, for example, a sizeable number of students undertake voluntary eight-week courses in the Dharma, which equip them to teach in the villages during their vacations. This commitment of time, which is called *grishma-sila,* or summer vows, is devoted to holding meetings, teaching Buddhist songs, reading from *The Buddha and*

His Dhamma, and organizing the construction or maintenance of a small *vihara.*

In sum, this revisioning of the Buddhist past relates to the life situation of the converts. The Dharma's origins in social concern, its non-Aryan character, and the ambiguous role of the Sangha are departures from traditional views which make Buddhism seem all the more relevant to the converts. One may wonder whether the divergences from scripture will cause eventual problems in the development of a strong tradition or whether the relative independence felt by the laity will impede the growth of a traditional Sangha. But, within this period at least, it is clear that the historical perspective Ambedkar afforded is meaningful and useful to his followers.

DOCTRINE

Two characteristics of the Buddha's teachings were perceived, prized, and proclaimed by Ambedkar above all others: their rationality on one hand, and their social message on the other. "Buddhism is nothing if not rationalism," he writes and describes the Buddha as:

> a reformer, full of the most earnest moral purpose and trained in all the intellectual culture of his time, who had the originality and the courage to put forth deliberately and with a knowledge of opposing views, the doctrine of a salvation to be found here, in this life, in inward change of heart to be brought about by the practice of self-culture and self-control.

The alleged rationalism of the Buddha serves chiefly, in Ambedkar's Bible, to deny the existence of God and soul. Where the Buddha of the Pali Canon appears to maintain an agnostic silence, Ambedkar's Buddha is certain and explicit. His teachings are assembled and interpreted, along with other philosophic arguments, to demonstrate conclusively that neither God nor soul exists. "He began by saying that his Dhamma had nothing to do with God and soul. His Dhamma had nothing to do with life after death," wrote Ambedkar of the Buddha's first sermon. And so do present-day ex-Untouchable Buddhists begin, for in their eyes the greatest danger of belief in God and soul is the basis it provides for belief in caste. In their teaching activities, this appears to be Lesson One. There is no God who created from his body the four *varnas* (classes), no God who ordained as part of his sacred order this cruel division of society. There is no soul to transmigrate and visit the sins of one life upon the next, no inherent or implicit blame in being born without privilege. This doctrine brings to the convert a psychological release, altering his self-image, even where society continues to regard him as Untouchable. Hence its "atheism" is seen as a key element of the Buddha Dharma, as much a hallmark as its rationality and egalitarianism. Within a Hindu context, such an interpretation of the anatman concept is understandable and perhaps even necessary, given the movement's aims. But within the context of traditional Buddhist doctrine, problems arise when the Buddha's ultimate silence on this question is overlooked.

In rejecting the existence of a "soul," as he put it, Ambedkar also rejected "belief in Samsara or wandering together, i.e. transmigration of the soul," "belief in Moksha or Salvation of the Soul, i.e., its ceasing to be born again," and "belief in karma (as) the determination of man's position in present life by deeds done by him in his past life."

The Buddha "denied the fatalistic view of karma. He replaced (it) by a much more scientific view of karma. He put new wine in (an) old bottle." According to this "scientific" view, rebirth as a concept applies only to the natural components of a being. When the body dies, the four elements disperse and live on and the body's energy is freed and never lost. While any psychological or spiritual dimension to the concept of rebirth is denied, karma as moral law is acknowledged, but it is operative only within one's present life and "the general moral order."

For Ambedkar and his followers, the denial of rebirth frees people from the weight of an imaginary past, unlike the Hindu karma which was devised to "sap the spirit of revolt," so that "the state can escape responsibility for the poor and the lowly."

"Once it is realized that Buddhism is a social gospel, its revival would be an everlasting event," said Ambedkar and, understandably, accords in his Bible great weight to the egalitarian aspect of the Buddha's life and message. The scriptural stories of the Buddha's acceptance of and regard for the low and outcaste followers, such as the sweeper Sumita, the barber Upali, the Untouchables Sopaka and Suppiya, and others, were featured in Ambedkar's Bible. Known by heart, recounted at gatherings with drama and relish, these accounts form an important part of the converts' Dharma. Although he stressed the Buddha's attack on caste and the Untouchables' historical connection with Buddhism, it should be noted that Ambedkar did not, however, identify the Buddha's message and movement solely in terms of a revolt against the caste system; as evident in the story of the Going Forth, the social concerns were wider.

If the Buddha's gospel is seen as essentially social, then so is *dukkha*, the central Buddhist notion of suffering or sorrow. "The recognition of suffering [is] the real basis of religion," writes Ambedkar in his version of the Buddha's first sermon. But this suffering is the condition of "misery and poverty," wrought by social and economic injustice. "Man's misery is the result of man's inequity to man." It is what we do to each other rather than what we do to ourselves. No reference is made to that inner dimension in which we enslave ourselves through our own misperceptions and misidentifications.

The view of suffering as primarily social entails a substantial amount of surgery on the Four Noble Truths. For, if one's suffering is inflicted from without, then its cause and alleviation do not relate directly to one's desire or craving. Ambedkar omitted them because he found them pessimistic. "The Four Aryan Truths deny hope to man...Do they form part of the original gospel or are they a later accretion by the monks?" In his version of the Buddha's first sermon, "the recognition of human suffering" and "the removal of this misery" are taught and can be seen as functional equivalents to the first and fourth Noble Truths. But as for the second and third Noble Truths, this sermon presents no analogous teachings, for no attention is given to the underlying cause of this sorrow nor any mention made of craving or desire. Elsewhere in the volume, however, craving does appear as a source of sorrow, but again its interpretation is social.

> "Why is this craving or greed to be condemned? Because of this," said the Buddha to Ananda, "many a bad and wicked state of things arises—blows and wounds, strife, contradiction and retorts, quarrelling, slander and lies." That this is the correct analysis of class struggle there can be no doubt. That is why the Buddha insisted upon the control of greed and craving.

Such being the perception of the human predicament, it is no surprise that the salvation to which the Buddha points is seen as a "kingdom of righteousness on earth," or that even the enlightenment itself is presented in a purely pragmatic perspective.

> On the night of the last day of the fourth week, light dawned upon him. He realized that there were two problems. The first problem was that there was suffering in the world and the second problem was how to remove this suffering and make mankind happy.

The jolt to a traditional, or even a contemporary Western Buddhist in reading such a description of the enlightenment, with its absence of a sense of radical transformation suggests the problems inherent in Ambedkar's "Turning of the Law." Given the drive for equality that motivated Ambedkar to lead his people into Buddhism, it is understandable why he interprets the Dharma purely in terms of social ethics. But the kind of liberation he sets forth, although invigorating as a call to ethical action, lacks the transcendent dimension of freedom which the Buddha also represented. This in turn raises questions about the durability of contemporary Indian Buddhism as a religious movement.

Such questions, however, must also take into account the vitality of the religious observances in the movement, as well as the growth in Pali studies. Since influential figures among the converts are enjoying increasing contact, both with the canonical scriptures and foreign-trained Buddhists, it is possible to suppose that the divergences of Ambedkar's Dharma belong to a transitional era. Certainly they belong to our time, as parallels with religious developments elsewhere in the world demonstrate.

The innovations evident in contemporary Indian Buddhism are not isolated phenomena. In the crucible of economic dislocation and ideological struggle, fresh views of the Buddhist social ethic have been expressed in the countries of South and Southeast Asia, from Sri Lanka to Vietnam. Perhaps only the Marxist Buddhists in these countries are comparable to Ambedkar in the degree of divergence from traditional doctrine, but non-Marxists also are reinterpreting basic Buddhist concepts in terms calling for social action and responsibility. This doctrinal ferment and the new emphasis on the role of the laity, persuade us that Ambedkar and his views can be seen to be a part of a larger phenomenon. This phenomenon is not limited to the Buddhist world. When we look at some of the strongest and most innovative currents in the religious consciousness of our time, we can see that Ambedkar's work and the faith of the new Indian Buddhism fit in the context of liberation theology. As in other forms of liberation theology, the revisioning of history and doctrine can help renew the religion's relevance to human need. From this perspective, such innovation can testify to the continuity and power of a tradition.

Daya Pawar, a Mahar poet, writes of a turning point in his life, when a friend had told him that Marxist and Buddhist philosophies could "in a certain sense" be accepted together. "His opinion was different from that of the doctrinaire Marxist, it gave me a new vision. Everything fell into place in my mind. [I had just] read earlier the article, "Buddha and Marx," by Dr. Ambedkar. The sorrow that is envisioned by the Buddha is not the sorrow of soul, or re-birth, of the law of karma, but the sorrow of the present injustices performed by the established class....I cannot look at the Buddha in a traditional way. I wrote about the Buddha:

> I never see you
> In Jetavana's garden
> Sitting with closed eyes
> In meditation, in the lotus position
> Or
> In the caves of Ajanta and Ellora
> With stony lips sewn shut
> Taking the last sleep of your life.
> I see you
> Walking, talking,
> Breathing softly, healingly,
> On the sorrow of the poor, the weak,
> Going from hut to hut
> In the life-destroying darkness
> Torch in hand,
> Giving the sorrow that drains the blood
> Like a contagious disease
> A new meaning.

CHAPTER FIFTEEN

Perseverance for the Long Haul:
A Dharma Lesson from Tibet

On the flight from Beijing to San Francisco, my husband, our daughter, and I compared memories of the seven-week trip we had just completed into Tibet. It was late September 1987, just days before the Chinese Government's crackdown in Lhasa that would virtually close Tibet to independent foreign travel. We had journeyed on our own through Szechwan province into Kham, the easternmost province of the Autonomous Region of Tibet, to join Tibetan friends whom we'd known for over twenty years in northern India. They were monks and lamas of Tashi Jong, the refugee community in the foothills of the Indian Himalayas where, after fleeing the Chinese occupation of Tibet, they had preserved their culture in exile.

A shift in Chinese policy in the early 1980s had allowed them to return to Tibet—some to visit, some to stay. We had gone to meet them on their home turf and visit the ruins of their monasteries. We had gone to see at long last with our own eyes the land they had so often and vividly described to us. We had gone because they asked us to come see the work they were undertaking to restore their Tibetan Buddhist culture and economy in the place of its birth, after three long decades of devastation and oppression.

The packs we carefully carried with us onto the plane held rolls of film and sheaves of notes about the Eastern Tibet Self-Help Project, for which we hoped to garner support in the West. Our talk held gratitude and laughter as we recalled our recent adventures. Yet, as the cabin lights dimmed and passengers dozed, my mind reached for something else underneath the exotic trappings of our trip. I was bringing back adventure stories to recount and a worthy project to serve, but what had I learned on a deeper level?

Then, in my mind's eye, I saw Bongpa Tulku on the earthen ramparts of Khampagar monastery. I whispered the words "the Dharma for the Long Haul"—and knew then what I had harvested and what I would carry into my life. Here is how this gift was given.

*   *   *

From the main truck road through Kham, it is a full day's ride to the great monastery of Khampagar. Here the hills and mountains are greener than the more arid plateaus of central Tibet. As our caravan of sturdy Khampa ponies left the road behind, we paused on a high grassy shoulder to look back. The road glinted like a ribbon in the morning light, as it curved and cut through the vast green billows of land. "Chinese made," said Nyija, one of the local monks. "Many die." I recalled hearing that forced labor on the road inflicted moral as well as physical suffering, for the Tibetans believed it wrong— bad karma—to blast and cut into the earth. We gazed in silence, then Nyija reached over to adjust my reins and laughed, "We go?" He turned his horse to lead us onward into a terrain less marked by time.

We rode in a company of ten lamas. Above the familiar maroon robes, they wore jaunty, brimmed riding hats which I had only seen in old paintings—white ones for the monks and yellow ones distinguishing the three tulkus or incarnate lamas in our midst. Several among them were old friends from the refugee community of Tashi Jong, like Bongpa Tulku and Lama Kaju who returned from exile to help rebuild and teach. Among the rest, who had never left Tibet, some, like Abu Nyendrak Rinpoche, had spent years in prison camps, others, younger, were recently ordained, and one, bright-eyed under a yellow brimmed hat, his horse on a lead, was a seven-year-old tulku, little Dergen Rinpoche.

Settling into a steady pace, we wound our way single file across the green highlands. Up we rode across slides of shale and hillsides of thick turf, down rocky gullies and up again—most of the journey above the tree line. Wild and majestic expanses spread before our eyes, flickering in the light show made by sun and scudding clouds. Two or three hours from the road brought us into a wide grassy bowl where we spied the black yak-hair tents of nomads. Khampa herders, their long braids wound up in red-tassels, strode out to meet us and help us dismount. Fresh-churned yak butter tea had been prepared, and crocks of thick, creamy yak curd, and carpets spread for us to sit on.

Already a little sore from the wooden saddle, it felt good to climb off and stretch and ease my sit-bones on the spongy ground. Our picnic was served with both reverence and humor. Our hosts exchanged news with our party, relaying messages from travelers who had passed through that week. Blocks of cut turf a foot high made seats and tables to honor our Rinpoches, and each of us drank from fine, oriental bowls. I had downed several servings of tea and curds before a sudden low massing of clouds began to spit rain. The drops became a deluge. Amidst laughter our hosts brought out Tibetan raincoats for the three Americans. Huge white circular affairs of heavy matted wool, they were awkward to manage on foot, but once we were hoisted back in the saddle, they covered most of the horse as well as the rider and the effect was quite stunning. We wore them for the next few miles until the rain eased off.

When the clouds dispersed, high rocky peaks appeared above us, and a dramatic gorge opened to the right, where cliffs as twisting as on a painted scroll plunged down into half-hidden groves of trees. Bongpa Tulku had us dismount to walk up to the edge and peer over into that dizzying, exquisite scene. There, he gestured, somewhere down there hidden in caves and crannies were ancient relics and treasures of Khampagar monastery—brought by faithful laypeople during the Cultural Revolution to save them from destruction by the Red Guards. "Do you know where they are?" I asked. "Well, not exactly. You see, the people who saved them died. But sometime we will find them."

Remounting, we took a more gentle descent to the left, across an immense grassy hillside strewn with red and purple wildflowers and thick silvery patches of edelweiss. Rivulets sparkled down it to feed into a rushing stream, and where it widened in a flatter stretch, we crossed. Our ponies' hooves slipped on the rocks, splashing and jerking us about, until they clambered up to find dry footing on the opposite bank; then we followed the waterway westward toward a horizon where rose the bare rock peak of a distant mountain. "The mountain over Khampagar," said Bongpa Tulku, pointing. I glanced at it briefly, then looked back over my shoulder to see how little Dergen Rinpoche had fared in the fording. His horse was riderless. But behind it rode the strapping monk Nyija, and cradled in his arms under a yellow riding hat was a small boy sound asleep.

I stood in my stirrups to tug at the woven saddle carpet, pulling it back again between me and the wooden frame. I thought, "This is the happiest day of my life." To ride along hour after hour in the file of mounted lamas stirred something within me that felt like memory. The steady pace of our Khampa ponies, the jingling of their brass bells amidst the vast surrounding silence, the maroon robes and murmured mantras, all invited me to imagine that I was once again doing what I had done for times as measureless as the land we had entered.

The scenes that our family had struggled through over the past weeks evaporated like a bad dream. The Chinese armed border patrols; the squalid barracks of the People's Liberation Army, the truck compounds awash with mud, oil and excrement; the choking exhaust in the wake of military convoys—they lost reality now, swallowed up into larger and more reassuring dimensions of time.

My mental pictures of Khampagar belonged to those dimensions. I had harvested them at Tashi Jong over the twenty-two years that I had known and worked with the refugee community; for its lamas and laypeople came from this land of Kham, and the monastery they had built in exile was a modest replica of Khampagar and bore the same name. Tashi Jong's temple and Institute of Higher Studies, its rituals, art, and masked dances, all evoked their source in that once great center of the Dragon Kargyu lineage of Tibetan Buddhism. The focal point of 200 branch monasteries and retreat centers, Khampagar had been called the "Glorious Divine Isle of the Wheel of the Law." The refugees' stories and paintings conveyed so vividly to me its happy magnificence that it became part of my own interior world, like some Shangri La which I too had known, and for which I too began to yearn.

As our train of ponies carried us westward toward the mountain at whose base it lay, I recalled again the memories of Khampagar which the Tibetans had shared with me. Beyond grand painted gateways and the flutter of prayer flags, the curving gilded roofs of temples and assembly halls shone golden through the trees. Around large plazas for processions and lama dances rose libraries, schools, and artists' workshops, their bright walls punctuated with bold colors.

Two-story dwellings for the monks, each row with its garden and stable, climbed up the hillside. While higher still, beyond the far-flung monastery walls, hermitages nestled amid rocks and trees.

This was the world to which Bongpa Tulku, as a newly discovered incarnate lama, was brought at the age of six. This was the world in which he grew up, honored and diligently trained as a scholar, meditator, artist, and administrator. And this was the world he left behind two decades later when, under the pressures of the Chinese occupation, he accompanied Khamtul Rinpoche, the head of the Dragon Kargyu lineage, into exile. When I knew him in India, I had no idea that political conditions would ever permit his return to Tibet; but now here he was, riding ahead of me in the caravan, taking us back with him to Khampagar. On this his third trip back, he had settled in for several years to oversee the reconstruction of the temple and the training of new monks.

Slowly the mountain before us grew nearer and daylight began to dim. As our ponies edged around a steep embankment to follow the river northward, the high shoulder above us emitted a thin white column of smoke. Soon I saw a similar smoke-stream rising from the next hillside ahead, and then farther on I glimpsed flame as another was ignited. "They are greeting us," said Lama Kaju smiling, "It is the custom. The fragrance is to please." Monks of Khampagar, their figures indiscernible, burned juniper branches to signal our welcome. No greeting ever stirred me more. Around a third bend in the river, monks became visible now, approaching across a low bridge. Coming up to us, they bowed and the white scarves they offered were bright in the dusk. When they took our reins to lead us over the bridge, a strong wild sound filled the valley and echoed between the mountainsides. The long horns of Khampagar were blowing.

It began again to rain, as we were led up from the bridge toward several dozen monks standing amid weeds and rocks. The low, uneven, mud-colored walls behind them were so nondescript that it seemed at first there was nothing there beyond the robed figures and strings sagging with wet prayer flags. The monks, mostly young, greeted us with smiles and stares. The reverence betokened by the long horns was for the honored tulkus of our party, but the curiosity was for our family of three, the first Westerners ever to come to Khampagar. Eager hands reached to help us dismount and unstrap our gear.

Others grasped our arms to lead us through an opening into a yard of liquid mud and guide us across teetering narrow planks. On the far side, we entered the low-ceilinged, candle-lit room that had been prepared for our family.

Store-bought fabric of huge, gaudy red roses totally covered the walls. Against them stood beds under traditional carpets, and on the floor waited washing basins of hot water. We had reached our destination. We had made it to Khampagar, the Glorious Divine Isle of the Wheel of the Law.

In the privacy of our quarters, we peeled off damp clothes to examine the bruises and chaffed places inflicted by the wooden saddles, and luxuriated, sparingly, with the warm water. We had just finished when we heard a knock on the door and an official visit was announced. In walked Bongpa Tulku and Abu Nyendrak Rinpoche, offering more white scarves of greeting and followed by monks bearing tea. Formally they greeted us and bade us welcome. Confused by fatigue, it took us a moment to register the fact that these two companions of our journey were appearing now in another role, as presiding officials of the establishment, receiving us into their domain. We had come to a great monastery, and if it was to live again, it must be treated as such. The exquisite etiquette of the Rinpoches was not a denial of the muddy shambles of the place, it was a statement of its enduring purpose.

Receiving us graciously, they inquired about any needs we might have for our health and comfort; dinner would be served shortly and tomorrow there would be a tour of the monastery. When we expressed appreciation for our room, the only part of the complex we had seen, they told us its history. After the successive waves of the Chinese Army and then the Red Guards, this storeroom of the old kitchens was the only chamber left intact. It served then as a detention cell for arrested monks before they were driven on foot to distant jails and labor camps. Later on, it functioned as an office for the Chinese government's attempt to organize a collective farm. The attempt was short-lived because many of the local herders disappeared, either dying of starvation when their goods and flocks were expropriated, or leaving to join forces with the Khampa resistance fighters. Now, as a more relaxed period of Chinese occupation policy permitted the rebuilding of monasteries and the return of their lamas from exile, it served as the establishment's guest room.

Having heard tales of torture, we inquired further about the sufferings that had been inflicted upon the Tibetans, but Bongpa Tulku turned our questions aside. As he had demonstrated on earlier occasions, he had little inclination to dwell on the past actions of the Chinese. He was evidently reluctant to express any blame or to arouse it in us.

We were the first Westerners Abu Nyendrak Rinpoche had known, and the round-faced, young abbot, who had never left Tibet, was moved by our visit. He had not accompanied Bongpa Tulku and the others into exile because he was only seven years old at the time and still lived at home with his family. Being educated and affluent, the entire family was arrested and sentenced to hard labor. "So I am ignorant," he said matter-of-factly, "a Rinpoche never able to study Dharma. I want now to learn the scriptures and do practice but no time now. First it is my duty to build again the monastery." To help pay for supplies and workers' meals, he earns small amounts of money performing the prayers and rituals he knows for villagers and nomads of the region.

Sleep came slowly that night and then, for a long while, only in snatches. I reckoned it was the altitude. I stared a lot into the dark, listening to the wind and the rain and the barking of dogs. I wondered about the monks who had been imprisoned in this room and if any still lived. I wondered if I could find my way to the distant privy we had used, if I needed to go again during the night. I turned gingerly in my sleeping bag and considered ways to fasten a pillow on my saddle for the onward journey.

We were awakened by chanting, cymbals, and drums. The sun was shining. Climbing the ladder near our door to a recently constructed second-story terrace, my husband and I peered into an upper room resounding with loud, eager voices. Lama Kaju, a stocky figure familiar to me from my first days with the refugees back in 1965, and one of the best dancers of Tashi Jong, was sitting with the thirty young monks of Khampagar. His deep tones audible beneath the general exuberance, he led them in the chanted prayers that he had helped preserve in exile.

From the terrace we looked down into the muddy, busy court-yard. Two large hairy beasts, led in by Khampa laymen, waited patiently by the kitchen door with their cargo of fresh red joints of meat. "Yak on yak," said my husband with delight and clicked his camera. Since nearly every dish of every meal in Kham included yak meat, it was just as well that we were not very strict as vegetarians.

By mid-morning we were off on a tour of the monastery complex. Seen in daylight the low, crumbling ruins bore little relation to my fantasies. I was glad to be guided by Bongpa Tulku himself, for his memories of his twenty-two years of Khampagar life serve as a blueprint for its reconstruction. Exiting from our now familiar courtyard, we re-entered the site—"the main South gate stood here." We found ourselves in a vast, drab complex, like a combination of construction yard and archaeological dig. Ladders, saw horses, and stacks of fresh-cut lumber were scattered along foundation walls, amidst mounds of ancient masonry. As we walked around them, Bongpa Tulku pointed to identify: "Here the painters' studios, there the library, over there the monastic college...." But in the dun-colored rubble it all looked depressingly the same; my powers of imagination deserted me.

Bongpa Tulku's pace quickened when he led us across an open space—"This was the main dancing ground"—to a partly scaffolded, multi-story edifice where carpenters could be seen at work. With the help of Abu Nyendrak's hard-earned fees and a small grant from the Chinese government, the central temple was under reconstruction.

The structure for the main prayer hall, built up from two partially remaining walls, is spacious, its quadruple rows of high pillars rising to catch the light from windows off upper loggias. On doorways and embrasures, intricate geometric woodwork is already in place, to be painted eventually in bright patterns of color. Bongpa Tulku pointed to high moldings where brocaded banners will hang and the walls where altars and Buddha figures will be placed. I tried to see the raw, bare hall through his eyes. Familiar with the temple in Tashi Jong and other Tibetan monasteries, I could almost imagine it, the brocades and painted statues and brass ritual objects glowing in the flickering light shed by banks of butter lamps. We watched Chinese carpenters working a two-man saw. They were hired out of the disbursement received from the provincial government, because they—the same people who had laid waste to Khampagar—provide a skill no longer available among the local Tibetans. Little Dergen Rinpoche, shyly accompanying us all morning, saw that we were impressed with his playground. Scooping up wood shavings, he tossed them in the air.

As we followed Bongpa Tulku about, we expressed respect for the work accomplished and the plans in store. But the scale of these plans daunted my heart. With pathetically meager resources, he was acting as if he could restore Khampagar. I was tempted to caution him. I wanted to remind him that his efforts could come to nought, that a change in Chinese policy could reduce his plans to empty dreams. But, of course, he knew that already, knew it better than I.

Climbing a stairway to the loggia and from there a ladder on up to a roof terrace, he showed us upper chambers designated for special shrine rooms. On that story only a single wall was in place, with windows already mounted in it. Standing on the outer parapet, I looked through them, and instead of an interior saw the green mountains of Kham. I turned my gaze to Bongpa Tulku himself, as we paused there for long moments that are with me still.

That tall, composed figure had been for me a familiar part of Tashi Jong; for years I had seen him moving sedately to execute the social and ritual privileges of his status as an incarnate lama. There he had helped rebuild a Khampagar in exile. There he could still be living now in comfort, enjoying the library and the ceremonial functions, and receiving the services of a hundred devoted monks. After the losses and hardships he had known during his flight from Tibet and after all he had done for the refugees, he deserved that ease and security. But now, unquestioningly, as if it were the most natural, logical thing in the world, he was here—in the ruins of his original monastery. With quiet, single-minded persistence, he was undertaking an endeavor that, given the political and economic context, seemed impossible, or foolhardy at best. But perhaps, I reflected, it was no more impossible or foolhardy than the building of Tashi Jong, that vital island of Tibetan culture on Indian soil. Perhaps, for that matter, it was no more unlikely than the creation of Khampagar itself, a wonder of art and learning amidst the rough nomadic peoples of eastern Tibet.

As we stood on the outer wall, I watched Bongpa Tulku smile calmly as my husband queried him about Chinese policies and the prospects of another period of repression. I saw that such calculations were conjectural to him, as were any guarantees of success. Who knows? And since you cannot know, you simply proceed. You know what you have to do. You put one stone on another and another on top of that. If the stones are knocked down, you begin again, because if you don't, nothing will get built. You persist. Through the vagaries of social events and the seesaw of government policies you persist, because in the long run it is persistence that shapes the future.

Behind the Tulku's demeanor I glimpsed urgency and humility combined. He was not afraid of failure. There was too much to restore for the sake of future generations, to let possibilities of failure stay his hand. There was too much at stake to let the past lure him into bitterness. No one had better reason to nurture righteous anger at the Chinese than Bongpa Tulku and his fellow lamas; but they seemed to have found better uses of the mind.

Two days later we took leave of Khampagar. We had watched how stones were laid and walls of rammed earth erected. We had joined the laypeople who came at sunset to circumambulate the ruins, murmuring prayers. We had walked the hillsides amidst wildflowers, and looked down at the sprawl of mud and masonry, squinting our eyes to imagine golden towers glinting there. Now, climbing on our horses, we prepared to ride South with Nyija and a small party. Abu Nyendrak Rinpoche and little Dergen Rinpoche and Lama Kaju—indeed everyone at Khampagar—assembled to see us off. Bongpa Tulku stepped forward to bestow white scarves in farewell. From the far side of the bridge, when we turned and waved a last goodbye, his tall figure was still standing there, calmly, by the rubble of the outer walls.

*   *   *

As I write these recollections three years later, he is still there. Friends in Tashi Jong, who regularly harvest news through the reliable grapevine of Tibetan travelers, say that the recent Chinese crackdown in central Tibet has had less effect in Kham. They expect a visit from Bongpa

Tulku this fall, in time for the November lama dances. I reckon he will stay there in northern India for the winter. I hope so, for wintertime travel in Tibet is hard, and he is over sixty now.

Whether or not Chinese policies will eventually permit that site to rise again in any semblance of its former glory, Bongpa Tulku, Abu Nyendrak Rinpoche, and the others proceed. However slow the task and however distant in time its completion, that daily, yearly effort is their sufficient purpose. It is what they are about. They are builders and restorers. And perhaps, in the world of today, that very persistence is the real glory of Khampagar.

I don't know if I will see it again. I don't know if I will ever ride again over the green hills of Kham to that company of monks and hear their long horns sound. Present Chinese policy forbids me to travel there; but it cannot block the memory of it. That memory is precious to me, because I know that we too, in our Western world, have to rebuild what has been destroyed.

I don't know where we are going to find the will and stamina to restore our contaminated waters and clear-cut forests, our dying inner cities and the eroded, poisoned soils of our farmlands—if not in the steadiness of heart that I saw in Bongpa Tulku and in his capacity to let go of blame.

When anger arises over stupid, destructive policies, and the pollution of our world tempts me to hopelessness, I remember his smile on the parapet of Khampagar. And when I catch myself looking for a quick fix, or assurances of success, or simply a mood of optimism before doing what needs to be done, I think of him and hear words that he never spoke.

Don't wait, just do it. A better opportunity may not come along. Place one stone on top of another. Don't waste your spirit trying to compute your short-term chances of success, because you are in it for the long haul. And it will *be* a long haul, with inevitable risks and hardships ahead for all. So just keep on, steady and spunky like a Khampa pony crossing the mountains. And then keep on keeping on, because in the long run it's perseverance that counts.

CHAPTER SIXTEEN

The Shambhala Warriors:
A Prophecy

I often tell this story in workshops, for it describes the work we aim to do and the training we engage in. It is from a prophecy that arose in Tibetan Buddhism over twelve centuries ago. I learned of it from my Tibetan friends in India when, in 1980, I heard many of them speaking of this ancient prophecy as coming true in our time. The signs it foretold, they said, are recognizable now, in our generation. Since this prophecy speaks of a time of great danger—of apocalypse—I was, as you can imagine, very interested to find out about it.

There are varying interpretations of this prophecy. Some portray the coming of the kingdom of Shambhala as an internal event, a metaphor for one's inner spiritual journey independent of the world around us. Others present it as an entirely external event that will unfold in our world independent of what we may choose to do or what our participation may be in the healing of our world. A third version of the prophecy was given to me by my friend and teacher Choegyal Rinpoche of the Tashi Jong community in northern India.

There comes a time when all life on Earth is in danger. In this era, great barbarian powers have arisen. One is in the western hemisphere and one in the center of the Eurasian land mass. Although these two powers have spent their wealth in preparations to annihilate each other, they have much in common: weapons of unfathomable destructive power, and technologies that lay waste our world. In this era, when the whole future of sentient life seems to hang by the frailest of threads, the kingdom of Shambhala begins to emerge.

You can't go there, for it is not a place, it is not a geopolitical entity. It exists in the hearts and minds of the Shambhala warriors —that is the term Choegyal used, "warriors." Nor can you recognize a Shambhala warrior when you see her or him, for they wear no uniform, or insignia, and they carry no banners. They have no barricades on which to climb to threaten the enemy, or behind which they can hide to rest or regroup. They do not even have any home turf. Always they must move on the terrain of the barbarians themselves.

Now the time comes when great courage—moral and physical— is required of the Shambhala warriors, for they must go into the very heart of the barbarian power, into the pits and pockets and citadels where the weapons are kept to dismantle them. To dismantle weapons, in every sense of the word, they must go into the corridors of power where decisions are made.

The Shambhala warriors have the courage to do this because they know that these weapons are *manomaya*. They are "mind-made." Made by the human mind, they can be unmade by the human mind. The Shambhala warriors know the dangers that threaten life on Earth are not visited upon us by any extraterrestrial powers, satanic deities, or preordained evil fate. They arise from our own decisions, our own lifestyles, and our own relationships.

So in this time, the Shambhala warriors go into training. When Choegyal said this, I asked, "How do they train?" They train, he said, in the use of two weapons. "What weapons?" I asked, and he held up his hands in the way the lamas hold the ritual objects of bell and dorje in the lama dance.

The weapons are compassion and insight. Both are necessary, he said. You have to have compassion because it gives you the juice, the power, the passion to move. When you open to the pain of the world you move, you act. But that weapon by itself is not enough. It can burn you out, so you need the other—you need insight into the radical interdependence of all phenomena. With that wisdom you know that it is not a battle between good guys and bad guys, but that the line between good and evil runs through the landscape of every human heart. With insight into our profound interrelatedness, you know that actions undertaken with pure intent have repercussions throughout the web of life, beyond what you can measure or discern. By itself, that insight may appear too cool, too conceptual, to sustain you and keep you moving, so you need the heat of the compassion. Together, within each Shambhala warrior and among the warriors themselves, these two can sustain us as agents of wholesome change. They are gifts for us to claim now in the healing of our world.

PART FOUR

Opening New Doors

CHAPTER SEVENTEEN

The Greening of the Self

Something important is happening in our world that you are not going to read about in the newspapers. I consider it the most fascinating and hopeful development of our time, and it is one of the reasons I am so glad to be alive today. It has to do with what is occurring to the notion of the *self*.

The self is the metaphoric construct of identity and agency, the hypothetical piece of turf on which we construct our strategies for survival, the notion around which we focus our instincts for self-preservation, our needs for self-approval, and the boundaries of our self-interest. Something is shifting here.

The conventional notion of the self with which we have been raised and to which we have been conditioned by mainstream culture is being undermined. What Alan Watts called "the skin-encapsulated ego" and Gregory Bateson referred to as "the epistemological error of Occidental civilization" is being unhinged, peeled off. It is being replaced by wider constructs of identity and self-interest—by what you might call the ecological self or the eco-self, co-extensive with other beings and the life of our planet. It is what I will call "the greening of the self."

At a recent lecture on a college campus, I gave the students examples of activities which are currently being undertaken in defense of life on Earth—actions in which people risk their comfort and even their lives to protect other species. In the Chipko, or tree-hugging, movement in north India, for example, villagers fight the deforestation of their remaining woodlands. On the open seas, Greenpeace activists are intervening to protect marine mammals from slaughter. After that talk, I received a letter from a student I'll call Michael. He wrote:

Lecture at the University of Colorado, January 1989, published in *Dharma Gaia* (Berkeley: Parallax Press, 1990), pp. 53-63.

> I think of the tree-huggers hugging my trunk, blocking the chain-
> saws with their bodies. I feel their fingers digging into my bark
> to stop the steel and let me breathe. I hear the bodhisattvas in their
> rubber boats as they put themselves between the harpoons and
> me, so I can escape to the depths of the sea. I give thanks for your
> life and mine, and for life itself. I give thanks for realizing that I
> too have the powers of the tree-huggers and the bodhisattvas.

What is striking about Michael's words is the shift in identification. Michael is able to extend his sense of self to encompass the self of the tree and of the whale. Tree and whale are no longer removed, separate, disposable objects pertaining to a world "out there"; they are intrinsic to his own vitality. Through the power of his caring, his experience of self is expanded far beyond that skin-encapsulated ego. I quote Michael's words not because they are unusual, but to the contrary, because they express a desire and a capacity that is being released from the prison-cell of old constructs of self. This desire and capacity are arising in more and more people today as, out of deep concern for what is happening to our world, they begin to speak and act on its behalf.

Among those who are shedding these old constructs of self, like old skin or a confining shell, is John Seed, director of the Rainforest Information Center in Australia. One day we were walking through the rainforest in New South Wales, where he has his office, and I asked him, "You talk about the struggle against the lumbering interests and politicians to save the remaining rainforest in Australia. How do you deal with the despair?"

He replied, "I try to remember that it's not me, John Seed, trying to protect the rainforest. Rather, I am part of the rainforest protecting itself. I am that part of the rainforest recently emerged into human thinking." This is what I mean by the greening of the self. It involves a combining of the mystical with the practical and the pragmatic, transcending separateness, alienation, and fragmentation. It is a shift that Seed himself calls "a spiritual change," generating a sense of profound interconnectedness with all life.

This is hardly new to our species. In the past poets and mystics have been speaking and writing about these ideas, but not people on the barricades agitating for social change. Now the sense of an encompassing self, that deep identity with the wider reaches of life, is a motivation for action. It is a source of courage that helps us stand up to the powers that are still, through force of inertia, working for the destruction of our world. This expanded sense of self serves to empower effective action.

When you look at what is happening to our world—and it is hard to look at what's happening to our water, our air, our trees, our fellow species—it becomes clear that unless you have some roots in a spiritual practice that holds life sacred and encourages joyful communion with all your fellow beings, facing the enormous challenges ahead becomes nearly impossible.

Robert Bellah's book *Habits of the Heart* is not a place where you are going to read about the greening of the self. But it is where you will read *why* there has to be a greening of the self, because it describes the cramp that our society has gotten itself into with its rampant, indeed pathological, individualism. Bellah points out that the individualism that sprang from the Romantic movement of the eighteenth and nineteenth centuries (the seeds of which were planted much earlier than that) is accelerating and causing great suffering, alienation and fragmentation in our century. Bellah calls for a moral ecology which he defines as a moral connectedness or interdependence. He says, "We have to treat others as part of who we are, rather than as a 'them' with whom we are in constant competition."

To Robert Bellah, I respond, "It is happening." It is happening in the arising of the ecological self. And it is happening because of three converging developments. First, the conventional small self, or ego-self is being impinged upon by the psychological and spiritual effects we are suffering from facing the dangers of mass annihilation. The second thing working to dismantle the ego-self is a way of seeing that has arisen out of science itself. It is called the systems view, stemming from general systems theory or cybernetics. From this perspective, life is seen as dynamically composed of self-organizing systems, patterns that are sustained in and by their relationships. The third force is the resurgence in our time of nondualistic spiritualities. Here I am speaking from my own experience with Buddhism, but it is also happening in other faithsystems and religions, such as "creation spirituality" in Christianity. These developments are impinging on the self in ways that are undermining it, or helping it to break out of its boundaries and old definitions. Instead of ego-self, we witness the emergence of an eco-self!

The move to a wider ecological sense of self is in large part a function of the dangers that are threatening to overwhelm us. Given nuclear proliferation and the progressive destruction of our biosphere, polls show that people today are aware that the world, as they know it, may come to an end. I am convinced that this loss of certainty that there will be a future is the pivotal psychological reality of our time. The fact that it is not talked about very much makes it all the more pivotal, because nothing is more preoccupying or energy-draining than that which we repress.

Why do I claim that this erodes the old sense of self? Because once we stop denying the crises of our time and let ourselves experience the depth of our own responses to the pain of our world—whether it is the burning of the Amazon rainforest, the famines of Africa, or the homeless in our own cities—the grief or anger or fear we experience cannot be reduced to concerns for our own individual skin.

When we mourn the destruction of our biosphere, it is categorically distinct from mourning over our own individual death. We suffer with our world—that is the literal meaning of compassion. It isn't some private craziness. Yet, when I was weeping over the napalming of villages in Vietnam twenty years ago, I was told that I was suffering from a hangover of Puritan guilt. When I expressed myself against President Reagan, they said I had unresolved problems regarding my own father. How often have you had your concerns for political and ecological realities subjected to reductionistic pop-therapy? How often have you heard, "What are you running away from in your life that you are letting yourself get so concerned about those homeless people? Perhaps you have some unresolved issues? Maybe you're sexually unfulfilled?" It can go on and on. But increasingly it is being recognized that a compassionate response is neither craziness nor a dodge. It is the opposite; it is a signal of our own evolution, a measure of our humanity.

We are capable of suffering with our world, and that is the true meaning of compassion. It enables us to recognize our profound interconnectedness with all beings. Don't ever apologize for crying for the trees burning in the Amazon or over the waters polluted from mines in the Rockies. Don't apologize for the sorrow, grief, and rage you feel. It is a measure of your humanity and your maturity. It is a measure of your open heart, and as your heart breaks open there will be room for the world to heal. That is what is happening as we see people honestly confronting the sorrows of our time. And it is an adaptive response.

The crisis that threatens our planet, whether seen from its military, ecological, or social aspect, derives from a dysfunctional and pathological notion of the self. It derives from a mistake about our place in the order of things. It is a delusion that the self is so separate and fragile that we must delineate and defend its boundaries, that it is so small and so needy that we must endlessly acquire and endlessly consume, and that it is so aloof that as individuals, corporations, nation-states, or species, we can be immune to what we do to other beings.

This view of human nature is not new, of course. Many have felt the imperative to extend self-interest to embrace the whole. What is notable in our situation is that this extension of identity can come not through an effort to be noble or good or altruistic, but simply to be present and own our pain. And that is why this shift in the sense of self is credible to people. As the poet Theodore Roethke said, "I believe my pain."

This "despair and empowerment" work derives from two other forces I mentioned earlier: systems theory, or cybernetics, and nondualistic spirituality, particularly Buddhism. I will now turn to what we could call the cybernetics of the self.

The findings of twentieth-century science undermine the notion of a separate self distinct from the world it observes and acts upon. Einstein showed that the self's perceptions are shaped by its changing position in relation to other phenomena. And Heisenberg, in his uncertainty principle, demonstrated that the very act of observation changes what is observed.

Contemporary science, and systems science in particular, goes farther in challenging old assumptions about a distinct, separate, continuous self, by showing that there is no logical or scientific basis for construing one part of the experienced world as "me" and the rest as "other." That is so because as open, self-organizing systems, our very breathing, acting and thinking arise in interaction with our shared world through the currents of matter, energy, and information that move through us and sustain us. In the web of relationships that sustain these activities there is no clear line demarcating a separate, continuous self.

As systems theorists say, "There is no categorical 'I' set over against a categorical 'you' or 'it.'" One of the clearer expositions of this is found in the writings of Gregory Bateson, whom I earlier quoted as saying that the abstraction of a separate "I" is the epistemological fallacy of Western civilization. He says that the process that decides and acts cannot be neatly identified with the isolated subjectivity of the individual or located within the confines of the skin. He contends that "the total self-corrective unit that processes information is a system whose boundaries do not at all coincide with the boundaries either of the body or what is popularly called 'self' or 'consciousness.'" He goes on to say, "The self is ordinarily understood as only a small part of a much larger trial-and-error system which does the thinking, acting, and deciding."

Bateson offers two helpful examples. One is the woodcutter, about to fell a tree. His hands grip the handle of the axe, there is the head of the axe, the trunk of the tree. Whump, he makes a cut, and then whump, another cut. What is the feedback circuit, where is the information that is guiding that cutting down of the tree? It is a whole circle; you can begin at any point. It moves from the eye of the woodcutter, to the hand, to the axe, and back to the cut in the tree. That is the self-correcting unit, that is what is doing the chopping down of the tree.

In another illustration, a blind person with a cane is walking along the sidewalk. Tap, tap, whoops, there's a fire hydrant, there's a curb. What is doing the walking? Where is the self then of the blind person? What is doing the perceiving and deciding? That self-corrective feedback circuit is the arm, the hand, the cane, the curb, the ear. At that moment that is the self that is walking. Bateson's point is that the self is a false reification of an improperly delimited part of a much larger field of interlocking processes. And he goes on to maintain that this false reification of the self is basic to the planetary ecological crisis in which we find ourselves. We have imagined that we are a unit of survival and we have to see to our own survival, and we imagine that the unit of survival is the separate individual or a separate species, whereas in reality through the history of evolution, it is the individual plus the environment, the species plus the environment, for they are essentially symbiotic.

The self is a metaphor. We can decide to limit it to our skin, our person, our family, our organization, or our species. We can select its boundaries in objective reality. As the systems theorists see it, our consciousness illuminates a small arc in the wider currents and loops of knowing that interconnect us. It is just as plausible to conceive of mind as coexistent with these larger circuits, the entire "pattern that connects," as Bateson said.

Do not think that to broaden the construct of self this way involves an eclipse of one's distinctiveness. Do not think that you will lose your identity like a drop in the ocean merging into the oneness of Brahma. From the systems perspective this interaction, creating larger wholes and patterns, allows for and even requires diversity. You become more yourself. Integration and differentiation go hand in hand.

The third factor that is aiding in the dismantling of the ego-self and the creation of the eco-self is the resurgence of nondualistic spiritualities. Buddhism is distinctive in the clarity and sophistication with which it deals with the constructs and the dynamics of self. In much the same way as systems theory does, Buddhism undermines categorical distinctions between self and other and belies the concept of a continuous, self-existent entity. It then goes farther than systems theory in showing the pathogenic character of any reifications of the self. It goes farther still in offering methods for transcending these difficulties and healing this suffering. What the Buddha woke up to under the Bodhi tree was the paticca samuppada, the dependent co-arising of phenomena, in which you cannot isolate a separate, continuous self.

We think, "What do we do with the self, this clamorous 'I,' always wanting attention, always wanting its goodies? Do we crucify it, sacrifice it, mortify it, punish it, or do we make it noble?" Upon awaking we realize, "Oh, it just isn't there." It's a convention, just a convenient convention. When you take it too seriously, when you suppose that it is something enduring which you have to defend and promote, it becomes the foundation of delusion, the motive behind our attachments and our aversions.

For a beautiful illustration of a deviation-amplifying feedback loop, consider *Yama* holding the wheel of life. There are the domains, the various realms of beings, and at the center of that wheel of suffering are three figures: the snake, the rooster and the pig—delusion, greed and aversion—and they just chase each other around and around. The linchpin is the notion of our self, the notion that we have to protect that self or punish it or do *something* with it.

Oh, the sweetness of being able to realize: I am my experience. I am this breathing. I am this moment, and it is changing, continually arising in the fountain of life. We do not need to be doomed to the perpetual rat-race. The vicious circle can be broken by the wisdom, prajña, that arises when we see that "self" is just an idea; by the practice of meditation, *dhyana;* and by the practice of morality, *sila,* where attention to our experience and to our actions reveals that they do not need to be in bondage to a separate self.

Far from the nihilism and escapism that is often imputed to the Buddhist path, this liberation, this awakening puts one *into* the world with a livelier, more caring sense of social engagement. The sense of interconnectedness that can then arise, is imaged—one of the most beautiful images coming out of the Mahayana—as the jeweled net of Indra. It is a vision of reality structured very much like the holographic view of the universe, so that each being is at each node of the net, each jewel reflects all the others, reflecting back and catching the reflection, just as systems theory sees that the part contains the whole.

The awakening to our true self is the awakening to that entirety, breaking out of the prison-self of separate ego. The one who perceives this is the bodhisattva—and we are all bodhisattvas because we are all capable of experiencing that—it is our true nature. We are profoundly interconnected and therefore we are all able to recognize and act upon our deep, intricate, and intimate inter-existence with each other and all beings. That true nature of ours is already present in our pain for the world. When we turn our eyes away from that homeless figure, are we indifferent or is the pain of seeing him or her too great? Do not be easily duped about the apparent indifference of those around you.

What looks like apathy is really the fear of suffering. But the bodhisattva knows that to experience the pain of all beings is necessary to experience their joy. It says in the *Lotus Sutra* that the bodhisattva hears the music of the spheres, and understands the language of the birds, while hearing the cries in the deepest levels of hell.

One of the things I like best about the green self, the ecological self that is arising in our time, is that it is making moral exhortation irrelevant. Sermonizing is both boring and ineffective. This is pointed out by Arne Naess, the Norwegian philosopher who coined the phrase *deep ecology*. This great systems view of the world helps us recognize our imbeddedness in nature, overcomes our alienation from the rest of creation, and changes the way we can experience our self through an ever-widening process of identification.

Naess calls this self-realization, a progression "where the self to be realized extends further and further beyond the separate ego and includes more and more of the phenomenal world." And he says,

> In this process, notions such as altruism and moral duty are left behind. It is tacitly based on the Latin term 'ego' which has as its opposite the 'alter.' Altruism implies that the ego sacrifices its interests in favor of the other, the alter. The motivation is primarily that of duty. It is said we *ought* to love others as strongly as we love our self. There are, however, very limited numbers among humanity capable of loving from mere duty or from moral exhortation.
>
> Unfortunately, the extensive moralizing within the ecological movement has given the public the false impression that they are being asked to make a sacrifice—to show more responsibility, more concern, and a nicer moral standard. But all of that would flow naturally and easily if the self were widened and deepened so that the protection of nature was felt and perceived as protection of our very selves.

Note that virtue is *not* required for the greening of the self or the emergence of the ecological self. The shift in identification at this point in our history is required precisely *because* moral exhortation doesn't work, and because sermons seldom hinder us from following our self-interest as we conceive it.

The obvious choice, then, is to extend our notions of self-interest. For example, it would not occur to me to plead with you, "Oh, don't saw off your leg. That would be an act of violence." It wouldn't occur to me because your leg is part of your body. Well, so are the trees in the Amazon rain basin. They are our external lungs. And we are beginning to realize that the world is our body.

This ecological self, like any notion of selfhood, is a metaphoric construct and a dynamic one. It involves choice; choices can be made to identify at different moments, with different dimensions or aspects of our systemically interrelated existence—be they hunted whales or homeless humans or the planet itself. In doing this the extended self brings into play wider resources—courage, endurance, ingenuity—like a nerve cell in a neural net opening to the charge of the other neurons.

There is the sense of being acted through and sustained by those very beings on whose behalf one acts. This is very close to the religious concept of grace. In systems language we can talk about it as synergy. With this extension, this greening of the self, we can find a sense of buoyancy and resilience that comes from letting flow through us strengths and resources that come to us with continuous surprise and sense of blessing.

We know that we are not limited by the accident of our birth or the timing of it, and we recognize the truth that we have always been around. We can reinhabit time and own our story as a species. We were present back there in the fireball and the rains that streamed down on this still molten planet, and in the primordial seas. We remember that in our mother's womb, where we wear vestigial gills and tail and fins for hands. We remember that. That information is in us and there is a deep, deep kinship in us, beneath the outer layers of our neocortex or what we learned in school. There is a deep wisdom, a bondedness with our creation, and an ingenuity far beyond what we think we have. And when we expand our notions of what we are to include in this story, we will have a wonderful time and we will survive.

CHAPTER EIGHTEEN

Bestiary

S hort tailed albatross
whooping crane
gray wolf
peregrine falcon
hawksbill turtle
jaguar
rhinoceros

In Geneva, the international tally of endangered species, kept up-to-date in looseleaf volumes, is becoming too heavy to lift. Where do we now record the passing of life? What funerals or farewells are appropriate?

reed warbler
swallow-tail butterfly
Manx shearwater
Indian python
howler monkey
sperm whale
blue whale

Dive me deep, brother whale, in this time we have left. Deep in our mother ocean where once I swam, gilled and finned. The salt from those early seas still runs in my tears. Tears are too meager now. Give me a song…a song for a sadness too vast for my heart, for a rage too wild for my throat.

This chapter is from *Thinking Like a Mountain* (Philadelphia: New Society Publishers, 1988).

anteater
    antelope
        grizzly bear
            brown bear
                Bactrian camel
                    Nile crocodile
                        American alligator

Ooze me, alligator, in the mud whence I came. Belly me slow in the rich primordial soup, cradle of our molecules. Let me wallow again, before we drain your swamp, before we pave it over and blast it to ash.

gray bat
    ocelot
        marsh mouse
            blue pike
                red kangaroo
                    Aleutian goose
                        Audouin's seagull

Quick, lift off. Sweep me high over the coast and out, farther out. Don't land here. Oil spills coat the beach, rocks, sea. I cannot spread my wings glued with tar. Fly me from what we have done, fly me far.

golden parakeet
    African ostrich
        Florida panther
            Galapagos penguin
                Imperial pheasant
                    leopard
                        Utah prairie dog

Hide me in a hedgerow, badger. Can't you find one? Dig me a tunnel through leaf mold and roots, under the trees that once defined our fields. My heart is bulldozed and plowed over. Burrow me a labyrinth deeper than longing.

> thick-billed parrot
>> zone-tailed pigeon
>>> desert bandicoot
>>>> Southern bald eagle
>>>>> California condor
>>>>>> lotus blue butterfly

Crawl me out of here, caterpillar. Spin me a cocoon. Wind me to sleep in a shroud of silk, where in patience my bones will dissolve. I'll wait as long as all creation if only it will come again—and I take wing.

> Atlantic Ridley turtle
>> pearly mussel
>>> helmeted hornbill
>>>> sea otter
>>>>> humpback whale
>>>>>> monk seal
>>>>>>> harp seal

Swim me out beyond the ice floes, mama. Where are you? Boots squeeze me ribs, clubs drum my fur, the white world goes black with the taste of my blood.

gorilla
   gibbon
      sand gazelle
        swamp deer
          musk deer
            cheetah
              chinchilla
                Asian elephant
                  African elephant

Sway me slowly through the jungle. There still must be jungle somewhere, my heart drips with green secrets. Hose me down by the waterhole, there is buckshot in my hide. Tell me old stories while you can remember.

fan-tailed flycatcher
   flapshell tortoise
      crested ibis
        hook-billed kite
          bobcat
            frigate bird

In the time when his world, like ours, was ending, Noah had a list of the animals, too. We picture him standing by the gangplank, calling their names, checking them off on his scroll. Now we also are checking them off.

ivory-billed woodpecker
   brown pelican
      Florida manatee
        Canada goose

We reenact Noah's ancient drama, but in reverse, like a film running backwards, the animals exiting.

ferret
    curlew
        cougar
            wolf

Your tracks are growing fainter. Wait. Wait. This is a hard time. Don't leave us alone in a world we have wrecked.

CHAPTER NINETEEN

The Council of All Beings

Listen, humans, this is our world. For hundreds of millions of years we have been evolving our ways, rich in our own wisdom. Now our days are coming to a close because of what you are doing. It is time for you to hear us.

I am lichen. I turn rock into soil. I worked as the glaciers retreated, as other life-forms came and went. I thought nothing could stop me...until now. Now I am being poisoned by acid rain.

Your pesticides are in me now. The eggshells are so fragile they break under my weight, break before my young are ready to hatch.

Listen, humans. I am raccoon, I speak for the raccoon people. See my hand? It is like yours. On soft ground you see its imprint, and know I've passed. What marks on this world are you leaving behind you?

The people seated in a circle are speaking extemporaneously. Stepping aside from their identification as humans, they are letting themselves be spokespersons for other life-forms. They are meeting in the Council of All Beings, a central part of the workshop they attend. These men, women, and young people have gathered in this workshop to share concerns for their planet. They have met to tell the truth about what they see happening to their world and to move beyond despair.

As the workshop began, they spoke out about developments that are familiar to us all, though they usually seem too vast, too pervasive to address. They spoke of poisons exuding from toxic waste dumps...the pollution of air, water, soil...extinction of plant and animal species... deforestation...spreading deserts...the suffering in animal laboratories

From *ReVision*, 1987.

and farm factories...chemical additives in food and drink...friends and relatives dying from spreading epidemics of cancer.

The ecological crisis these developments reflect is the ultimate expression of a human mistake—a mistake about our place in the order of things. It is the delusion that we can set ourselves apart, immune to what we do to other beings. It is the denial of our deep, systemic interdependence.

Fortunately, another perspective is emerging, a healing corrective. Ecology teaches us that we humans are neither the rulers nor the center of the universe, but imbedded in a vast living matrix and subject to its laws of reciprocity. "Deep ecology" is a term coined by Norwegian philosopher Arne Naess to contrast with "shallow environmentalism," a band-aid approach applying piecemeal technological fixes for short-term human goals. Its meaning for me has become analogous to the Buddha's teaching of dependent co-arising, or "interbeing" to use Thich Nhat Hanh's phrase. Deep ecology represents a basic shift in ways of seeing, and valuing, and being in this world. It calls us home to our true nature as interwoven strands in the web of life.

There are many ways to provoke this change in perspective, ranging from prayer to poetry, from wilderness vision quests to the induction of altered states of consciousness. The most effective is direct action in defense of Earth. In recent years an additional means has arisen, a do-it-yourself group process or ritual form called the Council of All Beings. Designed to heal our separation from the natural world, it lets deep ecology become an experiential reality so that it can take power in our lives.

The Council of All Beings first took place when I was in Australia in 1985, and in the intervening years has spread to the United States, Canada, Europe, and the USSR. It has been held in a wide variety of settings, indoors and out, from the Grand Canyon to a college student lounge, from churches to a grove of redwoods, to a police armory. Numbers of participants have ranged from a dozen to more than a hundred and included people of all ages. Simultaneously solemn and playful, it allows us to honor our pain for the world and our interconnectedness with all life—a sacred interconnectedness that steadies the heart and empowers subsequent actions in defense of Earth.

The Council of All Beings is most effective when it can unfold in three stages. These are the mourning, the remembering, then the speaking on behalf of other life-forms.

MOURNING

Deep ecology remains an abstract concept, without power to transform unless we allow ourselves to feel—which includes feeling the pain within us over what is happening to our world. The workshop serves as a safe place where this pain can be acknowledged and expressed. A sharing of personal experiences, a reading aloud from the list of endangered species (like "Bestiary," Chapter 18)...the best methods are simple ones, for it is natural to mourn and important to speak, at last, our sorrow. Often it arises as a deep sense of loss over what is slipping away—ancient forests, clean rivers, birdsongs, and breathable air. We honor that by saying good-bye to what is disappearing from our lives. This can be done in a circle. One by one, people bring forward a stone or twig or flower and, laying it in the center, name what it represents for them—something disappearing from their lives, the meadow become a shopping mall, a paved-over creek, safe food...And in the ritual naming of these losses, we retrieve our capacity to care.

Yes, in the grief and anger that well up, we rediscover a passionate caring. And this caring springs from our interconnectedness. Why else do we weep for other beings and those not yet born? There's no cause for so great a sadness if at root we are not one. Deep ecology serves as the explanatory principle both for the pain we experience on behalf of our planet and its beings and also for the sense of belonging that arises when we stop repressing that pain and let it reconnect us with our world.

REMEMBERING

As organic manifestations of life on Earth, we have a long and panoramic history. We are not limited to this one brief moment of our planet's story; our roots go back to the beginning of time. We can learn to remember them. The knowledge is in us. As in our mothers' wombs our embryonic bodies recapitulated the evolution of cellular life on earth, so we can do it now consciously, harnessing intellect and the power of imagination. We can reclaim our history in order to know afresh our deep ecology.

Certain methods help trigger this remembering. Guided visualizations can take us through our four and a half billion year story, making it present and vivid. Sometimes we use a drum to sound a heartbeat, affirming our connection with the pulse of life in all beings through time. Our evolutionary journey can also be explored through body movement. Nosing, crawling, wriggling, pushing up, we can actually begin to feel the inner body sense of amphibian and reptile and lower mammal, because these earlier stages of our life are imbedded in our neurological system. It is not necessary, therefore, to induce an altered state of consciousness to remember our human past. It is interesting to note, however, that when consciousness is altered by psychotropic chemicals or sustained, deep, accelerated breathing, nonhuman memories can surface with particular intensity and authenticity. For example, Stanislav and Christina Grof, having developed what they call holotropic breathing to help people recapture significant experiences surrounding their birth, have found that the material recovered often goes beyond the biographical and even the human realm—to include phylogenetic sequences and episodes conveying the experience of other species. These are so real as to produce remarkable insights into specificities of animal behavior, botanical processes, and even inorganic interactions of inanimate matter.

Ordinary consciousness is certainly sufficient, however, to allow us to shake off for awhile our solely human identification and imaginatively to enter the experience of other life-forms. It is as satisfying to do this as to resurrect a half-forgotten skill or sing, after years, a once familiar song. We let hoots and howls, wind and water noises, come through our throats, we hearken to inner intuitions, we stretch to see and feel what lies just barely beyond our human knowings.

One afternoon at his residence in Dharamsala, India, I told His Holiness the Dalai Lama how Buddhist teachings have inspired my work to empower social and environmental activists. I told him how they help us experience our interexistence with all beings. In Northern California, for example, in direct actions on behalf of the old-growth forests, they help us confront the loggers and lumber company executives without fear or blame, because we can remind ourselves now of our deep interconnections throughout our former lives.

"How can Western people know this if they do not believe in rebirth?" His Holiness asked.

"For rebirth we substitute evolution," I said. And to illustrate I took his hand and led him on a two-minute evolutionary remembering. "Each atom in each cell in this hand goes back to the beginning of time"...to the first explosion of light and energy, to the formation of the galaxies and solar systems, to the fires and rains that bathed our planet, and the life-forms that issued from its primordial seas..."We have met and been together many times."

"Yes, of course," he said quietly. "Very good."

SPEAKING FOR OTHER LIFE-FORMS

The Council of All Beings itself is the culminating ritual in which participants formally speak on behalf of other life-forms. This feels good to do, because the beings who coexist with us in the web of life are deeply affected by our actions, yet without a voice in our deliberations and plans. Because it is created to allow for spontaneous expression, each council has its own character; some are solemn and emotionally intense, some erupt in bursts of hilarity, almost all yield moments of memorable power and beauty.

We begin by allowing ourselves to be chosen by another life-form. When meeting outdoors in nature, people can go off alone to find the identity they will assume; when indoors, some moments of silence suffice as people relax, sometimes lying down, to wait with open, non-discursive mind the presence of another life-form. It is wise to stay with the first impulse that arises, for it is not a question of choosing a species one knows a lot about, but rather allowing oneself to be surprised—whether by plant or animal or ecological feature such as a mountain, swamp, or body of water.

We take time to see this life-form in our mind's eye, carefully and from every angle, and to enter it, imaginatively sensing its body from within, and to ask its permission to speak for it in the Council.

When time permits and supplies are at hand, we make simple masks or breastplates to portray our adopted identity. We do this in companionable silence to sounds of nature, actual or taped. Also when time permits, we cluster in small groups of three or four to practice speaking for our life-form, putting into human speech how it feels to be a hawk, a river, an otter or a willow. This helps stretch and sharpen our imaginative awareness, further dislodging us from the usual human roles we play.

Now the creatures gather in a circle and the Council of All Beings formally commences. Prayers and invocations help create a sacred space. Native American elements, such as smudging with sage or cedar and calling on the Four Directions, may be appropriate. After each comer to the Council identifies himself or herself in turn ("Wolf is here, I speak for all wolves." "The Nile is here, I speak for all rivers."), the ritual leader opens the proceedings. "We meet in Council because our planet is in trouble. It is fitting now, and it is important, that each of us be heard. For there is much now that needs to be said and much that needs to be heard." He or she invites the beings to speak spontaneously, and they do. There is much that wolf and Nile, hawk and lichen, have to say.

Soon it is evident that humans should be present to hear, and they are invited to come into the center of the circle to listen in silence. This means that participants in the ritual, five or six at a time, put aside their masks and move into the center to sit back to back facing outwards; and the Council continues with the manifold life-forms addressing the humans—and humans, for once, being quiet. Periodically, say every ten minutes or so, the ritual leader beats a drum to signal that the humans can return to take up their adopted identities in the wider circle and others replace them in the center. This enables everyone to participate both as human and nonhuman.

The testimony of the beings is often almost overwhelming; with poignancy and eloquence they report how rapidly and radically humans are affecting their lives and their chances of survival.

It is not all that strange to imagine ourselves in nonhuman forms and draw fresh understandings from them. Poets and children do it, shamans and primal people know that gift. The Lord Buddha himself, it is believed, developed his perfection of compassion through numerous animal incarnations; the Jataka or "birth" tales of his lives in such forms as rabbit, monkey, tiger, elephant, serve still as models of bravery and selflessness. The interconnectedness—or, more precisely, the interexistence—of all beings is expressed in the Buddhist vision of reality known as the Jeweled Net of Indra, where, at each node of the net, each being like a gem reflects all the others. Today explorations into quantum physics, systems theory, holography and morpho-genetic fields offer similar perspectives on the structure of the universe. The many transbiographical and trans-species experiences occurring throughout his years of psychophysical work with people have led Dr. Grof to conclude that:

> In a yet unexplained way each human being contains the information about the entire universe or all of existence, has potential experiential access to all its parts, and in a sense is the whole cosmic network, as much as he or she is just an infinitesimal part of it, a separate and insignificant biological entity.

It follows then that deep ecology can empower us. As we open to the radical interrelatedness of all that is, fresh vision and vigor can be gained for our work in the world. Actions on behalf of Earth are strengthened, less limited by self-doubt, self-interest, and discouragement. And it is good that that is so, for the crises we confront in this planet-time demand more of us than business-as-usual. They require reaches of wisdom and courage that appear to exceed our individual resources. These become available to us, as we break open to our deep ecology.

In religious language and experience, the sense of being sustained by a source beyond our self, by a power that is not our own possession, is known as grace. In this time of almost overwhelming peril, grace comes—as indeed it always has—in many forms. One of them is the Council of All Beings when, near the end, a shift occurs. Realizing that the fate of the Earth depends now on human decisions, the beings in the Council rally to find ways to strengthen the humans. The ritual leader can cue this shift: "Many humans know now that their ways are destroying the Earth. They feel overwhelmed by what they have unleashed. Yet our fate is in their hands. O fellow beings, what powers of ours can we share with them, what strengths of ours can we give?"

No other announcement is usually necessary for the beings in the Council to respond spontaneously.

I, lichen, work slowly, very slowly. Time is my friend. This is what I give you: patience for the long haul and perseverance.

By offering them, naming them, the participants in the ritual invoke the powers within themselves that they want strengthened. These powers are available to us all because they inhere in the web of life and because, in the final analysis, that web is what we are. By virtue of the long planetary journey we have made, and the processes still at work within us, that deep ecology is our true nature. We can draw upon it now in this time of danger.

It is a dark time. As deep-diving trout I offer you my fearlessness of the dark.

I, lion, give you my roar, the voice to speak out and be heard.

As rainforest, I offer you my powers to create harmony, enabling many life-forms to live together. Out of this balance and symbiosis new, diverse life can spring.

I am caterpillar. The leaves I eat taste bitter now. But dimly I sense a great change coming. What I offer you, humans, is my willingness to dissolve and transform. I do that without knowing what the end-result will be; so I share with you my courage too.

CHAPTER TWENTY

To Reinhabit Time

Both the progressive destruction of our world and our capacity to slow down and stop that destruction can be understood as a function of our experience of time.

We members of post-industrial societies in the closing years of the twentieth century have an idiosyncratic and probably unprecedented experience of time. It can be likened to an ever-shrinking box, in which we race on a treadmill at increasingly frenetic speeds. Cutting us off from other rhythms of life, this box cuts us off from the past and future as well. It blocks our perceptual field of time while allowing only the briefest experience of time.

Until we break out of this temporal trap, we will not be able to fully perceive or adequately address the crisis we have created for ourselves and the generations to come. Yet reflections on our relationship to time and some promising new approaches for changing it suggest that we may be able to inhabit time in a healthier, saner fashion. By opening up our experience of time in organic, ecological, and even geological terms and in revitalizing relationship with other species, other eras—we can allow life to continue on Earth.

THE BEINGS OF THE THREE TIMES

Let us begin as we often begin our workshops on empowerment for social action—with an invocation of the beings of the three times. We invoke them because, at this brink of time, we need them.

We call first on the beings of the past: *Be with us now all you who have gone before, you our ancestors and teachers. You who walked and loved and faithfully tended this Earth be present to us now that we may carry on the legacy you bequeathed us. Aloud and silently in our hearts we say your names and see your faces...*

Adapted from a presentation at the Conference on the Post-Modern Presidency, Santa Barbara, California, July 1989.

We call also on the beings of the present: *All you with whom we live and work on this endangered planet, all you with whom we share this brink of time, be with us now. Fellow humans and brothers and sisters of other species, help us open to our collective will and wisdom. Aloud and silently we say your names and picture your faces...*

Lastly we call on the beings of the future: *All you who will come after us on this Earth, be with us now. All you who are waiting to be born in the ages to come, it is for your sakes too, that we work to heal our world. We cannot picture your faces or say your names—you have none yet—but we would feel the reality of your claim on life. It helps us to be faithful in the task that must be done, so that there will be for you, as there was for our ancestors, blue sky, fruitful land, clear waters.*

THE READING OF THE WILL

In contrast to this prayer, our true regard for the beings of the future is portrayed in a recent cartoon by Tom Toles of the *Buffalo News*. To a group sitting before him expectantly, a lawyer is reading a will. It says:

Dear kids,

We, the generation in power since World War II, seem to have used up pretty much everything ourselves. We kind of drained all the resources out of our manufacturing industries, so there's not much left there. The beautiful old buildings that were built to last for centuries, we tore down and replaced with characterless but inexpensive structures, and you can have them. Except everything we built has a lifespan about the same as ours, so, like the interstate highway system we built, they're all falling apart now and you'll have to deal with that. We used up as much of our natural resources as we could, without providing for renewable ones, so you're probably only good until about a week from Thursday. We did build a generous Social Security and pension system, but that was just for us. In fact, the only really durable thing we built was toxic dumps. You can have those. So think of your inheritance as a challenge. The challenge of starting from scratch. You can begin as soon as—oh, one last thing—as soon as you pay off the two trillion dollar debt we left you.

Signed, Your Parents.

What is staggering about this cartoon, to the point of being funny, is not any exaggeration, for there is none, but the sheer enormity of the reality it portrays and our apparent insouciance in the face of it. This state of affairs can be approached, of course, from a moralistic perspective, in terms of the selfishness of our generation. But I find it more helpful to understand it in terms of our experience of time; for it reveals a blindness, a pathetically shrunken sense of time, that amounts to a pathological denial of the reality and ongoingness of time.

This disregard for the future is all the more astonishing since it runs counter to our nature as biological systems. Living organisms are built to propagate, and to invest a great deal of time and energy in the complex set of behaviors that effort requires. Through these behaviors, which usually have no direct survival value to the individual, the future is wired in. There is, as systems-thinker Tyrone Cashman points out, "this spilling out into the future that is the entire essence of organisms. Any plant or animal for whom, throughout its species history, this was not its most essential characteristic would not exist at all. This wired-in relationship to time is alterable only at the price of extinction. Of course, this time-thrust, this into-the-future-ness of all living beings can be lost by a species. But then, immediately, the species itself disappears, forever."

THE BROKEN CONNECTION

This systems design common to all organisms is clearly evident throughout human history. At great personal cost men and women have labored to create monuments of art and learning that would endure far beyond their individual lives. It makes our present generation's disregard for the future appear amazing, indeed. What developments can account for it? What has happened to our relationship to time?

For one thing, the bomb has happened. The advent of nuclear weapons has ruptured our sense of biological continuity and our felt connections with both past and future. Arguing this point, Robert J. Lifton says, "We need not enter the debate as to whether nuclear war would or would not eliminate *all* human life. The fact that there is such a debate in itself confirms the importance of *imagery* of total biological destruction, or radically impaired imagination of human continuity." This impairment reaches backward as well as forward, "since our sense of connection with prior generations...depends on feeling part of a continuing sequence of generations. The image of a destructive force of unlimited dimensions...enters into every relationship involving parents, children, grandparents, and imagined great-grandparents and great-grandchildren....We are thus among the first to live with a recurrent sense of biological severance."

From the workshops I have facilitated with thousands of people, designed to overcome psychic numbing and feelings of powerlessness, I know this to be true. When people feel safe to express their inner responses to the nuclear and the ecological crises, it is the threatened death of all life that surfaces as their deepest and most pervasive anguish. It is an anguish far deeper than their fears for their personal, individual well-being.

THE FUTURE CANCELLED

The sense of biological severance of which Lifton speaks found form and reinforcement in U.S. Government policies of the 1980s. It was reinforced not only by the saber-rattling of the Cold War, but even more by the frontier mentality that came to the fore in the Reagan and Bush administrations. This mentality denies any need to husband the Earth for the future, because there would always be fresh, unlimited land to move on to. Tyrone Cashman explains the connection:

> When the frontier was over, when there was no more empty land, no more unexplored territory, the engine of American ambition had no place to go. What we have done, and elected Ronald Reagan to stand as symbol for, is to cancel the future.
>
> Reagan essentially assured us, through his personal lack of concern for the future, his escalation of nuclear weapons production, and his own public comments about Armageddon and the end of history, that the future was cancelled, that we needn't concern ourselves about it any more. Thus, it became morally permissible to treat the lands we live on and the rivers and the soils and the forests much as we had treated them when we knew there was an unlimited open frontier in the West there for us to move to when the lands we were exploiting were exhausted, destroyed, and befouled.

When the future is cancelled, there is no need to care for the lands we live on. As former Secretary of Interior James Watt so clearly stated, we can use it all up now because we are the last generation. The great feeding frenzy of the 1980s when the economy was partly deregulated and the leveraged buy-outs and hostile take-overs were a daily occurrence—this resulted in part from the sense of the end of the era, and those who had the power to salt the stuff away before the whole thing went to hell, were out to do that.

THE TIME SQUEEZE

These developments are imbedded in and aggravated by a con-temporary lifestyle of increasing speed. We suffer ever more chronically from the loss not only of past and future, but of the present as well. We hurry. We complain about crowded schedules and the pressure of commitments, then check our watches and rush on. We experi-ence burn out and work hard to earn moments where time can cease and we can relax—then take our laptop computer along on vaca-tion. For we cannot waste the most precious commodity of all.

Time itself, both as a commodity and an experience, has become a scarcity; and many are aware of the irony that we who have more time-saving devices than any culture at any period appear the most time-harried and driven. The paradox is only apparent, however, for our time-scarcity is linked to the very time-efficiency of our technology. As Jeremy Rifkin chronicles in *Time Wars*, our measure of time that once was based on the changing seasons, then the wheeling stars, and then the ticking of the clock, is now parceled out in the nanoseconds of the computer—and we have lost time as an organically measurable experience.

The hurry in which we live invades our thought processes, our bodies, our relationships. In the present economy of time, "we suffer from a remarkable illness, a hectic fever. We don't take time to ponder things, to think them through to the end." Those are the words of Alfred Herehausen, chairman of the Board of the Deutsche Bank, assassinated by terrorists.

Larry Dossey, physician and author of *Space, Time and Medicine*, points out that this causes "hurry sickness." "Our perceptions of speeding clocks and vanishing time cause our own biological clocks to speed. The end result is frequently some form of hurry sickness—

expressed as heart disease, high blood pressure, or depression of our immune function, leading to an increased susceptibility to infection and cancer."

We find ourselves moving too fast for the cultivation of friendships, which have their own tempo and is not always time-efficient and time-predictable in the unfolding of trust and self-disclosure. Even classroom relationships suffer, the age-old relationship between student and teacher... "My teachers talk slower than my Atari," complains a nine-year-old, "so slow they make me mad sometimes. I think, 'Come on, enough of this, let me go home to my Atari. It tells me things faster.'"

The *Kali Yuga*—the "age of iron"—is ancient India's name for the final degenerative era of the world's cycles. One meaning of Kali Yuga is "the dregs of time": a temporal density, gritty and bitter as used coffee grounds. In this end-time, time gets extreme, speeding up, clogging our pores.

My second visit to my son on a wilderness farm in northern British Columbia was only one year after the first. As I trekked the last part of the twenty-five miles from the nearest public road, I looked up at the surrounding mountains and saw changes so startling they stopped me in my tracks. The once beautiful, wild, unbroken slopes and ridges of cedar and Douglas fir were now defaced by huge square areas —clear-cut, shaven, unsightly. "Pampers," said my son, when I asked, "it's a company that makes paper diapers."

All week, as I helped with the haying and the milking of the goats, I would look up at those slopes in anger and grief. "I never put paper diapers on *my* children," I muttered. Actually, there weren't any being mass produced, so as a matter of course I used cloth ones, soaking and washing them, as my mother had before me. To be honest, I have to admit that if I were a young mother today I'd be tempted to use the disposable ones, because, of course, I would be in a hurry. To save ten or twenty minutes, we cut down an old-growth forest.

Speed and haste, as many a wise one has pointed out, are inherently violent. The violence they inflict on our environment is not only because of our appetite for time-saving devices and materials, but also because they put us out of sync with the ecosystem. The natural systems that sustain us move at slower rhythms than we do. The feedback loop is longer, takes more time, than our interactions with our machines. We are like the hummingbird that moves so fast, with a metabolic rate so rapid, that it cannot see the movements of the bear coming slowly out of hibernation. To it, the bear appears as stationary as a glacier does to us. Our own accelerating speed puts us out of sync with more and more of the natural world and blinds us to many of our effects upon it.

By speed we strive to conquer time, we imagine we can escape the pressures of time. It doesn't take much subtlety to see that we get caught thereby in a vicious circle. The time-pressures we create in our computerized world, and the time-pressures we consequently experience, further inflame our desire to escape from time. In cybernetic terms, this is a classical deviation-amplifying feedback loop—and we are all victims of it. No matter how we writhe and turn to free ourselves from time, we twist ourselves more tightly in it. We become enslaved by what we would master, devoured by what we would consume, and increasingly view it—yes, view time itself—as the enemy.

SPIRITUALITY AS ESCAPE FROM TIME

Increasing numbers of us turn to spiritual practices, such as meditation, to find release from this rat-race. Closing our eyes, breathing deeply and slowly, we seek to rise above the pressures of our days into a timeless calm. This behavior can be helpful in slowing us down a bit, but it often perpetuates the notion of time as an enemy to be conquered or outwitted.

In many forms of Hinduism, time is considered to be unreal, a trap of illusion, a form of maya from which to escape into the greater reality of timelessness. In Buddhism more reality is accorded to time and change; yet Buddhist teachers often use the central notion of impermanence as a prod to practice—to arouse revulsion, or awareness of the unsatisfactoriness of life. See, what you prize soon passes. Flowers wilt, paint peels, lovers leave, your own body sags, wrinkles, decays. Ah, woe! Better fix your gaze on what is free from the ravages of time.

Western religions as well reveal this animosity to time. Reach for eternity. Keep your eyes on the pie in the sky. New Age spiritualities with their oft-repeated admonitions to "Be Here Now" can also serve to devalue chronological time and encourage disregard for past and future.

This mindset among people of different religious backgrounds was evident at a workshop where we discussed our experience of time. All the participants spoke feelingly about the frenzied and fragmented pace of their daily lives. When I invited them to hypothesize alternatives to the pace and pressure, only one alternative was voiced: escape into timelessness, into the mystical moment. The only way out they saw was a search for cessation through spiritual practice, aloof from chronological time.

This bothered me a lot, because I was working hard on the issue of nuclear wastes. I was looking for ways to relate to time that could help us face up to the challenge of their incredibly long-lived radioactivity. I wanted us to find the ability to inhabit time, longer stretches of time, not escape from time altogether.

It occurred to me then that our fear of time is, like our fear of matter, a legacy of the hierarchical, patriarchal mindset. As many have pointed out, this essentially dualistic mindset has tended to view the spiritual journey as an attempt to extricate spirit from the toils of matter. Setting one at odds with the very element on which one depends, it engenders a love-hate relationship with matter, where one seeks to conquer that which one fears. Has this mentality devalued chronological time in the same manner? Has it led us to perceive it as the enemy, fostering a love-hate relationship that enslaves us to futile efforts to conquer and escape from time? Can we not see an equation here? The formula would be this: As spirit is to matter, so eternity is to time. Each side of this equation represents that which we seek to escape *from* in relation to that which we seek to escape *to* and which we imagine to be more valuable.

$$\frac{\text{SPIRIT}}{\text{MATTER}} = \frac{\text{ETERNITY}}{\text{TIME}}$$

That equation triggers other reflections. If in our fear of time we strive to conquer time, we are, thanks to our technology, in great danger of succeeding. A distinctive feature of our nuclear war-making capacity is speed. The technological design thrust is ever to shorten the time of response to attack, and make launch-on-warning as instantaneous as possible. The time allowed for human appraisal and intervention—to see, for example, if the attack is real or the result of a computer misreading—is continually reduced. It is now reduced to the point where computer scientists at Stanford University have concluded from their models that the risk of an accidental nuclear war caused by computer malfunction will rise to 50% by the end of the 1990s. Our nuclear missiles may be the logical unfolding of our "spiritual" desire to escape from time—and the final, time-stopping blast the ultimate expression of that desire.

So we ask, how can we break free of our fear of time so that time may continue? Can we become friendly with time and reinhabit time, that our days on this Earth may be long?

TO RECLAIM TIME, RECLAIM STORY

To fall in love again with time, we need narrative. "It's all a question of story," says Thomas Berry. "We are in trouble just now because we do not have a good story." Though they are ineffective for us now, we had some good stories of our world in the past. "They did not necessarily make people good, nor did they take away the pains and stupidities of life or make for unfailing warmth in human association. They did provide a context in which life could function in a meaningful manner." And that is all we ask right now, that life function in a meaningful manner—or even function, period.

Berry and his fellow cosmologist, Brian Swimme, hold that the new story we need to guide us through the perils of this era must include the whole universe and all its beings. Only in that context can we perceive the long panorama and web of kinship that is basic to the creative commitment we are called now to make. Story nourishes, as they point out, a "time-developmental consciousness." And our particular story, Earth's and ours, has, of necessity, both grandeur and pain.

> Perhaps only by seeing the permanent destruction we have inflicted upon the Earth Community can we come to the realization that the Earth Community is in fact a dimension of ourselves. Perhaps only when that loss is felt personally, can the human realize the grandeur of the human in the grandeur of the Earth. Perhaps only by feeling directly the folly of destroying Earth's beauty can we

awaken to the simple truth that we are destroying our macrophase
self.

To appropriate the story of evolving Earth as our own can radically
expand our consciousness of time and our felt continuity with past
and future. In Deep Ecology workshops we set about this deliber-
ately and experientially. We engage, for example in "evolutionary
rememberings." We expand our sense of time to include the life
span of our planet. (See Chapter Twenty-two.) Our purpose is to
deepen our sense of what is personally at stake for us in issues of
planetary distress, and also to strengthen our sense of authority when
we act in defense of life on Earth. We act then not from the private
whim or personal nobility of our short-lived individual ego, but clothed
in the full authority of our five billion years.

BRIDGE TO THE FAR FUTURE

While the use of imagination to remember our evolution and reconnect with our ancestors can expand our awareness of the past,
analogous practices can extend our time-consciousness into the future.
Ecological restoration work brings a strong connection with coming
generations. To plant a tree extends one's sense of tenure on this
Earth. Careful, compelling novels like *Ridley Walker,* by Paul Hoban,
or *Always Coming Home,* by Ursula Leguin, can make far distant
generations and their claim on life seem more real to us. For me
the most lively link to beings of the future centuries and millennia
is provided by nuclear wastes. My involvement with this issue has
altered my experience of time. This is not surprising; for the radioactive
isotopes generated by our nuclear energy and weapons production
extend the effects of our actions into vast reaches of time, into *their*
life spans of thousands and even millions of years.

Surely the way we and other countries have produced and dis-
posed of nuclear wastes is, of all our behaviors, the most appalling
display of our denial of the future. For their radioactivity produces
not only disease, death, and sterility, it affects the genetic code itself.
Likened to a madman in a library, it can scramble and lose forever
the blueprints for life crafted by our long evolutionary journey. Yet,
knowing this, we dump millions of metric tons of this waste into

open unlined trenches, into the sea, into cardboard boxes, into tanks that crack and corrode within a decade or two.

The only permanent solution for high level waste that our government will provide is to hide it, out of sight and out of mind, in mammoth, deep geological repositories—although this strategy makes the leaking containers inaccessible for repair. The posture frequently taken by anti-nuclear citizens who protest the presence of this waste is in some ways analogous. For the NIMBY, or Not-In-My-Backyard, syndrome suggests a reluctance to acknowledge that our generation has really produced this material.

To see if we can come up with an alternative response to nuclear waste, I have experimented with ways that would help people experience on an immediate, intuitive or gut level its ongoingness through time. On one memorable occasion at an *ad hoc* "People's Council" near Los Alamos, when discussion about the waste was limited to wishing it away, I pulled out a small tape recorder. "Let's assume," I said, "if we can't stop the waste from going into the Carlsbad repository, that we can at least place this cassette there on the surface for future generations to find and listen to. What do we want to say to them?"

Passing the recorder among them, the men and women began to speak into it. "My name is George, I'm back in 1988 and trying to stop them from burying this radioactive waste. If they do and if you hear this, listen. This stuff is dangerous, don't dig here, stay away. It's really deadly, take care."

As the words came, the distant, unborn ones to whom they were addressed became more and more real and present to us. We began to inhabit large stretches of time. The NIMBY response evaporated and was replaced by a willingness to care for the waste in order to protect future generations. Several young people there even volunteered to live and work at a nuclear "Guardian Site." (See next chapter.)

Another experiment with time involves an enactment on the same theme, where we play the roles of the future ones, speaking *for* them instead of *to* them. At audio-visual presentations my colleagues and I take our audience with us on a fantasy journey to a Nuclear Guardian Site a century or two from now. From that vantage point we look back at the post-World War II generations that left behind the legacy of radioactive waste. We seek to understand what is required of those generations, in terms of creating institutions and practices for its responsible care. This exercise provides a fresh perspective on what our own generation has done and can do. This perspective can evoke a new sense of shock and shame, which is not inappropriate, and it is accompanied by a new sense of hope. Hope comes from glimpsing the possibility that we humans have the capacity to be faithful to life in dealing responsibly with what we have created.

The point I want to make here is that we have the ability, through our moral imagination, to break out of our temporal prison and let longer expanses of time become real to us. We can do it, we are good at it, and we like it.

Our radioactive legacy has had for me another peculiar effect on my experience of time. Suffering from the big squeeze as much as anyone, time's main meaning for me was scarcity and haste. Especially in social action, the clock was always ticking. Hurry, hurry to stop the next escalation of the arms race, to block the B-1 bomber or the Trident II. Make those calls, circulate those petitions, hurry to keep the world from blowing up, the countdown has started. When I began to focus on nuclear waste, when the longevity of its terrible toxicity dawned on me, when I glimpsed what this challenge would mean in terms of sustained human attention, the demands of time reversed themselves. The question of how fast one could get something done was replaced with the question of how long—how *lo-o-n-n-ng*— a period one could do it in. Will we actually be able to remember the danger of these wastes and protect ourselves for a hundred years, a thousand, a hundred thousand? As I pondered the likelihood of this, the challenge became duration not speed, the long haul, not the quick move. My breath slowed, the rib cage eased. The horror of the waste was helping me inhabit time.

POLITICS OF TIME

If, for a livable world, we must learn to reinhabit time, what changes are required in our system of self-governance? What political practices would reflect and encourage a sense of responsibility to coming generations? Such questions prompt a wide range of proposals. Extending the length of terms of legislative office would relieve harried representatives from the pressures of bi-annual electoral campaigns and allow them time to think. Alterations in executive budgetary requirements would free disbursements from having to be hastily made in a given fiscal year.

Let's create structures that would give voice to the interests of future generations. This is totally in keeping with our principle of no taxation without representation. Since we are taxing future generations by the exploitation of their resources, they should have their say in the process. Because they are not born yet, or too young to vote, offices should be instituted where pronouncements can be made on their behalf.

One possibility has a precedent in the Congressional offices of representatives of Puerto Rico and the District of Columbia. Though without a legislative vote, they are provided the means to bring views and needs of their constituencies to the attention of Congress. I propose a similar nonvoting representative for the people of the future, to promote their needs and bring a larger perspective on time into legislative debates. This representative could be selected at a special three-day convention in Washington, which would in itself be a salutary exercise in raising awareness of the effects of our present policies on coming generations.

A second possibility has even greater potential for changing our society's consciousness of time. Consider the establishment of a third house of Congress, a House of Spokespersons for the Future. Though without the power to pass laws, it would speak for the rights of coming generations. Its members, or "Spokes," would be high school seniors, two from each state, chosen at statewide conventions on Congressional election years. The House of Spokes would convene in Washington for a week three times a year, say in early January, spring, and summer, evaluate bills before Congress and suggest new legislation. During the balance of the year its members would still be heard from, as they point to the priorities they see appropriate for a healthy and decent future.

Our goals and values are increasingly shaped by our experience of time, and as this becomes more evident, the spectrum of political identifications will be reconceptualized—from spatial to temporal terms. Jeremy Rifkin suggests that political persuasions and loyalties formerly assigned to categories of "left" and "right" will sort themselves out more accurately and usefully in terms of their orientation to rhythms and duration of time. He sees the emerging political spectrum as moving between "power rhythms" at one pole and "empathetic rhythms" at the other. The latter, oriented to an ecological vision of life, would reintegrate our social and economic tempos with the tempos of the natural world so that the ecosystem can "heal itself and become a vibrant, living organism once again."

Since we as a species have no future apart from the health of that organism, this return to a more organic, ecological experience of time is a matter of survival. And we don't need to wait till we have created new institutions. We can begin now; by choice and mindfulness of our experience of time, we can become friendly with time. We can watch its rhythm in the breathing of the moment, and sense how its very passage, far from robbing us of life, connects us with the past and future ones. They become to us like unseen companions, as we reinhabit time.

CHAPTER TWENTY-ONE

In League With the Beings of the Future

For thou shalt be in league with the stones of the field, and
the beasts of the field shall be at peace with thee.

—Job 5:23

This verse of the Bible delighted me as a child and stayed with
me as I grew up. It promised a way I wanted to live—in
complicity with creation. It still comes to mind when I hear
about people taking action on behalf of other species. When our
brothers and sisters of Greenpeace or Earth First! put their lives on
the line to save the whales or the old-growth forests, I think, "Ah,
they're in league."

To be "in league" in that way seems wonderful. There is a
comfortable, cosmic collegiality to it—like coming home to conspire once more with our beloved and age-old companions, with
the stones and the beasts of the field, and the sun that rises and
the stars revolving in the sky.

Now the work of restoring our ravaged Earth offers us that—
and with a new dimension. It not only puts us in league with the
stones and the beasts, but also in league with the beings of the future.
All that we do for the mending of our planet is for their sake, too.
Their chance to live and love our world depends in large measure
on us and our often uncertain efforts.

I sense those beings of the future times hovering, like a cloud
of witnesses. Sometimes I fancy that if I were to turn my head suddenly,
I would glimpse them over my shoulder—they and their claim on
life have become that real to me. Philosophers and mystics say that
chronological time is a construct, a function of our mentality; there
is also, they say, a dimension in which all time is simultaneous, where
we co-exist with past and future. Perhaps because I am so time-ridden,
hurrying to meet this deadline and that appointment, I am drawn to
that notion. The dimension of simultaneity, where we stand shoulder
to shoulder with our ancestors and descendants, is appealing to me,
it gives context and momentum to work for social change.

First appeared in *Creation Magazine*, March 1989.

In that context it is plausible to me that the generations of the future want to lend us courage for what we do for their sake. I imagine them saying "thanks" for our dogged efforts to protect the rainforests. Thanks for our citizen campaigns on behalf of the seas and rivers. Thanks for working on renewable energy sources, so that those who come after us can have breathable air.

The imagined presence of these future ones comes to me like grace and works upon my life. That is one reason why I have been increasingly drawn to the issue of radioactive waste. Of the many causes that pull us into league with the future, this one, in terms of time and toxicity, is the most enduring legacy our generation will leave behind.

More than ten years ago I engaged in a citizens' lawsuit to stop faulty storage of high-level waste at a nearby nuclear reactor. Night after night, to substantiate our legal claims, I sat up studying the statistics, trying to understand the phenomenon called ionizing radiation. I poured over the research, revealing the mounting incidence of miscarriages, birth defects, leukemia and other cancers in the proximity of nuclear plants. Learning that genetic damage would accelerate over time, I strained to conceive of *spans* of time like a quarter million years, the hazardous life of plutonium.

During that period I had a dream so vivid that it is still etched in my mind. Before going to bed, I had leafed through baby picures of our three children to find a snapshot for my daughter's high school yearbook.

In the dream I behold the three of them as they appeared in the old photos, and am struck most by the sweet wholesomeness of their flesh. My husband and I are journeying with them across an unfamiliar landscape. The land is becoming dreary, treeless and strewn with rocks; Peggy, the youngest, can barely clamber over the boulders in the path. Just as the going is getting very difficult, even frightening, I suddenly realize that by some thoughtless but unalterable pre-arrangement, their father and I must leave them. I can see the grimness of the way that lies ahead for them, bleak as a red moonscape and with a flesh-burning sickness in the air. I am maddened with sorrow that my children must face this without me. I kiss each of them and tell them we will meet again, but I know no place to name where we will meet. Perhaps another planet, I say. Innocent of terror, they try to reassure me, ready to be off. Removed and from a height in the sky, I watch them go—three small figures trudging across that angry wasteland, holding each other by the hand and not stopping to look back. In spite of the widening distance, I see with a surrealist's precision the ulcerating of their flesh. I see how the skin bubbles and curls back to expose raw tissue, as they dog-gedly go forward, the boys helping their little sister across the rocks.

I woke up, brushed my teeth, showered, and tried to wash those images away. But when I roused Peggy for school, I sank beside her bed. "Hold me," I said, "I had a bad dream." With my face in her warm nightie, inhaling her fragrance, I found myself sobbing. I sobbed against her body, against her seventeen-year-old womb, as the knowledge of all that assails it surfaced in me. The statistical studies on the effects of ionizing radiation, the dry columns of figures, their import beyond utterance, turned now to tears, speechless, wracking.

Our citizens' group lost its suit against the Virginia Electric Power Company, but it taught me a lot. It taught me that all the children for centuries to come are my children. It taught me about the misuse of our technology and the obscenity of the legacy it bequeaths future generation—lessons confirmed by recent media exposés about mismanagement of nuclear wastes.

Hundreds of thousands of metric tons of radioactive waste have been generated by our production of nuclear power and nuclear weapons. The toxicity of these wastes requires them to be kept out of the biosphere for many times longer than recorded history. "Temporarily" stored in tanks, trenches, pools, and even cardboard boxes, it is leaking into the air, soil, aquifers, and rivers in thirty-four out of fifty states. No permanent repositories are operative. As a "final solution," two mammoth burial sites are being prepared in New Mexico and Nevada.

If we think on behalf of future beings, this last fact is the most alarming of all. Eager to put it out of sight and out of mind, our government intends to bury the waste. As we discover in other aspects of our lives, hiding does not work in the long run. This is especially true of nuclear materials because, irradiated by their contents, containers corrode, and because the Earth's strata shift and water seeps, the radioactivity will shift and seep with them — into the aquifers, into the biosphere, into the lungs and wombs of those who come after. Indeed, the two designated repositories are already presenting problems: salt brine is leaking into the New Mexico site and the other adjoining the Nevada testing site is geologically at risk.

When I asked officials at the designated repository in New Mexico how future generations would be protected, they said the site would be safe for a hundred years or so. "And after that?" I asked. They look at me blankly, as if puzzled by such an exotic question.

Standing there in the briefing room, I wondered how that question would be answered if we were to inhabit our Earth with a sense of time and of our unfolding story. If our long, ongoing evolutionary journey were real to us, if we felt the aliveness of our planet home and a living connection with those who come after, would we still want to sweep these wastes under the rug, hide them like a secret shame and go on about our business as before?

A different approach to nuclear waste came to mind in Great Britain five years ago as I visited Greenham Common and other citizen encampments surrounding U.S. nuclear missile bases. These encampments with their dogged dedication and strong spiritual flavor reminded me of the monasteries that kept the lamp of learning alive through the dark ages. I realized that we need communities with the same dedication to guard the centers of radioactivity that we bequeath for thousands of years to future generations.

In my mind's eye I could see surveillance communities forming around today's nuclear facilities—Guardian Sites which are centers of reflection and pilgrimage, where the waste containers are monitored and repaired religiously, and where the wisdom traditions of our planet offer contexts of meaning and disciplines of vigilance. Here "remembering" is undertaken —the crucial task of continuous mindfulness of the radioactive presence and danger. Here those who come for varying periods of time participate in an active learning community—to receive training and take their turn at nuclear guardianship.

The vision has remained with me. It compelled study of the whole issue of radioactive wastes, of the terrible negligence in current practices and of the requirements for longterm responsible care. Out of this study—undertaken with others, for it is too despairing to do alone—has emerged the Nuclear Guardianship Project which promotes on-site, above ground storage of the wastes. The Project also promotes citizen training in the technical knowledge and moral vigilance necessary for guardianship. For to keep these wastes out of the biosphere, human attention is required. No containments last as long as the "poison fire" itself, so we cannot hide them anywhere and walk away. But we do have reliable means for monitoring and repair, if only we pay attention. If only we sustain the gaze and stay mindful. To do that, and to carry that responsibility through the social and economic dislocations that are inevitably in store, faithful commitment is essential—and community to sustain it. So we begin now to build that commitment and community.

When I think about how the beings of the future will relate to our radioactive legacy, an unexpected danger occurs to me: the danger that they may not take seriously the toxicity of these wastes. That is because it will probably be hard for them to accept the fact that we, their ancestors, would knowingly fabricate and leave behind materials that would cripple and kill for millennia to come. How will they believe that we would do that? Such criminality may be hard for them to accept. They may be tempted to deny it, just as a growing number of people today want to deny the reality of the holocaust.

The challenge for them, therefore, in protecting themselves from these wastes will have to begin with acceptance of what we, their ancestors, have done. As I ponder that, it seems that in order for that acceptance to occur, a measure of forgiveness will be necessary. Our generation's crime against the future will be too terrible to be believed unless it is already acknowledged by us in a concrete way.

When and how should acceptance and forgiveness begin? It begins with ourselves; we can stop trying to hide our guilt and bury our shame. Our intention to be guardians heals our relationship to the future and to ourselves.

Such are the reflections that turn in my mind. They bring the future beings very close, as if they are right here, in conversation. These beings teach me about the acceptance and forgiveness that are needed if healing is to occur. Sometimes I imagine I can see their faces—some are human like mine, others furred or feathered.

My heart is warm in their company. That warmth encourages me to continue to work for guardianship of nuclear wastes.

At a recent meeting of educators, my friend Brian Swimme was asked to introduce me. He did so, saying, "She has a lot of friends. Most of them aren't born yet." The same is true for Brian. It is true for all of you who choose to take part in the mending of our world.

For then, thou shalt be in league with the beings of the future, and the generations to come after shall be at peace with thee.

CHAPTER TWENTY-TWO

Meditations in Deep Time

To enter into our healing as self, as world, let us move out into Deep Time. Let the reaches of time that we inhabit with our ancestors and those to come become real to us, as our birthright and wider home. Let us step out of the tiny, hurried compartment of time, where our culture and habits would enclose us. Let us breathe deep and ease into the vaster horizons of our larger story and our true, shared being.

Here are some practices to help us reinhabit time. We do not seek to escape from time, or cease its flow or declare it unreal. We would rather dance with time, embracing its mighty roll through the ages—with awe and even a kind of affectionate conspiracy.

OUR LIFE AS GAIA*

The meditation as written here is done with a group and a drum. It can also, of course, be done alone in stillness or interwoven with our daily activities.

Come back with me into a story we all share, a story whose rhythm beats in us still. The story belongs to each of us and to all of us, like the beat of this drum, like the heartbeat of our living universe.

There is science now to construct the story of the journey we have made on this Earth, the story that connects us with all beings. There is also great yearning and great need to own that story—to break out of our isolation as persons and as a species and recover through that story our larger identity. The challenge to do that now, and burst out of the separate prison cells of our contrivings, is perhaps the most wonderful aspect of our being alive today.

Right now on our planet we need to remember that story—we are in a hard time, the knowledge of the bigger story can carry us through. It can

---

* Taken from *Thinking Like a Mountain*, pp. 57-65.

give us the courage, and even the hilarity, to dance our people into sanity and solidarity. Let us remember it together.

With the heartbeat of the drum we hear the rhythm that underlies all our days and doings. Throughout our sleeping and rising, through all our working and loving, our heart has been beating steadily. That steady sturdy inner sound has accompanied us all the way. And so it can take us back now, back through our lives, back through our childhood, back through our birth. In our mother's womb there was that same sound, that same beat, as we floated in the fluid right under her heart.

Let that beat take us back farther still. Let's go back, back far beyond our conception in this body, back to the first splitting and spinning of the stars. As scientists measure now, it is fifteen billion years ago we manifested as a universe—in what they call the Big Bang.

There we were, careening out with the speed of light, through space and time, creating space and time. Gradually, in vast curls of flame and darkness, we reached for form. We were then great swirls of clouds of gas and dancing particles—can you imagine you remember? And the particles, as they circled in the dance, desired each other and formed atoms. It is the same desire for form that beats now in this drum and in our hearts.

Ten billion years later, one of the more beautiful swirls of those swirling masses split off from its blazing sun—the sun we feel now on our faces— and became the form we know best. And our lifetime as Gaia began.

Touch our Earth, touch Gaia. Touch Gaia again by touching your face, that is Gaia. Touch Gaia again by touching your sister or brother. That is Gaia, too.

In the immediate planet-time of ours, Gaia is becoming aware of herself, she is finding out who she is. How rich she is in the multitudinous and exquisite forms she takes.

Let us imagine that her life—our life as a planet—could be condensed into twenty-four hours, beginning at midnight. Until five o'clock the following afternoon all her adventures are geological. All was volcanic flamings and steaming rains washing over the shifting bones of the continents into the shifting seas—only at five o'clock comes organic life.

To the heartbeat of life in you and this drum, you, too, right now, can shift a bit—shift free from identifying solely with your latest human form. The fire of those early volcanoes, the strength of those tectonic plates, is in us still. For in our very bodies, we carry traces of Gaia's story as organic life. We were aquatic first, as we remember in our mother's womb, growing vestigial gills and fins. The salt from those early seas flows still in our sweat and tears. And the age of the dinosaurs we carry with us, too, in our reptilian brain, situated so conveniently at the end of our spinal column. Complex organic life was learning to protect itself and it is all there in our neurological system, in the rush of the instinct to flee or fight.

And when did we appear as mammals? In those twenty-four hours of Gaia's life, it was at 11:30 P.M.! And when did we become human? One second to midnight.

Now let us take that second to midnight that is our story as humans and reckon that, in turn, as twenty-four hours. Let's look back through the twenty-four hours that we have been human.

Beginning at midnight and until two o'clock in the afternoon, we live in small groups in Africa. Can you imagine you remember? We feel pretty vulnerable; we haven't the speed of the other creatures, or their claws or fangs or natural armor. But we have our remarkable hands, opposable thumbs to help shape tools and weapons. And we have in our throats and frontal lobes the capacity for speech. Grunts and shouts turn into language as we collaborate in strategies and rituals. Those days and nights on the verge of the forests, as we weave baskets and stories around our fires, represent the longest chapter of our human experience.

Then in small bands we begin branching out. We move across the face of Gaia; we learn to face the cold and hunt the mammoth and name the trees of the northern forest, the flowers and seasons of the tundra. We know it is Gaia by whom we live and we carve her in awe and fear and gratitude, giving her our breasts and hips. When we settle into agriculture, when we begin domesticating animals and fencing off our croplands and deciding that they could be owned as private property, when we build great cities with granaries and temples and observatories to chart the stars, the time is eleven fifty-eight. Two minutes to midnight.

At eleven fifty-nine comes a time of quickening change: We want to chart the stars within as well as those we see in the skies; we want to seek the authority of inner experience. To free the questing mind we set it apart from Gaia. We make conjectures and rules and heroes to help us chart our freedom to think and act. Major religious systems arise. At six seconds to midnight comes a man called Buddha, and shortly after another called Jesus of Nazareth.

What now shapes our world—our industrial society with its bombs and bulldozers—has taken place in the last few microseconds of the day we have known as humans. Yet those few microseconds bring us right to the brink of time. For the forces our technologies have unleashed, and the power they give to our fears and greeds, threatens all life. Each of us knows that at some level of our awareness.

We are now at a point unlike any other in our story. Perhaps we have, in some way, chosen to be here at this culminating chapter or turning point. We have opted to be alive when the stakes are high, to test everything we have ever learned about interconnectedness, about courage—to test it now when it could be curtains for conscious life on this beautiful water planet hanging there like a jewel in space.

In primal societies rites of passage are held for adolescents, because it is in adolescence that the fact of personal death or mortality is integrated into the personality. The individual goes through the prescribed ordeal of the initiation rite in order to integrate that knowledge, so that he or she can assume the rights and responsibilities of adulthood. That is what we are doing right now on the collective level, in this planet-time. We are confronting and integrating into our awareness our collective mortality as a species. We must do that so that we can wake up and assume the rights and responsibilities of planetary adulthood—so that we can grow up! That is, in a sense, what we are doing here.

When you go out from here, please keep listening to the drum beat. You will hear it in your heart. And as you hear it, remember that it is the heartbeat of the universe as well, and of Gaia your planet, and your larger Self.

When you return to your communities to organize, saying no to the machinery of death and yes to life, remember your true identity. Remember your story, our story. Clothe yourself in your authority. You speak not only as yourself or for yourself. You were not born yesterday. You have been through many dyings and know in your heartbeat and bones the precarious, exquisite balance of life. Out of that knowledge you can speak and act. You will speak and act with the courage and endurance that has been yours through the long, beautiful aeons of your life story as Gaia.

BREATHING WITH THE BEINGS OF ALL TIME
Wild air, world-mothering air, nestling me everywhere...

—*Gerard Manley Hopkins*

The sheer chemistry of life gives us cause to meditate on our interexistence with all beings through time. Consider our breathing, which might appear the most personal and intimate of acts, since the atoms of oxygen we draw into our lungs move on to sustain each cell in our innermost body and brain. Yet that very breathing links us directly and immediately with beings of the past and future; in each sniff and sigh and lungful they participate.

Wondrous are the mathematical givens of our presence to each other in this way. Reflect on the fact that the average breath you breathe contains about ten sextillion atoms, or ten to the twenty-second power. Now reflect on the amazing fact that the Earth's atmosphere itself is of a size to contain the same number of breaths. This remarkable symmetry, which places you midway between atom and world, also means that with each inhalation you take in an average of one atom from each of the breaths in our world, and with each exhalation send back the same average of an atom to each breath. This exchange repeated twenty thousand times a day by each of the Earth's billions of people produces such an "interbreathing" that, as scientists conclude, "each breath you breathe must contain a quadrillion atoms breathed by the rest of humankind within the past few weeks and more than a million atoms breathed personally sometime by each and any person on earth."

The circulation of air through normal atmospheric turbulence provides the diffusion that allows this to be so, as scientist Guy Murchie explains. And he goes on to evoke what this can mean: "Your next breath will include a million odd atoms of oxygen and nitrogen once breathed by Pythagoras, Socrates, Confucius, Moses, Columbus, Einstein, or anyone you can think of...And going on to animals, you may add a few million molecules from the mighty blowings of the whale that swallowed Jonah, from the snorts of Mohammed's white mare, from the restive raven that Noah sent forth from the ark..."

By the same token atoms of each breath you breathe will find their way into the lungs of beings yet to come, in whatever century they may walk this Earth.

So we can delight in this exchange, when we remember to re-member. We can bow to those atoms coursing through us with each inhalation and exhalation, and greet them like so many messages coming in from times past and going out to times future. Sustained within the web of life, we breathe with each other. We conspire.

HARVESTING THE GIFTS OF THE ANCESTORS

To inhabit broader reaches of time, let us sense the companionship of those who have gone before. They are with us, you know. Even as you read this page, your ancestors are present—in your curiosity or the set of your jaw.

Harvest their gifts.

Here is a process I learned from my friend Friedemann Wieland. When we do it in workshops, we stand and move to music, walking backwards and then forwards with eyes closed. Engaging the body helps, but you can also stay still. Take at least half an hour.

From this present moment you will walk backwards through time. Move back through the events and encounters of this day...this week...this month...this year...Walk back through the decades into your young adulthood, your adolescence, your childhood...Soon you are a baby in your mother's arms, now back in her womb, and returning to the climactic point of this life's conception...But what lives in you did not begin then. Walk back into your parents, into their lives, their meeting, their youth and teenage years and infancy...back into the wombs that bore them, back into your grandparents...Continue slowly back, into and through the nineteenth century, into ancestors whose names you no longer know, but a gesture of theirs, a smile or turn of the head, lives on in you.

Keep moving back upstream in this river of life, back through the industrial era...back into simpler, harsher times marked by the seasons, back into the Middle Ages...Walk back through the lives of men and women— peasants and magistrates, scholars, artists, scoundrels, who even then bore you within them like a future seed...Move back through times of plague and pilgrimage into lives of ancestors with hands, like yours, that chiseled the stones of great cathedrals and eyes, like yours, that tracked the movements of the stars...Keep going back...back...back to the dawning of the civilizations we know, and enter the early, wandering times...the small bands in forest settlements, their feasts and rituals around the sacred fire, and their long marches in the ages of ice.

Back through the millennia you walk with them, to your beginnings in the heartland of Africa. And now with the very first ones you stand at the edge of the forest.

Pause now, looking out over the savannah. The journey of your people lies ahead. Walk forward on it now. Retrace your steps, returning through time. Each ancestor has a gift to bestow; open your arms and hands to receive it, as you walk up through the centuries.

They who passed on to you the texture of your skin, the shape of your back, the marrow in your bones, also have courage to bequeath and stubbornness and laughter. These gifts are yours for the taking.

Garner them, as you come forward through the years to this present moment, this brink of time. They who loved and tended this Earth bequeath you the strength and wisdom you will need now, to do what must be done—so their journey and yours may continue.

LISTENING TO THE BEINGS OF THE FUTURE

Just as the life that pulses in our bodies goes back to the beginnings of Earth, so does that same heartbeat carry the pulse of those to come after. By the power of our imagination, we can sense them breathing with the rhythm of our own breath, or feel them hovering like a cloud of witnesses.

Given the power of the life that links us, it is plausible to me that these future generations want to lend us courage for what we do for their sake. I imagine them looking back across time to this critical period, when we are inflicting so much on our world that is irremediable—looking back and wishing they could help and be heard. So I listen to them in my mind.

What I imagine I hear them say keeps me going. Sometimes it's just a whisper of "thanks," when I crawl out of bed an hour early to finish a report, or squeeze in a late night meeting with environmental activists. I hear them thanking my activist colleagues, too, who also get tired and discouraged. Sometimes the comments of the future ones erupt unbidden. More than once I have been tempted to throw in the sponge on the Nuclear Guardianship Project (see Chapter Twenty-one), because I lack organizational and technical skills. "I'm no expert on radioactive wastes," I mutter; "It's not *my* job to store them. It's depressing and I'm tired and I have better things to do with my life."

Then comes this presence at my shoulder, and I feel an almost physical nudge. "Come on now. Just do what you can. This poison fire is going to be around for so long; help your people contain it while they still can." And there's an edge of laughter in the words I imagine I hear: "After all, *you* are the one who's alive now!"

There are countless ways to harness our imagination to let the future beings become real and to listen to what they have to say to us. These practices perform a function equivalent to the House of Spokespersons for the Future, proposed in Chapter Twenty.

Sometimes in workshops on Deep Time participants are invited to close their eyes and journey forward through coming generations and identify with a future being. They need not determine this person's circumstances, but only imagine that he or she is looking back at *them* in this present juncture of time at the close of the twentieth century. And they are asked to imagine what this being would want to say to them. After a period of silent listening (nonprogrammatic music helps free the mind), the participants write down what came to them. In other words, they write a letter to themselves from the future. Leave ample time, for messages can come from beneath our normal, self-identified consciousness and tap into the collective wisdom of our planet people. Later on, when they are shared aloud, at choice, they are often helpful and deeply inspiring to others in the group as well.

Identifying imaginatively with future beings can also help us tackle specific tasks with more purposefulness and buoyancy than is usually at hand. Here is an example from an early meeting of our local Nuclear Guardianship group. I put a sign on the front door of my house that said, "Chernobyl Time Lab: 2088" and I put on Ukrainian liturgical music in the background. As people came in, I said, "Welcome! Our work here at the time laboratory of this Guardian Site is based on the importance of being able to journey backward through time. This is because the decisions made by people in the late twentieth century on how to deal with the poison fire has such longterm effects. We must help them make the right decisions. So you have been selected to go back in time to a particular group in Berkeley, California, that has come to our attention. They are meeting exactly a hundred years ago today, to try to understand, with their very limited mentality, about the containment of the poison fire. It's easy for them to feel stupid and discouraged, so from our vantage point in the year 2088 and with our accumulated wisdom here at the Chernobyl Lab we're going to go backward in time to enter their bodies as they proceed with their study, so they will not get disheartened."

After that introduction, I simply proceeded, matter-of-factly, with the teach-in I had prepared on methods of containment for nuclear waste. No one felt called upon to play the role or speak on behalf of a future being; we simply concentrated on the material. But each of us, I think, sensed within ourself a presence that cared desperately that we understand about the poison fire and that we not feel limited by our own notions of our intelligence and courage.

Based, like other environmental actions, on concern for future generations, the Nuclear Guardianship Project has used imagination to look forward to time in order to look back at our present situation with a fresh perspective. (see Chapter Twenty-one). One product of such efforts is the "Remembering" we often use at our presentation of the Guardian Site concept:

THE STANDARD REMEMBERING OF OUR ANCESTORS
IN THE TIMES OF NUCLEAR PERIL

I ask you to breathe and open,
as we do when we remember times that are very far past,
Times that are very hard for us to imagine.
Hard for us to go back to the time
when the poison fire was made on the planet.

We in the twenty-second century are accustomed to the
     danger.
But the people of that time,
mid-twentieth century, were so innocent, dangerously
     innocent.

And as we remember the old stories,
we remember how it began in the press of war.
O, our ancestors in the press of war
were seeking new and larger ways to kill.

And they opened the nucleus of the atom.
And with great effort and with great acumen

and with great applications of their brains,
they made and exploded the first nuclear weapon,
and the project, God forgive them,
they called Trinity
in the desert of Alamo Gordo.

And the stories come down to us of a president
 called True Man
at a place called Pots Dam
receiving a telegram:
"Baby safely delivered!"

That baby was the poison fire.
And then in that very year, in that very month,
yes, the poison fire was first used as weapons.
Against great cities of a great people.
And we know the names and you can say them in your
 heart,
—we shall not forget them:
Hero Shimah, Nagah Saki.
A quarter million people burned at once,
then many more who sickened slowly,
for that is how it destroys, slowly, hidden.

And then our ancestors of that time, the stories tell us
 —this is hard—
they used the poison fire to make electricity.
We know how easy it is
 to share the power with the sun,
 and with the wind,
 and with the biomass,
but they took it from the poison fire,
and they used it to boil water for steam.

O the lords of arrogance were riding high then.
It was a dark time, the times of nuclear peril.

And the signs of sickening grew.
For at every step along the way the poison fire
    proliferated.

And there were epidemics of cancer
and there were epidemics of viruses
and immune deficiency
and deformity
and still births
and sterility.

O we know them well now.
And we know their source.
But for those ancestors
it was mysterious
whence came these sickenings of spirit and flesh.

And some,
sensing their connection with the poison fire,
with huge accumulation of its wastes,
wanted to wish it away.

The Governments tried to bury it—
There were places called Carl's Bad, Yucca Mountain
—deep holes half a mile down.
They wanted to bury it
as if the Earth were not alive.

And those who did not agree with the Governments said
"Not in my backyard."
Their pain and their despair were so great,
they wanted it out of their sight,
out of their minds.

We remember that in the story.
Because it was in those dark times
that our ancestors began to meet and take council,
groups coming together in where they lived.

They looked into their hearts
and thought:
"We can guard the poison fire.
We can overcome our fear of guarding it and be mindful.
Only in that way can the beings of the future be
    protected."

They remembered us!

How clear it is to us today.
But it was new in that time.

What inspired them?
What did they draw on in those closing years of the
twentieth century to hit upon this idea to inspire
    themselves,
and indeed then to carry it forward?

CHAPTER TWENTY-THREE

The Third Turning of the Wheel

The turning wheel is a powerful symbol of the mystery at the heart of life. Planets and solar systems and electrons in their orbits are wheels revolving within larger wheels, just as the hours and seasons of day and year rotate too, and the circulation of the blood in the body, and the vast hydrological cycles that sustain our living world. Like the sacred hoop of the Native Americans and the round dances and mandalas of ancient peoples, the wheel reminds us that all is alive and moving, interconnected and intersecting. Little wonder, then, that the wheel has served to symbolize the Dharma, the teachings of the Buddha. For the Buddha taught, in his central doctrine, the dependent co-arising of all things, how they continually change and condition each other in interconnections as real as the spokes in a wheel. The Buddha said, "He who sees the Dharma sees dependent co-arising, and he who sees dependent co-arising sees the Dharma." Thus, when he taught, he was said to turn the Wheel of the Dharma.

As this book conveys, I have been deeply inspired by the Buddha's teaching of dependent co-arising. It fills me with a strong sense of connection and mutual responsibility with all beings. Helping me understand the non-hierarchical and self-organizing nature of life, it is the philosophic grounding of all my work.

I have described, in this book, two Turnings of the Wheel of the Dharma. The first occurred with the Buddha's own teachings, recorded in the early scriptures. When he set forth the Dharma of dependent co-arising, he likened it, as we saw, to discovering a forgotten city. The second turning occurred at the beginning of the Mahayana tradition, with scriptures honoring the Perfection of Wisdom, Mother of All Buddhas. Now, at the end of this book, I want to suggest that the cognitive shifts and spiritual openings taking place in our own time can be seen as the Third Turning of the Wheel, that is as dramatic re-emergence of the Dharma of dependent co-arising.

The insight into the nature of reality which the Buddha presented, in a wealth of metaphor, story, and philosophic argument, revealed the interdependence of all phenomena. In contrast to the thinkers of his time, he saw all things in process, intrinsically connected and sustaining each other in intricate patterns of mutual causality. To comprehend this co-arising was tantamount to wisdom, and its social implications were embodied in the Buddha's teachings of compassion, nonviolence, and sharing, and in the customs of the Sangha he founded.

Five centuries later, the Wheel of the Dharma is said to have turned again. The time had come to reclaim and recast in fresh thought and language the Buddha's core teaching, which had then become obscured for many by generations of scholastic thought. The thinkers of the Abhidharma had focused more on analyzing and enumerating the factors of existence than on perceiving their interrelations. The separate *factors* that co-arise became more interesting than the *fact* of co-arising itself; and as they were labeled, quantified, and categorized, hierarchical notions of reality crept into Buddhism.

Enter the Perfection of Wisdom, the Mother of All Buddhas. Her scriptures bring a strong corrective. Readjusting the lens through which we see reality, she offers a vision of interdependence so radical that, as we realize anew, no factor or no constituent element can be understood in isolation, in its own separate self-existence. With this Turning of the Wheel come new terms, like *emptiness* (for the other face of dependent co-arising is emptiness of own-being); new metaphors like *deep space*, a new playful, paradoxical style; and a new model, the *bodhisattva*. Knowing his interexistence with all beings, the bodhisattva seeks not perfection but wholeness and healing. As the core teaching of dependent co-arising is reclaimed and reframed, the world itself comes back into focus as the field of enlightenment, the arena for wisdom and compassion.

The recognition of our essential nonseparateness from the world, beyond the shaky walls erected of our fear and greed, is a Dharma gift occurring in every generation, in countless individual lives. Yet there are historical moments when this perspective arises in a more collective fashion and when, within Buddhism as a whole (if we can even talk of "Buddhism as a whole"!), there is a fresh reappropriation of the Buddha's central teaching. This seems to be occurring today. Along with the destructive, even suicidal nature of many of our public policies, social and intellectual developments are converging now to bring into bold relief the Buddha's teaching of dependent co-arising—and the wheel of the Dharma turns again.

Like all use of metaphor, it is somewhat fanciful, of course, to call it the Third, but what is happening today seems to me as momentous in the history of Buddhism as that great watershed called the Second Turning. In any case, this awakening to the living interconnectedness of our world is stirring in other religions too. There is, among people of all faiths, an urgency to taste and know this relatedness and to break down the old dichotomies between self and world, mind and nature, contemplation and action. Perhaps we suspect that our survival depends upon our doing that.

For the Buddhist world, it is high time that such a turning occur. For many generations now the doctrine of dependent co-arising has been often neglected or misinterpreted by Buddhist scholars, especially Western scholars conditioned by substantialist and hierarchical thinking, and by assumptions of one-way causality. Popular thinking about the Dharma, even among practicing Buddhists, has been confused by currents of subjective idealism flowing in from Hindu as well as classical Western thought. Notions have arisen, and even been ascribed to the Buddha, that the phenomenal world is not real, or that we create it unilaterally by the power of our projections, or that suffering is a spiritual mistake and the ideal of nonattachment refers not to the ego and its machinations, but to the world itself and the fate of all beings. These errors have perpetuated the popular stereotype of Buddhism as a world-denying religion, offering escape from this realm of suffering into some abstract, disembodied haven. In many places Buddhist teachings are still conveyed in this light, but a ground swell is rising, a tidal movement in the other direction.

The Turning of the Wheel in our time is evident in many ways. I see it in the return to the social teachings of the Buddha, in the revitalization of the bodhisattva ideal, in the rapid spread of "engaged Buddhism," be it among Sarvodayans in Sri Lanka, Ambedkarite Buddhists in India, or Dharma activists in Tibet, Thailand, or Southeast Asia. Western Buddhists, too, are taking Dharma practice out into the world, developing skillful means for embodying compassion as they take action to serve the homeless, restore creekbeds, or block weapons shipments. The vitality of Buddhism today is most clearly reflected in the way it is being brought to bear on social, economic, political, and environmental issues, leading people to become effective agents of change. The gate of the Dharma does not close behind us to secure us in a cloistered existence aloof from the turbulence and suffering of samsara, so much as it leads us out into a life of risk for the sake of all beings. As many Dharma brothers and sisters discover today, the world is our cloister.

Here new hands and minds, aware of the suffering caused by outmoded ways of thinking and dysfunctional power structures, help turn the wheel. Strong convergences are at play here, as Buddhist thought and practice interact with the organizing values of the Green movement, with Gandhian nonviolence, and humanistic psychology, with ecofeminism, and sustainable economics, with systems theory, deep ecology, and new paradigm science.

In his teaching of Interbeing, Vietnamese Zen master Thich Nhat Hanh captures the flavor of this turning. Not only does he model the many bodhisattva roles one life can play—scholar, activist, teacher, poet, meditator, and mediator; he opens as well through the concept and practice of Interbeing a wide gate into the Buddha's doctrine of dependent co-arising.

With this Third Turning, we see that everything we do impinges on all beings. The way you are with your child is a political act, and the products you buy and your efforts to recycle are part of it too. So is meditation—just trying to stay aware is a task of tremendous importance. We are trying to be present to ourselves and each other in a way that can save our planet. Saving the planet includes developing a strong, caring connection with future generations; for, in the Dharma of co-arising, we are here to sustain one another over great distances of space and time.

The Third Turning, I think, will be like what Robinson Jeffers called "falling in love outward." Our mission is not to escape from our world, or to fix things by remote control, looking at charts and pushing buttons, and pulling levers, but to fall in love with our world. We are made for that, because we co-arise with her—in a dance where we discover ourselves and lose ourselves over and over.

In this Third Turning we build community. Loneliness is one of the great sufferings of our time; we acknowledge that now, and recognize the need to take charge of our lives *together*, to manifest our interdependence in visible, palpable ways. We have to risk trusting each other, and build ourselves into each others' lives in new ways, allowing structures to arise by which we live together, work together, play, and pray together. Greed and fear are very isolating. They make us crazy. We have to see through them and refuse to be pitted against each other. Only through all beings and with all beings can we awaken to our peace and joy. Our daily adventure is to realize that.

The Dharma wheel, as it turns now, also tells us this: that we don't have to invent or construct our connections. They already exist. We already and indissolubly belong to each other, for that is the nature of life. So, even in our haste and hurry and occasional discouragement, we belong to each other. We can rest in that knowing, and stop and breathe, and let that breath connect us with the still center of the turning wheel.

Notes

All scriptural quotes are from the Pali Text Society editions.

Page   CHAPTER ONE

  9   *"Through the calculations . . ."*: Italo Calvino, *Cosmicomics* (New York:
      Harcourt Brace Jovanovich, 1968), pp. 43-47.

 14   *"Being rock, . . . died."*: Thich Nhat Hanh, *The Collected Poems of Thich
      Nhat Hanh* (Berkeley: Parallax Press, forthcoming 1992).

                                       CHAPTER FIVE

 53   *"they who . . ."*: Majjhima Nikaya II.32.

 55   *"There arose . . ."*: Samyutta Nikaya II.105.

 56   *"Coming to be . . ."*: Digha Nikaya II.33.

 57   *"I have penetrated this truth . . ."*: Ibid., II.36.
      "There are those . . . understand.": Ibid., II.37-39.
      "that is to say . . . away.": Ibid., II.41.

 58   *"This being . . . ceases."*: Samyutta Nikaya II.28, 65; Majjhima Nikaya
      II.32, etc.

 60   *"neither desire . . . verity."*: Anguttara Nikaya I.174.

 62   *"I say that liberation . . ."*: Samyutta Nikaya II.30.

 63   *"Wonderful, lord . . . faring on."*: Digha Nikaya II.91.

                                        CHAPTER SIX

 66   *"Is sensory experience . . ."*: Thomas S. Kuhn, *The Structure of Scientific
      Revolutions* (Chicago: University of Chicago Press, 1970) p. 126.

 67   *"Monks, as if . . . consciousness."*: Majjhima Nikaya I.259-60.
      "Apart from . . . consciousness.": Ibid., I.257.

 68   *"Were a man . . ."*: Samyutta Nikaya III.57.

 72   *"Whatever is . . ."*: Anguttara Nikaya II.24.

 73   *"Could there be . . . is nirvana."*: Ibid., V.7ff.

 76   *"just knowing"*: Ibid., V.9j.

Page

94 *"I will . . . 'intentions.'"* : O.H. Mowrer, "Ego Psychology, Cybernetics, and Learning Theory," Buckley, *Op. Cit.*, p. 338.

CHAPTER NINE

97 *"Ah, the savor of it!"* : Digha Nikaya III.86.

98 *"to be . . . censured."* : *Ibid.*, II.93.

"the vulgar . . . menials." : *Ibid.*, III.82.

100 *"Whosoever . . . righteousness."* : *Ibid.* I.99.

"So long . . . prosper." : *Ibid.*, II.77.

103 *"those men . . . realm."* : *Ibid.*, I.135.

"Then, Ananda . . . want." : *Ibid.*, II.180.

"so as . . . creation." : Jatakas 501, 540. cf. U.N. Ghosal, *A History of Indian Political Ideas* (London: Oxford University Press, 1959), pp. 70ff.

"Moreover I have . . . Dhamma." : Lucien Stryk, *World of the Buddha* (New York: Doubleday Anchor, 1968), p. 245 (Seventh Pillar Edict of Asoka).

104 *"Wherever there are . . . "* : P. Wheelwright, ed. and tr., *Aristotle: Natural Science, Psychology, and Nichomachean Ethics* (New York: Odyssey Press, 1935), p. 35.

105 *"glorious . . ."* : Vinaya, I.113.

CHAPTER TEN

112 *"to the Indian mind . . . dimension."* : A.K. Coomaraswamy, "Kha and Other Words Denoting Zero in Connection with the Metaphysics of Space," *Bulletin of the School of Oriental Studies*, London Institution, Vol., VII, Part 3, 1934, p. 496.

114 *"with her . . . "* : Richard Lannoy, *The Speaking Tree* (Oxford: Oxford University Press, 1971), p. 107.

CHAPTER THIRTEEN

134 *"This definition . . ."* : A.T. Ariyaratne, *In Search of Development* (Moratuwa, Sri Lanka: Sarvodaya Press, 1981), p. 32.

135 *"A Sarvodaya worker . . ."* : *Ibid.*, p. 33.

141 *"The ideas . . . group."* : A.K. Ariyaratne, *Collected Works I* (Netherlands: Sarvodaya Research Institute, 1979), p. 26.

143 *"for the haves . . ."* : Sarvodaya Movement Collective, "What is Self-Reliance?" *Annual Service Report 1980-1981* (Sarvodaya Shramadana Movement, April 1981), p. 70.

Page   CHAPTER FOURTEEN

157   *"There is one..."*: B.R. Ambedkar, *The Buddha and His Dhamma,* Second Edition (Bombay: Siddharth Publication, 1974), p. 254. P. Lakshmi Narusa had written much to the same effect: "The dictum accepted in all schools of Buddhism as the sole regulative principle is that nothing can be the teaching of the Master, which is not in strict accord with reason." [*The Essence of Buddhism* (Bombay: Thacker & Co., 1948), p. vii, emphasis added].

158   *"These are..."*: *Ibid.,* p. xi.

159   *"He had ... conflict."*: *Ibid.,* I.II.6.4-9.

161   *"It may be... strata."*: V.S. Paramar, "Was the Buddha an Aryan?", *The Illustrated Weekly of India,* May 16, 1976, p. 28ff.

     "the Buddha ... preached.": Ambedkar, *Op. Cit.,* V.IV. 3 8-10.

     "Is the bhikkhu ... is not a bhikkhu.": *Ibid.,* V.II. 4 17-22.

     "Except on ... upsaka.": *Ibid.,* II.I. 3-4.

162   *"the Vinaya ... laity."*: *Ibid.,* V.IV. 2.

     "Sangha-Diksha ... in India.": *Ibid.,* V.IV.1. 10-12.

     "neither learning... them.": Keer, Dhananjay. *Dr. Ambedkar, His Life and Mission,* Second Edition (Bombay: Popular Prakashan, 1962), p. 248.

163   *"a reformer... self-control."*: Ambedkar, *Op. Cit.,* II.II.7.7.

     "He began ... death.": *Ibid.,* II.II.2.14.

164   *"belief in ... past life."*: *Ibid.,* I.VII.1.1.

     "denied ... old bottle.": *Ibid.,* I.VII.2.3.

     "the general moral order.": *Ibid.,* II.III.5.10-12.

165   *"the recognition ... to man."*: *Ibid.,* III.V.2.16.

     "The Four Aryan Truths ... monks?": *Ibid.,* p. x, cited by Richard Taylor in "The Ambedkarite Buddhists," T.S. Wilkinson, ed., *Ambedkar and The Neo-Buddhist Movement* (Bangalore: Christian Institute for the Study of Religion and Society, 1972), p. 156.

     "'Why is this'... craving.": *Ibid.,* III.III.4.12-14.

166   *"kingdom ... earth."*: *Ibid.,* V.11.4.10.

167   *"I never ... new meaning."*: *Ibid.,* II.IV.2.9.

               CHAPTER NINETEEN

204   *"In a yet..."*: Stanislav Grof, "Modern Consciousness Research and Human Survival," in *ReVision,* Vol. 8, No. 1, Summer-Fall 1985.

Page   CHAPTER TWENTY

208   *"this spilling . . . forever."* : Tyrone Cashman, Unpublished manuscript, 1989.

      "We need not . . . severance." : Robert Jay Lifton, *The Broken Connection* (New York: Simon and Schuster, 1979), p. 338.

209   *"When the . . . do that."* : Cashman, *Op. Cit.*

210   *"Our perceptions . . . cancer."* : Larry Dossey, M.D. *Space, Time and Medicine.* (Boulder: Shambhala Publications, Inc., 1982), p. 49.

      "My teachers . . . faster." : Ariane Barth. "Im Reisswolf der Geschwindigkeit," *Der Spiegel,* Nov. 20, 1989, p. 210.

214   *"It's all . . . manner."* : Thomas Berry, *The Dream of the Earth* (San Francisco: Sierra Club, 1988), p. 123.

      "Perhaps only . . . self." : *Ibid.*, p. 127.

219   *"heal itself . . . again."* : Jeremy Rifkin, *Time Wars: The Primary Conflict in Human History* (New York: Henry Holt and Company, 1987)

CHAPTER TWENTY-TWO

230   *"Your next breath . . . ark..."* : Guy Murchie, *The Seven Mysteries of Life* (Boston: Houghton-Mifflin Co., 1978), p. 320-321.

Suggested Reading

In addition to the referenced Buddhist texts, here are some books that help us remember and learn about our interconnectedness with the world and its beings.

Badiner, Allen Hunt, ed. *Dharma Gaia: A Harvest of Essays in Buddhism and Ecology.* Berkeley: Parallax Press, 1990.

Bateson, Gregory. *Steps to an Ecology of Mind.* New York: Ballantine Books, 1972.

_____. *Mind in Nature: A Necessary Unity.* New York: Dutton, 1979.

Berry, Thomas. *The Dream of the Earth.* San Francisco: Sierra Club Books, 1988.

Buckley, Walter, ed. *Modern Systems Research for the Behavioral Scientist.* Chicago: Aldine Publishing, 1968.

Button, John, ed. *The Green Fuse: The Schumacher Lectures 1983-1988.* New York: Quartet Books, 1990.

Calvino, Italo. *Cosmicomics.* New York: Harcourt Brace Jovanovich, 1968.

Capra, Fritjof. *The Turning Point.* New York: Simon & Schuster, 1982.

Devall, Bill and George Sessions. *Deep Ecology: Living as if Nature Mattered.* Salt Lake City: Gibbs M. Smith, Inc., 1985.

Devereux, Paul, John Steele and David Kubrin. *Earthmind.* New York: Harper & Row, 1989.

Eppsteiner, Fred, ed. *The Path of Compassion: Writings on Socially Engaged Buddhism.* Berkeley: Co-published by Parallax Press and the Buddhist Peace Fellowship, 1988.

Gray, William and N. Rizzo. *Unity and Diversity.* New York: Gordon and Breach, 1973.

Griffin, Susan. *Woman and Nature: The Roaring Inside Her.* New York: Harper & Row, 1978.

Henderson, Hazel. *Creating Alternative Futures: The End of Economics.* New York: Berkeley Publishing Co., 1978.

_____. *Politics of the Solar Age.* New York: Doubleday, 1981.

Ingram, Catherine. *In the Footsteps of Gandhi: Conversations with Spiritual Social Activists.* Berkeley: Parallax Press, 1990.

Kalupahana, D.J. *Causality: The Central Philosophy of Buddhism.* Honolulu: University of Hawaii Press, 1976.

Koestler, Arthur, ed. *Beyond Reductionism: New Perspectives in the Life Sciences,* The Alpbach Symposium. London: Hutchinson & Co., 1969.

Kohn, Alfie. *No Contest.* Boston: Houghton Mifflin Co., 1986.

Kroptkin, Petr. *Mutual Aid.* Boston: Porter Sargent Publishers, n.d.

LaChapelle, Dolores. *Sacred Land, Sacred Sex, Rapture of the Deep: Concerning Deep Ecology and Celebrating Life.* Silverton, Colorado: Finn Hill Arts, 1988.

Laszlo, Ervin. *Introduction to Systems Philosophy.* New York: Harper Torchbook, 1973.

_____. *System, Structure, and Experience.* New York: George Braziller, 1974.

Lifton, Robert Jay. *The Broken Connection.* New York: Simon & Schuster, 1980.

Lovelock, J.E. *Gaia: A New Look at Life on Earth.* New York: Oxford University Press, 1982.

_____. *The Ages of Gaia: A Biography of Our Living Earth.* New York: W.W. Norton, 1988.

Macy, Joanna. *Despair and Personal Power in the Nuclear Age.* Philadelphia: New Society Publishers, 1983.

_____. *Dharma and Development.* West Hartford, Connecticut: Kumarian Press, 1983.

Margulis, Lynn and David Sagan. *Microcosmos: Four Billion Years of Evolution from our Microbial Ancestors.* London: Allen and Unwin, 1987.

Merchant, Carolyn. *The Death of Nature: Women, Ecology and the Scientific Revolution.* San Francisco: Harper & Row, 1980.

Milsum, John H. *Positive Feedback.* London: Pergamon Press, 1968.

Murchie, Guy. *The Seven Mysteries of Life: An Exploration in Science and Philosophy.* Boston: Houghton Mifflin Co., 1978.

Myers, Dr. Norman, ed. *Gaia: An Atlas of Planet Management.* Garden City: Anchor Press/Doubleday and Co., 1984.

Naess, Arne. *Ecology, Commmunity and Lifestyle.* Cambridge: Cambridge University Press, 1989.

Nhat Hanh, Thich. *Being Peace.* Berkeley: Parallax Press, 1987.

_____. *Interbeing: Commentaries on the Tiep Hien Precepts.* Berkeley: Parallax Press, 1987.

_____. *The Heart of Understanding: Commentaries on the Prajña-paramita Heart Sutra.* Berkeley: Parallax Press, 1988.

_____. *The Sun My Heart: From Mindfulness to Insight Contemplation.* Berkeley: Parallax Press, 1988.

_____. *Breathe! You are Alive: Sutra on the Full Awareness of Breathing.* Berkeley: Parallax Press, 1990.

_____. *Old Path White Clouds: Walking in the Footsteps of the Buddha.* Berkeley: Parallax Press, 1990.

_____. *Our Appointment With Life: Buddha's Teaching on Living in the Present.* Berkeley: Parallax Press, 1990.

_____. *Transformation and Healing: Sutra on the Four Establishments of Mindfulness.* Berkeley: Parallax Press, 1990.

Porritt, Jonathan and David Winner. *The Coming of the Greens.* London: Fontana Paperbacks, 1988.

Roszak, Theodore. *Person/Planet.* New York: Anchor Press/ Doubleday, 1979.

Russell, Peter. *The Global Brain: Speculations on the Evolutionary Leap to Planetary Consciousness.* Los Angeles: J.P. Tarcher, Inc., 1983.

Sahtouris, Elisabet. *Gaia: The Human Journey from Chaos to Cosmos.* New York: Pocket Books, Simon & Schuster, 1989.

Sayre, Kenneth. *Cybernetics and the Philosophy of Mind.* Atlantic Highlands, NJ: Humanities Press, 1976.

Schumacher, E.F. *Small is Beautiful: Economics as if People Mattered.* New York: Harper & Row, 1975.

Seed, John, Pat Fleming, Joanna Macy, and Arne Naess. *Thinking Like a Mountain: Towards a Council of All Beings.* Philadelphia: New Society Publishers, 1988.

Spretnak, Charlene, ed. *The Politics of Women's Spirituality: Essays on the Rise of Spiritual Power within the Feminist Movement.* Garden City: Doubleday/Anchor Books, 1982.

_____. *States of Grace: The Recovery of Meaning in the Postmodern Age.* San Francisco: HarperCollins, 1991.

Swimme, Brian. *The Universe is a Green Dragon, A Cosmic Creation Story.* Sante Fe, NM: Bear and Co., 1984.

Thomas, Lewis. *The Lives of a Cell.* New York: Bantam, 1975.

von Bertalanffy, Ludwig. *General Systems Theory.* New York: George Braziller, 1968.

Wachtel, Paul. *The Poverty of Affluence.* Philadelphia: New Society Publishers, 1989.

ABOUT THE AUTHOR

Joanna Macy, a scholar of Buddhism and general systems theory, is known in many countries for her workshops and trainings to empower creative, sustained social action. Her books include *Despair and Personal Power in the Nuclear Age* (New Society Publishers, 1983), *Dharma and Development: Religion as Resource in the Sarvodaya Self Help Movement in Sri Lanka* (Kumarian Press, 1985), *Thinking Like a Mountain: Toward a Council of All Beings,* co-authored with John Seed *et al* (New Society Publishers, 1988), and *Mutual Causality in Buddhism and General Systems Theory: The Dharma of Natural Systems* (SUNY Press, 1991). A mother of three grown children, she lives in Berkeley with her husband Francis, and teaches at the California Institute of Integral Studies and Starr King School for the Ministry.

ABOUT THE PUBLISHER

Parallax Press publishes books and tapes on socially engaged Buddhism. Some of our recent titles include:

Dharma Gaia: A Harvest of Essays in Buddhism and Ecology, edited by Allan Hunt Badiner

The First Buddhist Women: Translations and Commentary on the Therigatha, by Susan Murcott

Old Path White Clouds: Walking In the Footsteps of the Buddha, by Thich Nhat Hanh

Seeds of Peace: A Contemporary Vision for Renewing Society, by Sulak Sivaraksa

The Path of Compassion: Writings on Socially Engaged Buddhism, edited by Fred Eppsteiner

For a copy of our free catalog, please write to:

Parallax Press
P.O. Box 7355
Berkeley, CA 94707